X.media.publishing 

For further volumes:
http://www.springer.com/series/5175

Alberto Gil Solla • Rafael G. Sotelo Bovino

TV-Anytime

Paving the Way for Personalized TV

Alberto Gil Solla
University of Vigo
Vigo
Spain

Rafael G. Sotelo Bovino
Universidad de Montevideo
Montevideo
Uruguay

ISSN 1612-1449 X.media.publishing
ISBN 978-3-642-44468-5 ISBN 978-3-642-36766-3 (eBook)
DOI 10.1007/978-3-642-36766-3
Springer Heidelberg New York Dordrecht London

ACM Computing Classification (1998): H.5, H.3, C.3, I.3

Title of the Spanish original:

TV-Anytime: Hacia una TV personalizada

Printed on acid-free paper

Springer is part of Springer Science+Business Media (www.springer.com)

To our families

Preface

Television is a mature mass media that has been around for 55 years in Spain and Uruguay, while it has now been close to eight decades of regular broadcasts since its beginnings in the UK and the USA.

Spurred by the spectacular growth of the Internet and social networks, it has become more and more frequent in recent times to hear the echo of critical voices that question both the impact of television on new generations and the future projection of its influence in society. However, the decline of the influence television still exerts on most of the population is a conjecture all the same, supported by scant studies and without important numbers to rely on. Television in fact remains the leading channel for entertainment and information in any developed society, exerting an unparalleled influence on public opinion.

What is clear is that television has been, until recently, a media phenomenon with a rather slow evolution regarding the interaction with its users, and that this is beginning to change. Until now, viewers historically limited its use to the reception and playback of images complemented in many cases by the latest capability to record contents. The digital transition has rushed things, and the computational capacity of televisions and set-top boxes has increased the possibilities of communication and implementation of services of the users' equipment.

But to use this processing capacity effectively and elevate the discrete improvements we are experiencing today to the category of revolution, it is necessary for the software that provides intelligence to have within its reach information it can manipulate and understand, and not only signals to reproduce. It is essential to characterize the environment (content, users, devices, etc.) by means of formal descriptions, on which it is possible to apply the comparison and reasoning processes that allow the software to identify the most attractive contents for each user and properly resolve any issues so that they can be accessed transparently.

At the same time, to promote economies of scale that give a well-founded hope of recovering the necessary investments, it is essential to ensure interoperability between equipments (which entails sharing of information formats and protocols). By doing this, users can purchase equipment with the assurance that they will be able to have universal access to the services provided by operators or third parties, and not just to niches artificially established by the initiatives of manufacturers or TV platforms.

This book provides a general introduction to the resources and capabilities of the TV-Anytime standard, a regulating effort that is aimed at making a homogenizing proposal for certain information formats and communication protocols to create a framework on which to easily develop the intelligent services that are coming into the audiovisual market. The purpose of this standard is to achieve a consensus on the formats of the information that must feed the reasoning processes inherent to an intelligent system, thereby ensuring manufacturers and creators that their products will aspire to the widest possible market, without fear of being constrained by the wars of interest typical for emerging technologies.

Throughout the book, the successive chapters provide a detailed revision of the most important contributions of the standard. To start with, Chap. 1 focuses on the actual state and future trends of the television industry and on the vision and structure of the TV-Anytime standard. Then, Chap. 2 presents a general outline of the standard, showing the logical architecture of a possible platform that deploys TV-Anytime services and describing the main elements involved, together with the information they handle. It can be considered, partly, a summary of the book, where the contents of the following chapters are presented to get a general overview of their relationships.

The next chapters present the main tools provided by the standard. Chapter 3 is devoted to the mechanism defined in TV-Anytime for the unambiguous reference to contents and the resolution of such references to get locators that make it possible to acquire the contents. Chapter 4 is entirely focused on the description of metadata, which is standardized to describe audiovisual contents.

After introducing the main tools, several frameworks to support advanced audiovisual services are covered. Chapter 5 presents different elements and procedures to implement customized smart services related to audiovisual contents: features to manage the customization processes, mechanisms for the dynamic substitution of advertisements, and a coupon system to promote offers related to the announced contents or products. Following this, Chap. 6 deals with content packaging, a procedure to group and coordinate many contents aimed at being consumed in a joint and synchronized way.

Chapter 7 deals with different aspects of the delivery of TV-Anytime metadata in unidirectional contexts, at the destination.

The last chapters are devoted to issues related with the communication of TV-Anytime devices with the outside world. Chapter 8 deals with the characteristics of communication with external services that provide metadata, which are accessible through bidirectional networks, and the procedures for sharing user profiles. Chapter 9 covers the remote programming of a receiver (which belongs to a user or to a service provided by third parties) and the formats of information exchange with applications that do not meet the TV-Anytime regulations. Finally, Chap. 10 closes the book with brief conclusions.

This book is not a reference manual of the standard, and it does not contain complete and thorough descriptions of all aspects covered in the TV-Anytime specifications (unapproachable because of its length and inadvisable—in an informative work such as this one—because of the thoroughness that would be required). Its sole purpose is to arouse the reader's curiosity about the promising capabilities of this initiative, provide a brief description of the mechanisms and elements involved, and present simple examples to clarify what is described and to show its scope. We hope that this book helps readers resolve their doubts with respect to possible projects, or at least gain a more accurate vision of what the future may hold for them in this scenery.

Acknowledgments

We would like to thank Universidad de Montevideo and Universidad de Vigo for providing the conditions to complete this work. Finally, as several figures and examples in this book have been extracted from the TV-Anytime[1] specifications (in some cases with slight modifications and in others as is), we would like to thank the TV-Anytime Forum for their permission for reproduction and adaptation.

Contents

List of Figures

List of Listings

Introduction

1

1.1 And Television Awoke

1.1.1 An Unquestionable Importance

In spite of the substantial increase in the prominence reached by the Internet and videogames in the last few years, nobody really seriously questions yet the fact that television still plays a preponderant role in our homes whether as a service to which we devote a great deal of our leisure time or as the main channel to have access to the latest news.

No one can deny that television is extraordinarily important in our society, even though there is no agreement on how to measure its influence. In any case, this multipurpose and beloved invention occupies a prominent space in most homes, and it is the handiest source of entertainment, the main source of daily information, an essential distraction that keeps us company and an effective means for continuous education.

The strong expressiveness of the television images has a great influence on our perception of the reality that is beyond what is around us. Nowadays, many easily believe what they see on television to be true and are sceptical whenever something is not supported by it. That gives television a great controlling power, something that political and economic forces of all societies have always been aware of.

The wide versatility of television regarding the roles it plays in its everyday interaction with people guarantees it an extraordinary capacity to form opinions, generally stereotypes, especially among the young. This makes it a highly effective tool to promote certain ideologies or increase the possibility that some minority groups or viewpoints have of being accepted or rejected.

In the area of social micro-organization, television also has a wide array of effects in our everyday lives. It distinctly affects what we talk about daily with family and friends, and it even influences the arrangement of furniture in our

A. Gil Solla and R.G. Sotelo Bovino, *TV-Anytime*, X.media.publishing,
DOI 10.1007/978-3-642-36766-3_1, © Springer-Verlag Berlin Heidelberg 2013

homes, normally being the centre of attention in living rooms, around which the other articles are arranged.

In case its direct influence were not enough, television is an integrating macro-spectacle through which we enjoy almost all other spectacles (music, theatre, sports, etc.), which are definitely affected by the high figures that retransmission brings to their financing.

According to the latest General Media Study ("Estudio General de Medios", AIMC,[1] 2012), television reaches 89.1 % of the Spanish population over 14 daily, while the radio only reaches 61.9 %. As for the Internet, the daily access rate "only" reaches 46.7 % of this population group.

Although it is unquestionable that the Internet has evolved significantly over the last few years, with a 36-point increase in the penetration rate during the last decade, it is also true that this breakthrough has not happened mainly at the expense of television, which has only dropped one point during this period.

It could be said that the great breakthrough of the Internet in the last few years has caused a significant decline in the amount of time devoted to watching television. Nonetheless, the last data published regarding audience ratings does not allow us to draw that conclusion, given that the television's average daily consumption is still as high as 242 min per person.

Conversely, it is important to mention that a recent study by the AIMC (2010) reveals that almost half of the people who surf the Internet watch TV shows online assiduously, mostly because of the time flexibility the Internet offers. And 85 % of them say that this habit has not reduced their consumption of regular television.

Researchers could be led to believe the situation is very different among the younger age group (between 12 and 24), owing to the fact that various studies show the Internet is the main source of entertainment at these ages, when there is a rate of television consumption significantly lower than the average. Extrapolating, it could be inferred from this conjecture that the substitution will develop slowly until the Internet prevails over television as a source of information and entertainment.

However, a detailed analysis of available statistics in this respect (Lara, 2010) shows two conclusive facts that allow us to be sceptical about this hypothesis:

- Television consumption rates in the age group immediately below (4–12 years old) show similar numbers, and this cannot be attributed to Internet penetration rates, which are much lower in this age group.
- There is no significant decrease in the evolution of television consumption in the past 10 years among young people, as opposed to what could be assumed given the exponential increase of Internet consumption in those age groups that has occurred in the same period.

These two facts suggest, on the one hand, that the lower television consumption rate among young people is due to structural causes, which need more complex explanations than the explosive irruption of the Internet, and, on the other hand, that

[1] "Asociación para la investigación de medios de comunicación", a Spanish media research association

the significant increase in the amount of time young people devote to the Internet has not really taken place at the expense of television, but instead the time is distributed much more diffusely among the various entertainment options available to them (Lara, 2010).

Hence, there are no unequivocal signals to fear that the appearance of the Internet as a top-level player in the media and entertainment arena could pose an unsettling threat in the short or medium term to the impact of television in our society.

Conversely, there is an objective indicator that shows the impact that market studies have on those who make important decisions in this regard (economic decisions) and put the relative importance ascribed to all media nowadays in the right place. This indicator is advertising investments in conventional media, which reached 5,849.5 million Euros in Spain in 2010 (INFOADEX, 2011). From this amount, 2,471.9 million (42.3 %) were invested in television, while "only" 789.5 million (13.5 %) were invested in the Internet. Similar numbers can be found in the international advertising market, for example in the estimations for 2011 by Magna Global,[2] a consultancy firm: 169,000 million dollars invested in television advertising in 2011 and 71,000 million dollars in online publicity. And even though this consultancy firm expects a greater increase in online publicity investments than in television in general in the next 5 years, it also estimates that the greater increase will occur in Pay Television, prevailing even over online media. And in case there is doubt as to whether or not this difference is smaller in bigger markets, this example from the data provided by Nielsen[3] for the US market in 2011 could be illustrative: 72 billion dollars invested in television publicity compared to 6 billion dollars invested in Internet publicity.

1.1.1.1 Times of Change

Although it cannot be denied that television has long entered a phase of great changes, which take place seamlessly with no guarantee of continuity, the first four decades of existence of this medium—being a little over 50 years old in the authors' countries—were characterized by a certain technological stagnation due to the lack of significant change, disregarding the invention of colour and of the video recorder. During that period, even though there were constant breakthroughs in materials, components and the aesthetics of devices—as well as in the equipment necessary for production and transmission—there were no major changes with regard to the functionality provided to users nor were there any innovations having a significant impact on the way this medium affected the entertainment habits of citizens.

Conversely, the last decade has seen many technological changes that are altering the aesthetics and functionality of this means of entertainment and communication in a fast and profound way. On the one hand, it is essential to highlight

[2] http://www.magnaglobal.com

[3] http://www.nielsen.com

the emergence and stunning colonization of LCD and plasma technologies, which have deeply affected the physical appearance of television sets in our homes. This transcendental change in manufacturing technology has not only led to a substantial increase in the average size of the screens sold—together with a noticeable decline in prices—but it has also significantly risen the importance of aesthetics in the customers' feature checklist when it comes to purchasing a new television set. The result has been that this technological change has posed an extraordinary incentive to launch an accelerated renovation of the total number of conventional television sets that used to abound until recently.

On the other hand, in the last few years we have witnessed the beginning of the most important technological change that has taken place in this context: the transition from analogue to digital, another feature of the omnipresent digitalization that has been transforming our society for some time and to which television could not remain indifferent.

1.1.2 The Importance of the Digital Transition

This fundamental transition ended in the more developed countries from 2006 onwards (with the well-known analogue blackouts), while in the rest of the world it is, at least, still under planning. It was born from the change in the representation system for audiovisual signals, from analogue to digital, and the subsequent use of new modulations to send the digital signal carriers. This change has had extraordinary consequences, given that it has affected billions of people, and it has had a major economic impact both on end users, who must purchase new equipment or adapters, and on the signal distribution network, not to mention the disputed market of licences and broadcast concessions.

The reasons for this transition are the significant technological advantages associated with it, related in part to the substantial improvements of certain features that users have enjoyed for some time, but which are also catalysts for new services that, although foreseeable and already predicted in a more or less recent past, did not fully materialize due to the lack of an appropriate technological support. In the first case, we find consequences that may be transparent to users, for whom the changes or improvements in the quality of services often go unnoticed, or their origin is not directly associated with the digital transition. Thus, we can mention the improvement in signal reception quality, especially in mobility, as a result of the greater strength of the carriers that transport audiovisual signals, for example, against echoes; the improvement of error detection and recovery mechanisms for errors produced during the transmission; the greater ease to include better-quality audio systems; the capacity to process the signal in the receiver by decoding, modifying or creating customizable synthetic contents according to the geographical area or even each home; and the emergence of many more channels in the same bandwidth (or high-definition broadcasts), thanks to modern digital compression mechanisms that take advantage of the spatial-temporal redundancies of images.

But digitalization also brings many other benefits that directly affect the way we enjoy the service and the possibilities open to us that enrich our leisure and communication skills. This refers to the improvement of data protection mechanisms, which has a strong impact on the percentages of illegitimate access to paid contents and, therefore, on the business models that exist in the market; the widespread use of general-purpose computer hardware for TV signal processing, which enables significant cost savings and an increased repertoire of content-display devices (mobile phones, computers, tablets, etc.); the establishment of new distribution channels such as the Internet, cell phones or ADSL, thanks to the repackaging process facilities of the digital signal; a greater flexibility in the storage and location of contents, thanks to the possibility of adding metadata that describes them; and, in short, all the benefits associated with the digitalization of the hardware for content reception and playback, which turns modern televisions into real computers, capable of recording signals on a hard drive, connecting to the Internet, contacting devices surrounding them through typical computer networks and protocols or even running resident or downloaded applications together with audiovisual contents.

This last possibility, symbolized by several international standards with strong institutional support such as *MHP* (ETSI TS 102 727, 2010), *GEM* (ETSI TS 102 728, 2011), *Ginga* (ABNT NBR 15606, 2011) in South America, or private business initiatives like *Google TV*,[4] *Connected Yahoo*[5] or *Samsung Smart TV*,[6] or recent alliances between them as the *Smart TV Alliance*,[7] opens the door to the enjoyment in our living room of endless leisure and communication services, such as the ones provided through the Internet or available in the catalogues of mobile applications that have been revolutionizing lately the market of so-called smartphones.

We are, in short, in the presence of a new landscape conditioned by an infinitely more flexible technology, which in a few years has brought into our lives a multitude of new acronyms for standards, protocols, services or business models. Relatively recent terms already seem to be traditional technology (*DLNA*[8]), while others are consolidated as eternal promises (*GEM/MHP*). The magic words of today (*HD*, *3D*) will soon give way to new words that are already claiming preferential attention (*OLED*, *HbbTV*), not to mention the ever-present threat to the traditional model of linear television posed day by day by new concepts such as *over-the-top*, *catchup-tv* or *second screen* in a market that is nervous out of uncertainty and eager to consolidate changes as indisputable as unpredictable.

---

[4] http://www.google.com/tv

[5] http://connectedtv.yahoo.com

[6] http://www.samsung.com/smarttv

[7] http://www.smarttv-alliance.org

[8] http://www.dlna.org

1.1.3 The PDR and Non-linear Consumption of TV

Another one of the technological changes of the last decade that are having a significant impact on our television habits is the growing popularity of the DVR (Digital Video Recorder) or, using a more general term, the PDR (Personal Digital Recorder). After all, it is the modern version of the traditional video cassette recorder, now equipped with a hard drive, where the contents can be stored after being extracted from the transport stream (or after their digitalization, if receiving an analogue signal).

At first, this may seem to be a simple technological evolution, resulting just in quantitative improvements (more storage, better quality and reliability of the recordings or easier access to contents). However, it implies a great qualitative advance, with a much greater scope than it may seem, mainly due to the great flexibility that digital technologies offer to attach descriptive data to audiovisual information and to their later processing inside or outside the receiver, before, during or after the reproduction of contents.

This flexibility provides important advantages regarding the recording and enjoying of audiovisual contents:

- More ease to plan recordings, based on EPGs (Electronic Program Guides) that only require pressing a button and help us avoid having to fully indicate the recording period
- Direct access to stored contents, identified by a significant name, without searching and waiting times that discourage a quick, natural and spontaneous consumption
- Capacity to stop live content in a natural way and resume it afterwards (*time shifting*)
- Capacity to organize and classify recordings according to different criteria
- Capacity to edit recordings and extract them from the PDR into several formats and mediums (DVD, USB flash drive, etc.)

However, it also opens up a range of new possibilities directly derived from the capacities to interact with the environment that characterizes digital devices, such as:

- Capacity to exchange information with computers, not only to transfer our recordings to them, but also to import contents or reproduce them remotely
- Capacity to reproduce all kinds of multimedia contents, such as photos, music and radio
- Capacity to have direct access to contents provided by Internet services, some as well-known as *YouTube* or *Picasa*
- Capacity to take the initiative on behalf of the user in the process of selection or acquisition of contents

It is basically a collection of new or improved capacities in comparison to the previous situation, as a result of the process of convergence between smart devices favoured by digital technologies. If we focus on the truly differential aspects related to our leisure habits, this convergence opens the door to (although it does not necessarily directly imply) an extension of the traditional way of consuming television, which has been conventionally based on the linear distribution and visualization of contents, where these are sent massively to users from a central point, through an operator-controlled schedule, leaving a narrow margin of options for viewers.

In this new scenario, non-linear consumption of television gains importance, where the consumer uses these new devices to access contents different from the planned programming, extracted from multiple sources, some possibly on the device's own initiative. Moreover, it sets the basis to overcome the traditional isolation that has characterized entertainment platforms, unifying the consumption of audiovisual contents through broadcasting (television and radio) with the enjoyment of on-demand contents through streaming services, including access to the Internet and gaming platforms, centralizing everything in a way similar to what smartphones and multimedia tablets have already started implementing.

Early stages of these kind of devices have been entering the audiovisual market for some time, as is the case of *TiVO, ReplayTV* or *Windows Media Center*, which represent unified access points not only to different broadcast networks (DTT, cable or satellite) but also to contents available through streaming directly from the Internet (*YouTube*) or through video on-demand services of operators or third parties (*Netflix*). This is particularly true in the USA, where the latest data[9] reveals that 44 % of North American households own a device with these characteristics and watch recorded contents at an average close to half an hour a day. And, what is more important, this is the only device that shows a continuous increase in its penetration, doubling in the last 5 years. However, its acceptance in the rest of the markets has been very limited, and it has not achieved its objective of penetrating significantly the consumption habits of the general population.

They are, in any case, private initiatives developed through proprietary infrastructure (hardware, software and data formats) that lacks the main element that has guaranteed the success of technological deployments on a large scale in the past: the compatibility between sources of information and devices.

1.1.4 The Importance of Standardization

Looking at the attribute list of the PDRs presented in the previous section, we can see the clear abuse of the word "capacity". Far from evidencing the authors' limited vocabulary, which is a fact, it attempts to reflect our view that the potentialities of these devices are well beyond the functionalities they currently provide. The characteristics and capabilities of their CPU, memory and communication protocols allow them to support a wide array of services which are much more ambitious than the tasks they currently perform. This situation is mainly due to the lack of standardization of the elements that should fulfil these functionalities.

[9] Nielsen (http://www.nielsen.com)

Indeed, in order for these devices to fulfil the main role we have outlined, it is necessary for users to get a significant added value and strong guarantees of continuity, which are by no means independent issues, but they support and revalue each other in a natural way.

In order to adopt a technology, users need interesting functionalities, and the more service providers contributing with their proposals, the easier this is. They also appreciate a wide compatibility of devices that makes it possible to replace or extend part of their equipment in the most convenient way according to prices, functionalities and quality, assuring that they will not be caught up in captive markets.

This device compatibility is also an essential requirement for a large number of service providers to emerge and develop the value-added services we mentioned, given that the greater the universe of devices their services are aimed at, the lower their unit cost. Also, these providers need a standardization of the sources of information from which to develop such services.

Finally, prices need to be low and accessible for a critical user mass. This, of course, requires competition among several device manufacturers, which can only exist if the information processed by these devices is compatible, if there are several service providers that use them and, many times, if the integration of these devices in more complex environments is standardized.

Overall, the success of the coordinated incorporation of several cooperating agents into an important venture like this inevitably requires an important standardization process that guarantees an appropriate interoperability among devices, a correct communication within the services and a reliable processing of information generated by distinct providers.

This is why it is to be expected that the real boom of these devices will take place with open standards that will boost the entire chain of value by having common standards to regulate communication among devices as well as the syntax and semantics of exchanged information. This will allow for lower costs, a higher possibility of interconnection and the emergence of new service providers.

1.2 TV-Anytime

In the particular case of PDRs, they are devices whose aim is to work as a platform to provide users with new intelligent services having to do with audiovisual contents, based on an absolute independence between device manufacturers (hardware and software) and content creators, aggregators or distributors.

We are talking about going beyond the common functionalities provided by the current devices, which are mainly concerned with playing audiovisual contents in a variety of formats. This basic functionality is normally complemented with opportunities to acquire these contents by different means, which usually require the direct intervention of the user to identify the contents to be processed (and their source). All of this is based only on the name of the content. We could be processing a bunch of bytes corresponding to a shopping list, and our receiver would offer neither more nor less possibilities—that is, to acquire and store—than in the case of a movie (the later reproduction would logically entail differences).

On the contrary, the potential capacities of the hardware and software in current devices allow discerning a series of new functionalities that go beyond the routine options seen so far and which require an increase of the level of intelligence of the services provided. We are talking, for instance, about the possibility for users to program the system to record episodes or entire TV series without knowing the channel, date and time in which they will air (e.g. when seeing an episode they like); order the recording of all movies aired starring a particular actor; having the system select among similar contents taking into consideration the format and quality; that a service offered by a third party recommends contents according to the user's profile and consumption history; or that the operator customizes advertising for each individual consumer according to the same data, etc.

In order to achieve this, it is essential that the elements involved are perfectly described in a standardized way, in order for the software that offers the service to be able to compare, make decisions or build new and more complex services out of basic components. In these cases, it is vital to know just what kind of information is available, what its features are, what can be done with it and what requirements are necessary to proceed.

To attain this, as we said above, the main element is standardization, and especially that which relates to the information that describes the elements involved in the services to be developed (contents, users, consumption, networks, rights, etc.). This standardization is fundamental to be able to develop intelligent services which offer to the user some added value regarding the available audiovisual contents.

In 1999, the TV-Anytime[10] forum was created with the goal of contributing to this standardization. It was an association of over a hundred of the most important European, American and Asian organizations (government institutions and companies) in the audiovisual and consumer electronics sectors: broadcasters, content owners, service providers, telecommunication companies, device manufacturers, software developers, institutional regulators, etc. This new organization's ultimate goal was to establish richer relations among content producers, service providers and consumers, by means of identifying new and more ambitious business models based on a greater interactivity with users.

In the following years, a series of specifications were created under the cover of this forum to standardize different aspects related to the description, search and location, selection and acquisition of audiovisual contents (whether broadcast or accessible online on demand), trying to guarantee the independence between each of these stages. The intention was to promote a wide interoperability between teams that would facilitate the creation and generalized deployment of audiovisual services, among others, based on consumer devices with high storage capacity

[10] http://www.tv-anytime.org

(PDRs), all of this with absolute independence of the distribution mechanism. The end result should allow operators to describe audiovisual contents so these can be found and handled easily by users (with the assistance of their TV-Anytime PDR, of course), thus being able to reproduce them whenever and however they wish, without being forced to watch them when they air.

This standardization was mainly aimed at facilitating aspects related to:

- The processing and comparison of contents based on the declared (and formally described) features
- The identification, location and acquisition of contents transparently to users
- The customization and recommendation of contents according to users' profiles and consumption history
- The creation of a flexible framework for the customization of advertising, by means of the dynamic selection in real time of the more appropriate advertisements for each user
- The guarantees to creators and distributors regarding the content consumption rights
- The integration of interactive packages made up of various kinds of information

In order to achieve these goals, four fundamental objectives were formulated during the first stages of operation of the TV-Anytime forum:

1. Define specifications that will allow for the development of applications that will exploit the local storage in consumer electronic platforms.
2. Make the resulting services based on this standard independent of the network used to deliver the content to the consumer's electronic device, taking into account a number of well-known transport mechanisms (ATSC, DVB, DBS, Internet, etc.).
3. Develop specifications for interoperable and integrated systems, all along the chain of content providers and creators, service providers, network operators, software developers, hardware manufacturers and advertisers.
4. Specify the security structures to protect the interests of all those involved in an effective way.

Led by these objectives, four workgroups were created at the core of the forum (*"Business Models"*; *"Systems, Delivery Interfaces and Content Referencing"*; *"Metadata"*; *"Right Management and Protection"*) in order to reflect the most appropriate solutions in the corresponding specifications to achieve the goals that promoted the creation of the association and whose description is the main goal of this book.

1.3 New Business Models

One of the criteria that guided the work within the TV-Anytime forum was that the result had to be aimed at promoting new services that were, above all, economically profitable. This is why the contents of the first document that was created were devoted in whole to discuss the new business models that would result from or be favoured by the standardization processes to come.

In this regard, the first decision was to classify these business models into two groups, named Phase 1 and Phase 2. This division was initially based on the degree of bidirectionality that would be required of the devices in relation to service operators or providers: while business models in Phase 1 required devices with minimal bidirectional capacity, Phase 2 was designed for devices with full high-capacity connectivity in both directions. However, the work done within Phase 2 introduced new kinds of data and multiple advanced features, which were not necessarily conditioned by the bidirectionality requirement.

1.3.1 TV-Anytime Phase 1

In Phase 1, a wide range of new features and improvements on existing device characteristics were identified, and the following are worth noting:

- Consumers will be able to order the recording of content (or a set of contents grouped by the creator or provider) without knowing the specific details of its broadcast (channel, date, time, etc.), simply through a reference supplied by the service provider that the device will use for this task. This would include ordering the recording of the next broadcast of a programme that has already started or ordering a recording from an advertisement for a show.
- Consumers will be able to manage multiple personal profiles in the receiver, for example, for a number of household members, or different versions of the same user aimed at different service providers. They may allow a provider to access these profiles in the receiver in order to deliver customized services. They will even be able to transfer the profiles from device to device easily when buying or leasing a new receiver, while travelling, etc.
- Service providers or the receiver's own software will be able to recommend contents to the users based on their profile and consumption history. What is more, the consumer shall be able to give them permission to capture, store and update (free or paid) contents automatically in the receiver, to offer them to the user if they consider they may be of interest to them.
- Consumers will be able to allow the insertion of (possibly customized) pre-recorded announcements or promotional campaigns in commercial breaks, both in live and previously captured content.
- Whenever the provider gives the necessary information, consumers will be able to process the different segments that make up a particular content (for its reproduction, storage, etc.), including managing indexes that allow selective or partial viewings or the creation of new contents as a result of a customized reorganization, according to their wishes, needs, criteria, etc.
- Consumers will be able to order remote devices connected to a network (depending on the service they have subscribed to) to record the contents they want, for example, to continue recording if the storage capacity of their device runs out.
- Consumers will be able to access location resolution services provided by the operator or by third parties to find out where and how to acquire certain contents from a reference.

Clearly, we are talking about functionalities in which most of the movement of information (audiovisual contents) is performed through the broadcast channel, from the operator to the user's home. The need for a return channel is limited to sending commands or information about the user's profile, which does not require a large bandwidth.

1.3.2 TV-Anytime Phase 2

In turn, the work done within Phase 2 was then aimed at identifying and defining a set of new features focused on the full-connectivity requirement of the user's device, including the necessary mechanisms to carry out the corresponding exchanges of information.

However, this second phase was also used to add new elements that would allow the deployment of other types of services that did not require bidirectional communication. For example, new types of data (besides audiovisual data) were identified which the user's device had to be able to manage, mechanisms for packaging various pieces of information (aimed at being consumed jointly or synchronously) were defined and a step forward in the treatment of customized advertising was taken.

Among the features of Phase 2 whose deployment the forum wanted to facilitate, we can include the following:

- Consumers will be able to easily move the contents they capture (along with their associated metadata) among different devices, whether mobile or fixed, wired or wireless, owned or belonging to third parties, and enable other users to have access to those contents.
- Consumers will be able to order the capture of interactive packages, composed of audiovisual contents, applications, data, text, graphics, games and links to other contents. The device may guide the user on the best way to consume the contents included in the package.
- Consumers will be able to order their devices to capture in advance contents associated with a future event, so that they are available for a synchronized reproduction when the event takes place.
- The devices will be able to automatically update recorded contents that are sensitive to the passing of time (e.g. news or announcements).
- Consumers will be able to set up their devices to allow them to acquire contents that have specific features (audio and video format, aspect ratio, quality, etc.) as well as ensure that any captured contents are playable on their devices, or set them up, for instance, so that when recording any contents, the device selects (or finds and captures) the audio and subtitles corresponding to their preferred language.
- Consumers will be able to order recordings starting from the metadata provided by third parties (or available online) and make sure that any subsequent change in that metadata is automatically reflected in the schedule of their device.
- Consumers will be able to configure and view the settings and tasks of their devices from remote terminals, including mobile devices.
- Consumers who want to order more concurrent recordings than their devices can manage (or who have used up their storage space) will be able to indicate that

some contents are to be recorded by remote equipment of a service provider and then transferred to their devices.

- When an advertisement has additional contents associated or linked to it, consumers will be able to pause the content they are viewing, access the promotional information and then resume the content where they paused it.
- Viewers will be able to indicate the type of advertisements they want to receive. Both advertisers and users can set limits on the number of times the latter are offered a particular advertisement.
- Consumers will be able to choose among different payment models to pay for contents, for example, based on the number of advertisements that they are willing to accept during reproduction.
- Advertisers will be able to make sure that their advertisements are only shown in relevant places or to the right audience, or ensure that similar competitive products are not advertised in close intervals.
- Advertisers will be able to establish that advertisements inserted in pre-recorded content are replaced according to various criteria: time of year, time of day, number of times they have been seen, etc.

Clearly, a common feature of these new business models is the increased communication with providers, i.e., they involve more interactive services, which often require a high-capacity return channel to move contents from the user's device to the outside world.

We can also foresee a greater intelligence in the processes running in the receiver, such as the ability to customize contents and services or the possibility of integrating communications with third parties, enabling more open systems, which go beyond the closed dialogue between the user and the platform's operator. Even from the ambiguous statement about the "ability to run applications included in interactive packages", we see the need for a high degree of hardware/software resources to implement the frameworks to run the applications (which will be greater or lesser depending on their type). Finally, it is necessary to emphasize the great importance given to the dynamic and personalized management of advertising, where both the user and the provider are facing a new context which is much more flexible than the current one.

1.4 Organizing the Standard

The specifications created by the TV-Anytime forum to regulate the provision of the services detailed above were finally published by ETSI (*European Telecommunications Standards Institute*) in nine documents[11] called "parts", under the generic title "Broadcast and On-Line Services: Search, select and rightful use of content on personal storage systems ('TV-Anytime')" sharing the common identifier "ETSI TS 102 822".

[11] Documents available at http://www.etsi.org

The first two parts are merely informative, devoted to present the objectives of the standard and the elements that compose the architecture of the system:

Part 1 (ETSI TS 102 822–1, 2006): "*Benchmark features*"
This first document of the standard presents some of the features that the TV-Anytime set of standards intends to facilitate. In order to do this, it describes different business models that the standard intends to allow or encourage (some examples have been presented above).

Part 2 (ETSI TS 102 822–2, 2007): "*System description*"
The second document presents the general architecture of the system and the main elements involved in the deployment of the abovementioned business models. It is a general overview of the standard, which we will deal with in Chap. 2.
The other parts are regulatory (they present and regulate all the elements necessary to implement the framework that was described and achieve the objectives set in advance):

Part 3: "*Metadata*"
- Subpart 1 (ETSI TS 102 822-3-1, 2011): "*Phase 1—Metadata schemas*"
- Subpart 2 (ETSI TS 102 822-3-2, 2010): "*System aspects in a unidirectional environment*"
- Subpart 3 (ETSI TS 102 822-3-3, 2011): "*Phase 2—Extended metadata schema*"
- Subpart 4 (ETSI TS 102 822-3-4, 2011): "*Phase 2—Interstitial metadata*"

Part 4 (ETSI TS 102 822–4, 2011): "*Content referencing*"

Part 5: "*Rights management and protection (RMP)*"
- Subpart 1 (ETSI TS 102 822-5-1, 2011): "*Information for broadcast applications*"
- Subpart 2 (ETSI TS 102 822-5-2, 2006): "*RMPI binding*"

Part 6: "*Delivery of metadata over a bidirectional network*"
- Subpart 1 (ETSI TS 102 822-6-1, 2011): "*Service and transport*"
- Subpart 2 (ETSI TS 102 822-6-2, 2006): "*Phase 1—Service discovery*"
- Subpart 3 (ETSI TS 102 822-6-3, 2011): "*Phase 2—Exchange of personal profile*"

Part 7 (ETSI TS 102 822–7, 2003): "*Bidirectional metadata delivery protection*"

Part 8 (ETSI TS 102 822–8, 2011): "*Phase 2—Interchange data format*"

Part 9 (ETSI TS 102 822–9, 2011): "*Phase 2—Remote programming*"

Throughout all of these documents, a series of elements necessary to organize the standard are identified and described (participating entities, data formats, information exchange protocols, etc.). The elements related to Phase 1 can be summarized as follows:

CRID (*Content Reference IDentifier*). A CRID is an unambiguous identifier assigned to each content (or to a set of contents grouped according to some criteria), independent of its copy or specific location. It is described in Part 4 of the standard, together with a procedure to find the information required to acquire a copy of the content from the CRID (or to capture the CRIDs of each member of a given group from the group's CRID). Both issues (the characteristics of a CRID and its resolution process) will be described extensively in Chap. 3.

Classification Schemes. They are composed of various groups of controlled terminology, used to indicate the possible values of a content attribute and to classify contents hierarchically according to multiple dimensions, such as genre or format. They are described in Part 3-1 of the standard, and we will deal with them in Chap. 4.

Description Metadata: It covers a markup language used to structure different characterizations of contents, summarized below. It is described in Part 3-1 of the standard, and we will focus on this in Chap. 4. Basically, this metadata is divided into four sections:

- *Content description*. These are generic descriptions of contents, independent of the particular details of each specific copy, such as the video's aspect ratio or the encoding of audio.
- *Instance description*. It is specific information that characterizes specific instances of certain contents, which may be different in terms of the format, quality, acquisition information, etc.
- *Segmentation*. It describes specific information that allows identifying different individual segments of content, which can be separated for selective visualization, or following a customized order (e.g. news).
- *User preferences and consumption history*. It is specific information that describes each user's preferences and their content consumption history.

Encoding, Encapsulation and Indexing of Metadata Fragments. It is a set of mechanisms to manage the representation, transport, and use of metadata fragments, so that they can be processed individually, guaranteeing the detection of updates and favouring the reference to specific elements within great volumes of information. This is described in Part 3-2 of the standard. The main characteristics will be presented in Chap. 7.

Rights Management and Protection of Information. It is a set of usage rules and conditions to guarantee the preservation of the rights of the rightful owners of contents. It is described in Parts 5-1 and 5-2 of the standard and will not be analysed in this book.

Description of Third-Party Metadata Services. It standardizes the information necessary for clients (particularly the users' devices) to make correct requests to metadata service providers, including request and reply formats, and transport protocols (encoding and encapsulation) of metadata over IP networks. It is described in Part 6-1 of the standard and will be presented in Chap. 8.

Metadata Service Discovery. It sets the procedure according to which clients can find third-party metadata services. It is described in Part 6-2 of the standard and will be briefly described in Chap. 8.

Metadata Encryption and Authentication. It defines procedures to guarantee the privacy of information during delivery and the protection of consumption rights by those who are rightfully allowed to do so. It is described in Part 7 of the standard and will not be dealt with in this book.

Regarding Phase 2, the elements that are regulated in the different documents are as follows:

Packaging. It is a set of rules and procedures to describe each of the elements in a group of contents (and the relationships between them), created and grouped to be consumed together in a coordinated way. It is described in Part 3-3 of the standard, and we will devote Chap. 6 to it.

Targeting. It regulates the specific information that allows identifying and deciding the suitability between contents and users, based on user profiles. It is described in Part 3-3 of the standard, and it will be one of the sections analysed in depth in Chap. 5.

Coupons. It sets a framework to attach information about the price and discount coupons (or gifts) to audiovisual contents or products promoted in advertisements. It is described in Part 3-3 of the standard and will be dealt with in Chap. 5.

Terminal Capabilities. It defines the metadata necessary to describe the operative capabilities of devices, with the aim of guaranteeing the correct reproduction of acquired contents in the user's receiver. It is described in Part 3-3 of the standard.

New Content Types. It standardizes the identification of new content types, such as text, games or applications, so as to facilitate the correct specification of terminal capabilities. It is described in Part 3-3 of the standard.

Educational Metadata. It standardizes a set of metadata aimed at describing educational contents. It is described in Part 3-3 of the standard.

Interstitials. It defines a framework to allow the automatic substitution of advertisements during the pauses to the reproduction of content, following different criteria. It is described in Part 3-4 of the standard, and we will deal with it in Chap. 5.

Exchange of Profiles. It determines the necessary metadata for the correct transfer and exchange of user profiles. It is described in Part 6-3 of the standard, and we will indicate some of its characteristics in Chap. 8.

Interchange Data Format. It establishes a data format for information exchange between TV-Anytime devices and devices that do not follow the guidelines of this set of standards, mainly so that the latter can send information to the former, together with indications as to what should be done with it. It is described in Part 8 of the standard and will be dealt with in Chap. 9.

Remote Programming. It defines a communication protocol to access a TV-Anytime device remotely (whether the user's home device or one that belongs to an operator's service), in order to send it queries or order actions. It is described in Part 9 of the standard, and we will deal with it in Chap. 9.

1.5 Book Contents

As mentioned throughout this chapter, the rest of the chapters of this book analyse in detail the various parts of the TV-Anytime standard. In short:

- Chapter 2 presents a general outline of the standard, showing the logic architecture of a possible platform that deploys TV-Anytime services and describing the main elements involved, together with the information they handle. It can be considered, partly, a summary of the book, where the contents of the following chapters are presented to gain a general overview of their relationships.
- Chapter 3 is devoted to the mechanism defined in TV-Anytime for the unambiguous reference to contents and the resolution of such references to get locators that make it possible to acquire the contents.
- Chapter 4 is entirely focused on the description of metadata which is standardized to describe audiovisual contents.
- Chapter 5 presents different elements and procedures to implement customized smart services related to audiovisual contents: facilities to manage the customization processes, mechanisms for the dynamic substitution of advertisements, and a coupon system to promote offers related to the announced contents or products.
- Chapter 6 deals with the packaging of contents, a procedure to group and coordinate many contents aimed at being consumed in a joint and synchronized way.
- Chapter 7 handles different aspects of the delivery of TV-Anytime metadata in unidirectional contexts, including facilities to manage them at destination.
- Chapter 8 deals with the characteristics of communication with external services that provide metadata, which are accessible through bidirectional networks, and the procedures for sharing user profiles.
- Chapter 9 covers the remote programming of a receiver (which belongs to a user or to a service provided by third parties) and the formats of information exchange with applications that do not meet the TV-Anytime regulations.
- Finally, Chap. 10 closes the book with brief conclusions.

From this and from what was described in the previous section, it is clear that this book does not include a thorough treatment of all the aspects that are standardized in the TV-Anytime standard. Without doubt, this requires a more ambitious and, particularly, a lengthier work.

On the contrary, the aim of this text is simply to awaken the reader's curiosity about the standard, the services and business models it is trying to promote and the aspects about which it presents a standardized solution in an attempt to facilitate the deployment of smart audiovisual services.

Because of this, and in order to achieve a text that is easy to read and comprehend where technical details do not bore readers that approach the matter with certain curiosity, we have only gone in depth in those aspects that we find more interesting, because they deal with solutions explicitly related to the context we are dealing with, and because new mechanisms to solve the problems that arise during deployment are involved, and they are not only adaptations to generic technologies, such as rights management, or the encryption and authentication of information.

Also, in the abovementioned sections, especially in the description of different types of metadata, the examples provided are only aimed at illustrating the descriptive possibilities of the language and providing an overview of the characteristics of the contents we can include in the documents, which will later be processed by software applications. They are not in any case complete specifications of all the fields that can be used to describe content attributes, which would require a lot more space and would probably result in a more tedious text. If the examples presented here awaken the reader's curiosity to learn details of the descriptive options of a specific structure, simply reading the documents of the standard should answer any questions quickly and accurately. The aim of this book is precisely to try to make that reading simple, offering a panoramic outline of the parts of the standard, with the aims and bases of each of them, to pave the way for those who want to find out more about one or more aspects of the standard.

Architecture and Components

2

2.1 Introduction

Considering the presentation from the previous chapter, it can be said that TV-Anytime is a set of specifications aimed at promoting the development of audiovisual services with high added value by establishing a normalizing framework that guarantees interoperability between hardware/software from different manufacturers and the applications developed by service providers. To this end, the set of documents of the TV-Anytime standard identifies multiple tasks involved in providing these services, distinct entities that can participate in their deployment and different elements of information that they need to exchange to carry on their functions.

The purpose of this chapter is to present a general overview of the architecture suggested by TV-Anytime: which processes should be conducted, what information is needed in each of them and who may be responsible for managing these mechanisms or generating the information. Later, in the following chapters, we will go into the details of those elements that we consider more interesting because of their novelty or because they play a role with specific and relevant features in this new environment of advanced audiovisual services.

Thus, this chapter includes an overview of the TV-Anytime standard: a summary of everything that will be explained in more detail in subsequent chapters. This overview is also meant to help assimilate some concepts presented in the intermediate chapters, which are closely related to others which will be formally defined in later chapters.

Functionally, it can be said that a broadcast system that deploys the services outlined by TV-Anytime can be divided into three main elements: a service provider, which provides the functions described in the standard; a transport provider, which carries the TV-Anytime contents and information to the client's home; and the user's receiver device (PDR), which interacts with the viewers, presents the services to them, requests and/or captures contents, stores them and finally reproduces them.

A. Gil Solla and R.G. Sotelo Bovino, *TV-Anytime*, X.media.publishing,
DOI 10.1007/978-3-642-36766-3_2, © Springer-Verlag Berlin Heidelberg 2013

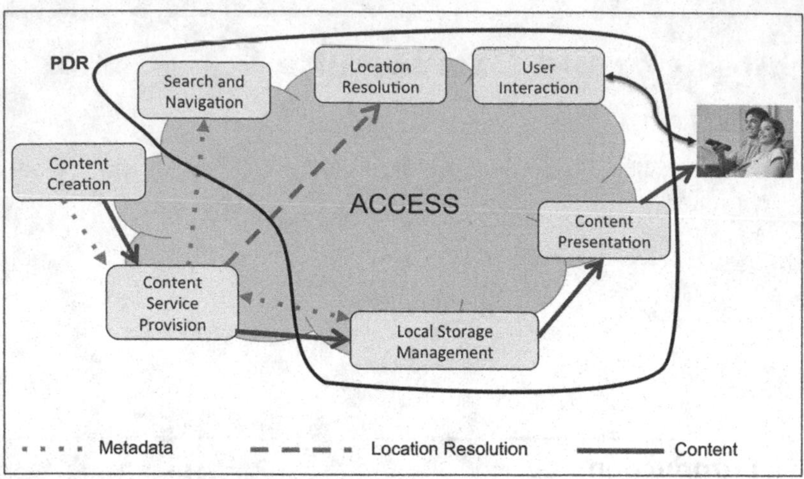

Fig. 2.1 Traditional broadcast model

These elements must be combined into a functional reference model or system architecture, where the various tasks to be performed by each entity are presented, identifying the possible function groupings that can be performed depending on who is in charge of solving each task. In the end, it is all about visualizing graphically the entities that generate and consume data (contents and metadata) and identifying the streams of information generated by each process, along with those responsible for their initiation.

2.1.1 Phase 1

A first model of this distribution of functions could be the one in Fig. 2.1, adapted from a similar one from (ETSI TS 102 822–2, 2007), which corresponds to a framework in which the connectivity requirements for the receiver are clearly minimum.

The model shown in Fig. 2.1 is therefore aimed at basically a traditional television environment, where most of the information gets to the receiver through the broadcast channel. The return channel is used only for very limited exchanges, primarily focused on the submission of information about the users (user preferences and consumption history) to providers, upon their consent, of course. This communication is illustrated by the bidirectional dotted green line between the two modules: local storage management and content service provision. Functionally speaking, it could be said that it is the model into which most of the capabilities and business models included in Phase 1 fit, which were summarized in the previous chapter.

Each of the boxes in Fig. 2.1 represents a function of a TV-Anytime system and can be implemented very differently depending on the interests of the manufacturer and the service provider, including the location of the hardware/software mechanisms that offer them. The various lines show the flow of information between each of the identified functions (contents, continuous blue lines; descriptions or auxiliary metadata, dotted green; and the signalling of location resolution, dashed red).

It can be seen in Fig. 2.1 that the stream of contents follows a traditional trajectory, typical of broadcast environments, from the creators of the contents to the users, through transport operators. Additionally, there is an associated flow of metadata that follows the same route and that at some points is unfolded to feed search and content location resolution services. This metadata is originally generated by the creator of the content, but it can be modified or expanded in the different stages of the route, for example, by the broadcaster or by services provided by third parties.

In this model, only three functions of the system are located outside the PDR: the creation of contents, which is done by movie studios, entertainment companies, organizers of sporting events, etc.; content provision services, offered by television broadcasters, for example; and the access mechanism, typically provided by cable, satellite or IPTV operators.

The remaining functions are implemented by the PDR. Although the user perceives that it is only a device to store and present contents, in this model the receiver also handles the various tasks involved in the processes of search and navigation among contents, resolution of their specific location, acquisition, rights management, etc.

All of this should help users with the tasks of searching, selecting, locating and acquiring all the contents which they are interested in, or even allow the system to do so on their behalf, guessing their interests. Most of these processes will be based on the existence of different metadata that accurately describe and characterize the contents: metadata provided by their creators, the operators that group them or even third-party services.

Searching for contents will be done using unique references to them, which will unambiguously identify them and will allow their location, for example, in a specific channel, date and time. It is precisely to this end that the metadata provided by the operator about the contents must include, in addition to their characterization, the necessary references for their unambiguous identification and the resolution information to enable their location and acquisition.

2.1.2 Phase 2

The business models covered in Phase 2 of TV-Anytime present as the main feature the requirement of full connectivity to the PDR. This frees the PDR from much of the abovementioned tasks and locates them in external services with greater resources. The functional model that could be considered in this case to implement TV-Anytime Phase 2 services is the one represented in Fig. 2.2, also from (ETSI TS 102 822–2, 2007), which, given the existence of a wide and permanent connectivity, could be called a "full interactive model".

Therefore, this new model supports (but does not require) the outsourcing of functions such as content search or location resolution after the corresponding

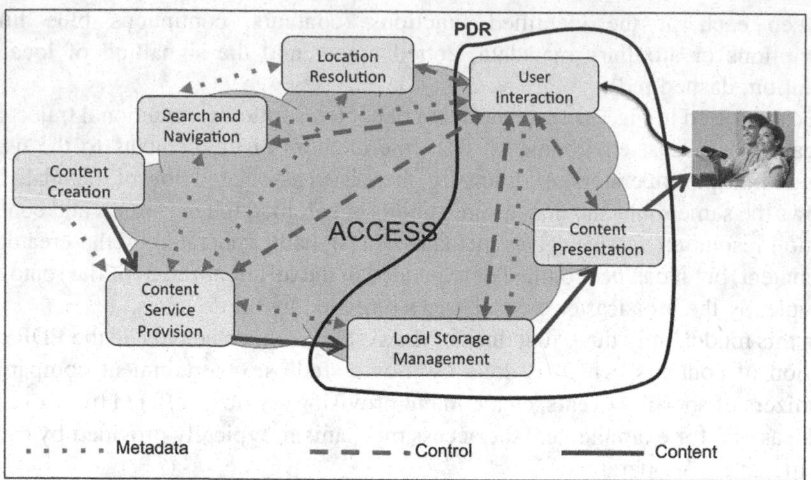

Fig. 2.2 Full interactive model

selection, which could be provided by third parties. It also expands the range of possible actors to carry out the other tasks, such as the creation of contents by the users themselves or the provision of services through Internet portals.

Figure 2.2 shows that although the content flow is still the same, both the streams of metadata and control signals are clearly enriched to reflect the exchange of information and commands between the software running on the PDR and the services provided by external agents.

Thus, we can see new lines of control between the "user interaction" module and some services now provided by external agents, such as those in charge of the search and navigation among contents or the content service provision. We can also notice the appearance of new lines of metadata transfer, both between the receiver and the new agents that provide outsourced services as well as among the latter.

In the following sections, we will examine the various elements required to implement the services presented in the previous chapter, focusing mainly on the mechanism to be able to unambiguously reference contents, the repertoire of metadata to describe them and the procedures for flexible and efficient transport to the receiver.

2.2 Content Reference IDentifier (CRID)

2.2.1 What Is a CRID?

As stated in the previous chapter, one of the basic elements required in the scenario detailed by TV-Anytime is the capacity to create unique references for every content, besides the specific information regarding their broadcast (such as channel, date and time) or the way to acquire it online (e.g. through a streaming service). This capacity of unambiguous identification combined with the ability to resolve that reference and obtain the specific location of a copy of that content would enable users to arrange recordings (acquisitions, in general) ignoring the details of the broadcast, not even knowing beforehand the length or the nature of what is to be recorded.

Let us imagine that the user sees the advertisement of a movie that will be aired soon, although at that time not even the operator knows the broadcast details yet. In order to enable the user to order the recording of the movie, the operator would only have to assign an unambiguous reference to it, which would be broadcast as metadata together with the advertisement. The PDR would have to monitor the reference, and once the operator decides and makes public the specific details of the broadcast, the PDR would be able to associate the reference to specific location data and schedule the recording.

Or it could happen that what is advertised is a series made up of various episodes which the operator wants to advertise immediately, even though it does not have yet any specific details about the episodes (they may not have been recorded yet, or the number of episodes may be even unknown). The operator would only have to assign a generic reference (group reference) to the series so the receiver would put it under watch. Once the operator had the information, it would reveal the list of episodes and provide a unique reference to each of the episodes, which would be monitored by the receiver. Finally, once knowing when and where the episodes will be broadcast, the operator would make public the necessary information to associate each of the references to the corresponding location data (e.g. channel, date and time). In other words, all the episodes of the series would be recorded requiring only minimum actions from the user: upon seeing an advertisement of the upcoming premiere of the series, he/she just needs to indicate to the PDR that he/she wants to record it. The rest of the process takes place without the user's intervention.

In TV-Anytime, this unambiguous reference to certain content is called CRID (*Content Reference IDentifier*) and allows differentiating the content identification (CRID) from the necessary information to find and acquire this content (locator). Each CRID can lead to one or multiple locators, which will represent different copies of the same content. Copies may or may not be identical, differing, for example, in the video signal resolution.

From a TV-Anytime-system perspective, a CRID is the result of a search and selection process and its syntax is the following:

```
crid://<authority>/<data>
```

The <*authority*> field represents the entity that created the CRID, and its format corresponds to that of a DNS mechanism identifier (IETF RFC 1591, 1994). The <*data*> field represents a chain of characters assigned by the authority itself. An example could be:

```
crid://www.C4.com/Lost/S1/E1
```

After the search and selection stage which concludes with a CRID, the resolution process may provide one or many CRIDs (e.g. if the original represents a group of contents) or directly one or various locators which contain the information to find and acquire the content. These locators are scarcely regulated in TV-Anytime, affecting only their format, which should follow the pattern:

Fig. 2.3 Example of a *RAR* table record

Field Name	Value
Authority name	C4.com
Resolution Provider	media3.com
URL	dvb://1.2ffe.4e7
Version number	6
Other	

<transport-mechanism>:<specific-data>

Regarding the first part, the only requirement is that there is a unique identifier for each transport mechanism. The format of the second part is specific for each transport mechanism, including the content's location and its temporal availability. The most frequently encountered situation is that of DVB locators to identify contents carried through the networks that adhere to the standard (ETSI TS 102 851, 2010), such as

dvb://112.4a2.5ec;2d22~20111012T220000Z–PT01H30M

for a television programme for which the channel, start time and duration are identified (as analysed in Chap. 3).

2.2.2 Resolution of a CRID

The CRID's resolution process involves the use of information contained in two tables. The first one is called *Resolving Authority Record* (*RAR*) and provides information regarding a set of authorities. Each record in the table contains information about a specific authority, for example the name of the provider of the resolution service that resolves that authority's CRIDs or the address to contact or listen to in order to get it.

A record from a *RAR* table is shown in Fig. 2.3. Here, an authority called "*C4.com*" is declared, whose resolution service provider is the entity named "*media3.com*", which provides resolution information through the transport stream identified by the URL "*dvb://1.2ffe.4e7*".

The second table mentioned above is the resolution table itself (named *ContentReferencingTable*) which, given a CRID of a programme, returns one or more locators through which that content can be acquired (or one or many new CRIDs, if the original CRID represented a grouping of contents).

In Listing 2.1, an example of the second table is given, in XML format, where two different sections are included (*<Result>* elements) with information describing each of the resolution cases[1]:

[1] Chapter 3 provides more details about some of the elements and attributes that may be included in this table.

```
1 <ContentReferencingTable version="1.0">
2   <Result CRID="crid://C4.com/Lost/S1/E1"
3           status="resolved" complete="true" acquire="any">
4     <LocationsResult>
5        <Locator>
6           dvb://1.4ee2.3f4;4f5~@2011-10-12T22:00:00.00+01:00/PT01H00M
7        </Locator>
8        <Locator>
9           dvb://1.4ee2.3f4;4f6~@2011-10-19T23:00:00.00+01:00/PT01H00M
10       </Locator>
11    </LocationsResult>
12  </Result>
13  <Result CRID="crid://C4.com/Lost/S1/E2"
14          status="resolved" complete="false" acquire="any">
15    <LocationsResult>
16       <Locator>
17          dvb://1.3de2.7c3;4f5~@2011-10-19T22:00:00.00+01:00/PT01H00M
18       </Locator>
19    </LocationsResult>
20  </Result>
21 </ContentReferencingTable>
```

Listing 2.1 Example of CRIDs resolution table

- The first case (line 2) declares how a CRID ("*crid://C4.com/Lost/S1/E1*") is resolved, corresponding to the series "*Lost*" (specifically, the first episode of the first season). The result of the resolution process is two DVB locators (the content of the two *<Locator>* elements within the *<LocationsResult>* element on lines 6 and 9) which tell us that the episode will air on channel "*1.4ee2.3f4*" on OCT/12/2011 at 10 p.m. and on OCT/19/2011 at 11 p.m.
- The second of the *<Result>* elements (line 13) resolves the CRID of the second episode of the first season providing a DVB locator (line 17) that informs the episode is going to air on OCT/19/2011 at 10 p.m. on channel "*1.3de2.7c3*".

Thus, combining the two tables (*RAR* and *ContentReferencingTable*), the process a receiver should follow to resolve a CRID can be derived as follows:

1. Through the authority included in the CRID, finding a *RAR* record that informs about it. For TV-Anytime, the procedure to send *RAR* records to the receiver depends on the platform, and its regulation corresponds to the platform itself.
2. Reading the information about the mechanism to obtain the resolution table in the *RAR* record.
3. Finally, making a query through that mechanism to obtain the *ContentReferencingTable* which includes the locators known to the CRID.

Chapter 3 will include an in-depth analysis of all of these issues: the necessary information structures (including the meaning of some attributes shown in Listing 2.1) and the resolution process. Two situations can be clearly distinguished there:

- The receiver is connected to a unidirectional network, so the query address specified in the *RAR* records must point somewhere within the transport streams received through the broadcast channel (or, at least, towards information located in a hypothetic local storage system), where the *ContentReferencingTable* should be found.

- The receiver is connected to a bidirectional network through which it can obtain external information. In this case, the receiver can start interactive queries with data servers which can be accessed through the network, resulting in greater flexibility to obtain different versions of the *ContentReferencingTable*, with more or less data according to the characteristics of the service accessed.

2.3 Metadata

Metadata basically consists of information about information, either to describe its features or structure, giving meaning to each part in order to make its appropriate processing easier, which is especially useful if this processing is to be carried out automatically by an intelligent agent.

In general, the most visible part of the metadata standardized in the TV-Anytime specifications consists of detailed characterizations or descriptions of audiovisual contents that users can access. These descriptions fulfil two goals: on the one hand, they provide viewers with elements to compare so that they can decide whether or not they are interested in viewing any given contents (or to work as indicators for the receiver's software, if it is intelligent recommendation mechanisms we are talking about); on the other hand, considering the operator, these descriptions work as a mechanism to advertise products and highlight their benefits to viewers. Overall, this is about luring the user towards contents, be it in a generic way or in a way customized for each viewer.

In addition, the TV-Anytime metadata repertoire also includes descriptive elements which have several aims, such as specifying possible content consumption models (so that the user can assess costs in each case), stating technical requirements the receiver must comply with in order to guarantee a correct display, or the thorough register of user preferences and their consumption history, with the purpose of facilitating the appropriate matching of users and contents by recommendation mechanisms.

In general, the metadata elements defined by TV-Anytime do not intend to specify all the possible ways in which service providers or operators may carry out their tasks but to provide a generic reference framework in which the different participants are free to define their operation rules according to their possibilities.

This metadata we are talking about may be originated in each stage of the distribution chain, from the creator of certain content to the viewer. In order to guarantee interoperability between such different participants, the chosen representation format is the XML metalanguage (W3C-XML, 2008), due to the many advantages related to its extensibility; its clear independence among documents, applications and platforms; its widely extended use; and the existence of a large amount of tools to facilitate its processing, efficient storage and simple query specification (XSL, XQL, etc.).

In order to state the specific XML language details through which metadata is structured, TV-Anytime adopts the DDL (*Description Definition Language*) (ISO/IEC 15938–2, 2001) created at the core of the MPEG-7 standard (ISO/IEC 15938–1, 2002) for a similar task: structuring and describing metadata about

```
1 <TVAMain xmlns="urn:tva:metadata:2007" version="03" xml:lang="en"
2          xmlns:mpeg7="urn:tva:mpeg7:schema:2005"
3          xmlns:xsi=http://www.w3.org/2001/XMLSchema-instance
4          xsi:schemaLocation=
5             "urn:tva:metadata:2007 schemas/tva_metadata_3-1_v141.xsd">
6    <CopyrightNotice> ... </CopyrightNotice>
7    <ProgramDescription>
8      <ProgramInformationTable> ... </ProgramInformationTable>
9      <GroupInformationTable>   ... </GroupInformationTable>
10     <ProgramLocationTable>    ... </ProgramLocationTable>
11     <ServiceInformationTable> ... </ServiceInformationTable>
12     <CreditsInformationTable> ... </CreditsInformationTable>
13     <ProgramReviewTable>      ... </ProgramReviewTable>
14     <PurchaseInformationTable>... </PurchaseInformationTable>
15   </ProgramDescription>
16   <UserDescription>
17     <UserPreferences> ... </UserPreferences>
18     <UsageHistory>    ... </UsageHistory>
19   </UserDescription>
20 </TVAMain>
```

Listing 2.2 Generic structure of a TV-Anytime document

Root Element "TVAMain"					
Cat1 Content Description Metadata	Cat2 Instance Description Metadata	Cat3 Consumer Metadata	Cat4 Segmentation Metadata	Cat5 Metadata Information Metadata	Cat6 Interstitial and Targeting Metadata

Fig. 2.4 TV-Anytime metadata categories

multimedia contents. This language gives syntax, structure and vocabulary to most of the descriptions which are necessary in TV-Anytime.

Listing 2.2 shows the generic structure of a typical document containing varied TV-Anytime information, all of which is organized under one main element or root called *<TVAMain>* (line 1).

In this listing two blocks can be clearly observed: one including the description of contents (the *<ProgramDescription>* element starting in line 7) and the other consisting of user descriptions (the *<UserDescription>* element in line 16). In most cases, information about programmes is structured in elements called "tables" (lines 8–14), many of which are optional (this is also the case with the content of each table, which is mostly optional).

Within a TV-Anytime document, the metadata is structured in several sections, mainly according to the kind of entity they describe and the viewpoint from which the description is made, especially conditioned by its objective or expected usefulness.

Figure 2.4 shows a chart that summarizes the main points of the defined metadata. It consists of six main categories, which include different descriptive elements, listed hierarchically under the root element *<TVAMain>*:

```
<ProgramInformationTable>
  <ProgramInformation programId="crid://C4.com/Lost/S1/E1">
    <BasicDescription>
      <Title type="main"> Pilot </Title>
      <Synopsis>
        The Oceanic Airlines Flight 815 suffered turbulence...
      </Synopsis>
      <Keyword> Lost </Keyword>
      <Keyword> Plane crash </Keyword>
      <Language type="original"> en </Language>
      <Genre href="urn:tva:metadata:cs:FormatCS:2007:3.5.7.3"
             type="main"/>
    </BasicDescription>
    <OtherIdentifier>
       urn:mpeg:mpeg21:diid:isan:29ef-94ba-53c4-3e7a-4ce8-e-5a45-98ecf
    </OtherIdentifier>
    <MemberOf crid="crid://C4.com/Lost/all" index="1"
              xsi:type="EpisodeOfType"/>
  </ProgramInformation>
</ProgramInformationTable>
```

Listing 2.3 Example of content description metadata

Cat1. Metadata describing in a generic way several content characteristics, normally unchanging, which are independent from any differences that may exist between the copies that the user can have access to

Cat2. Metadata describing specific content instances, with details, such as image format or price, characteristic to a specific copy the user can have access to

Cat3. Consumer descriptive metadata, with profile information (socio-demographic data, preferences, etc.), and content consumption history

Cat4. Segmentation metadata, with information about the different parts a given content may be divided into, as well as interest points within the content

Cat5. Metadata descriptive metadata (e.g. with information about the origin of the metadata)

Cat6. Metadata about the characteristics of commercial advertisements and content customization details, which can help to identify the most appropriate audience for them

2.3.1 Metadata Defined in Phase 1

In the documents standardized in Phase 1, the generic content description (Cat1) deals with the most traditional audiovisual formats, further including elements in tables to describe groups a given content can belong to, credit titles, reviews provided by critics or certain information to purchase it.

To illustrate this (Chap. 4 will go into further detail), Listing 2.3 shows an example of the kind of information about a programme that can be contained in the *<ProgramInformationTable>* element.

```
1  <ProgramLocationTable>
2      <BroadcastEvent serviceIDRef="C4100022311">
3        <Program crid="crid://C4.com/Lost/S1/E1"/>
4        <ProgramURL> dvb://1.4ee2.3f5/ </ProgramURL>
5        <PublishedStartTime> 2011-09-12T19:00:00 </PublishedStartTime>
6        <PublishedDuration> PT1H </PublishedDuration>
7        <Live value="false"/>
8        <Repeat value="true"/>
9        <FirstShowing value="false"/>
10       <LastShowing value="false"/>
11       <Free value="false"/>
12     </BroadcastEvent>
13 </ProgramLocationTable>
```

Listing 2.4 Example of instance description metadata

It is important to highlight the "*href*" attribute in the *<Genre>* element (line 11). It belongs to a type of value list known as *Classification Schemes*. These are groups of terms with predefined names, which help to characterize discretely the possible values of a given attribute, often arranging them in a hierarchical way. Several classification schemes have been defined in TV-Anytime in order to determine different value spaces applicable to the corresponding types of data. This mechanism (further dealt with in Chap. 4) provides a simple tool to compare contents by making it an obligation to describe them using a limited set of familiar terms.

A second descriptive point comprises the particular information that only affects a given content copy or instance (Cat2), which includes information quite specific like the format, quality, location data, available acquisition models and the reason for broadcast on that day (if there is one). This category also includes elements to describe the services (TV channels) available in the system.

Listing 2.4 shows an example of this kind of information, organized in the *<ProgramLocationTable>* element, which specifies a programme's broadcast data (line 3) in a given channel (line 2), including diverse information (lines 5–11) about the starting time and duration, if it is free, a replay, a live show, etc.

In any case, the information included in this structure about the broadcast of a programme is not aimed at aiding its acquisition (this is what the CRIDs resolution process is for) but to just inform the viewer about the broadcast schedule.

Thirdly, Phase 1 also includes metadata elements related to the viewer (Cat3), in order to be able to automatically identify the users to whom it would be appropriate to offer certain content, given the fact that they will be very likely to find it interesting. We are basically talking about the description of user preferences and their consumption history.

Listing 2.5 shows an example of such a user description, where preferences for news in English are specified in lines 8 and 9, as well as interest in comedies (line 12) rated by a well-known reviewer (line 13).

Lastly, an important element of the metadata defined in Phase 1 includes segmentation information (Cat4), which helps to identify time sequences within

```
<UserDescription>
  <UserPreferences>
    <mpeg7:UserIdentifier protected="true">
      <mpeg7:Name xml:lang="en"> John Smith </mpeg7:Name>
    </mpeg7:UserIdentifier>
    <mpeg7:FilteringAndSearchPreferences>
      <mpeg7:ClassificationPreferences preferenceValue="10">
        <mpeg7:Language> en </mpeg7:Language>
        <mpeg7:Genre href="urn:tva:metadata:cs:ContentCS:2011:3.1.1"/>
      </mpeg7:ClassificationPreferences>
      <mpeg7:ClassificationPreferences preferenceValue="12">
        <mpeg7:Genre href="urn:tva:metadata:ContentCS:2011:3.5.7"/>
        <mpeg7:Review>
          <mpeg7:Rating>
            <mpeg7:RatingValue> 7 </mpeg7:RatingValue>
            <mpeg7:RatingScheme best="10" worst="1"
                                style="higherBetter"/>
          </mpeg7:Rating>
          <mpeg7:Reviewer xsi:type="mpeg7:PersonType">
            <mpeg7:Name>
              <mpeg7:FamilyName> Doe </mpeg7:FamilyName>
              <mpeg7:GivenName> John < /mpeg7:GivenName>
            </mpeg7:Name>
          </mpeg7:Reviewer>
        </mpeg7:Review>
      </mpeg7:ClassificationPreferences>
    </mpeg7:FilteringAndSearchPreferences>
  </UserPreferences>
</UserDescription>
```

Listing 2.5 Example of user preferences

content or specific moments whose reference is interesting by virtue of some criteria. This makes it possible to specify the division of contents in different parts, whether organized or not, and to provide direct links to the most interesting parts, allowing for a personalized reproduction. This way, users may be offered the possibility to consume just part of the content, in any order, or even delegate the selection to intelligent agents that know their preferences.

All of these issues will be further dealt with in Chap. 4, which is specifically devoted to the description of the main core of descriptive metadata standardized in TV-Anytime Phase 1.

2.3.2 Metadata Defined in Phase 2

Phase 2 is thought to be an extension (mainly modular) of the specifications of Phase 1, and it also adds many new elements that mostly relate to the main idea of taking the traditional television model a step further. Although it is equally focused on the context of audiovisual contents, Phase 2 tries to keep in mind the repercussions and possibilities of a fully bidirectional context with the new digital distribution mechanisms that result from it.

As such an extension, a fundamental criterion was to keep the compatibility with everything that was standardized in Phase 1, so that it is not necessary to change the existing descriptions or tools to adapt to the guidelines of Phase 2. This second phase simply adds new descriptive resources and protocols for the representation and exchange of information to facilitate the deployment of certain types of services that had not been included in the previous phase.

The first element of this extension is the introduction of new types of data to describe contents and users, as well as the adoption of other types imported from the MPEG-21 standard (ISO/IEC 21000–2, 2005) to enable new functionalities. This includes the definition of new types of data to define new contents (games, applications, websites, etc.), or properties of these new contents that may have a special interpretation according to the context (e.g. in educational contexts), and, in general, any element that makes it possible to describe other data formats that can be associated with traditional audiovisual contents, with the purpose of providing more gratifying experiences.

Regarding descriptive metadata, Phase 2 introduces a series of new tools to promote the development of value-added services, among which we find:

- Tools to create groupings of several contents: traditional audiovisual contents, applications, games and websites. These elements are grouped in a package (*Packaging*, Cat1) in order to be consumed together, in a free or synchronized way or according to certain directives set up in the package, which can be fixed or depend on different criteria related to the device and/or the user. Chapter 6 will be devoted entirely to this topic.
- Information and procedures to estimate the suitability of each content for each user (*Targeting*, Cat6) in a way that new contents can be recommended and delivered automatically to users according to their profile (preferences, consumption history, receiver features, characteristics of the context where contents are consumed, etc.) or to make the search processes easier for viewers. This is dealt with in more depth in Chap. 5.
- A framework to process commercial advertisements (*Interstitials*, Cat6) and their real-time substitution (in live programmes or in reproductions of stored content) according to each viewer's particular criteria. This will also be dealt with in Chap. 5.
- A framework to include discount coupons or promotions (*Coupons*, Cat6) with available audiovisual contents (or announced products), indicate their existence and explain how to redeem them. This will also be dealt with in Chap. 5, where more details will be provided about this tool.

All of this translates into the definition of new metadata tables (or extensions of those defined in Phase 1) that are added to the different categories found in Fig. 2.4. In any case, as stated before, these new tables present a modular, incremental nature, which does not require in any case changes in the systems developed according to Phase 1.

2.4 Metadata Transport

As stated before, the specifications developed within TV-Anytime give a detailed description of the data structures that help implement unambiguous references to contents and to the metadata used to characterize them. However, the development of the services described in the introduction requires a whole series of procedures to send the information that TV-Anytime does not make reference to, which affect, for example, the effective transport both of the metadata and the contents and the indication to changes. Nonetheless, TV-Anytime does require certain functionalities of these mechanisms.

Although we will provide a more detailed analysis of this issue in Chap. 7, here is a summary of some interesting ideas to which TV-Anytime makes a contribution.

2.4.1 Requisites for Transport Mechanisms

The aim of TV-Anytime is to be completely independent from the transport mechanism used in the content delivery network. It is due to this that it does not regulate how the information must reach the receiver, which falls within the regulatory scope of the standards that each specific transport mechanism belongs to.

However, TV-Anytime does describe certain requisites demanded of the transport mechanism. In unidirectional environments, TV-Anytime determines that the underlying transport system must provide certain information to the upper-level services in charge of implementing the TV-Anytime functionalities. For instance:

- It must carry and deliver metadata in an asynchronous way, even when the submission is produced through several channels, which must be transparent to the applications receiving the metadata.
- It must provide a method to find out what kind of TV-Anytime metadata is available and how to get it. This includes both location resolution tables, presented in Sect. 2.2, and the descriptive metadata from Sect. 2.3.
- It must provide the locators of the concrete instances of broadcast contents.
- It must allow the cyclic transmission of TV-Anytime structures, with the frequencies the operator considers to be appropriate for each case.
- It must provide support for the selective update of the different metadata elements, without resulting in inconsistencies, even if some of them are lost.

The way each transport network makes available this information or manages to implement such processes is not relevant for TV-Anytime, being only important for the software executing on the equipment connected to such a network.

2.4.2 Segmentation and Delivery of TV-Anytime Information

In a unidirectional context, from the operator to the user, there is no return communication. Therefore, all the information, including metadata, is carried to the user through the broadcast channel, whichever it may be. This information can represent a significant amount of data, as sometimes descriptions spanning the programming of several channels over several days may be sent.

This is especially relevant in a context like the current one where receivers usually have a limited processing capacity, which makes managing this huge amount of data very difficult. On the other hand, this information must be cyclically

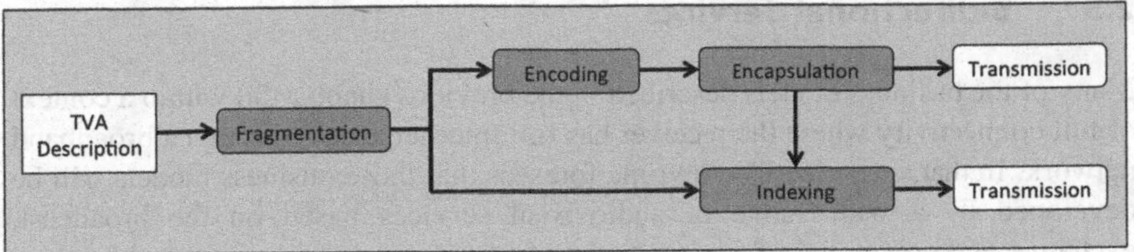

Fig. 2.5 Auxiliary procedures for information transport

repeated for it to be permanently accessible immediately after a receiver is connected. Therefore, the bandwidth assigned to metadata may be significant, requiring the usual trade-off between the cost of metadata transport and the minimum refresh rate established.

In order to deal with these matters, TV-Anytime defines a series of mechanisms to facilitate the submission and later processing of metadata describing contents. These tools are part of a set of processes, which can be seen in Fig. 2.5, where the intermediate steps are the only ones regulated by TV-Anytime.

Fragmentation is a procedure by which it is possible to break down a TV-Anytime document into a series of smaller self-contained and consistent units, called fragments. A fragment is the smallest part of a given description that can be delivered independently to a terminal and must be consistent in the following ways:

- It must be able to be updated independently from other fragments.
- Its processing must be independent from the order in which those fragments are received.
- Its decoding and aggregation must always lead to a valid description.

A series of fragments are defined in the standard, among which we may find *PersonName*, *ProgramInformation*, *GroupInformation*, *PurchaseInformation* and *Review*. In all cases, the names are clear enough regarding the content: they carry the structure of the homonymous information.

The second process, called *Encoding*, allows the efficient delivery (in terms of bandwidth) of metadata in unidirectional contexts. It consists, basically, of the delivery of metadata in a binary format, for which the BiM method (ISO/IEC 15938–1, 2002) has been chosen, as defined in MPEG-7, mainly due to interoperability issues.

The different encoded fragments are carried (individually or in grouped form) in a structure called "container", especially designed in the TV-Anytime standard.

Thirdly, *Encapsulation* is a mechanism that makes it possible to know the identifiers and version numbers of the fragments carried by a container without the need to open and analyse them individually. This declaration of identifiers and version numbers allows the receiver to make a simple query to monitor the updates made to the container's payload.

Lastly, *Indexing* is a mechanism aimed at enabling the processing of large fragment streams in receivers with lower resources. Receiving the right indexing information enables them to locate the desired information easily within descriptions of great size.

2.5 Bidirectional Services

Many of the business models described in the previous chapter fall within a context of full connectivity where the receiver has full Internet access through a broadband network. In that scenario, TV-Anytime foresees that those business models will be developed by a wide range of audiovisual services based on the broadcast, exchange and processing of various types of metadata, possibly provided by third parties.

Also, this bidirectional connectivity opens up possibilities for different types of remote access to our devices (or external devices offered by service providers), facilitating their consultation and programming regardless of where we are.

TV-Anytime also addresses the regulation of certain aspects of these communication processes in order to facilitate interoperability between different devices, belonging to users and providers.

2.5.1 Metadata Provision Services

To begin with, Phase 1 of TV-Anytime already considered the possible existence of third-party metadata provision services, capable of collecting and adding information from multiple sources and processing it in the interests of users. This metadata could certainly be more abundant and richer than the one received through the broadcast channel or simply be preferred by the viewer because he/she trusts the provider.

Users, in turn, would be able to connect to those services and request the raw metadata available or make queries about this information, for example, by asking about contents that meet certain requirements or requesting the content location information that they cannot find on their own.

In this regard, TV-Anytime's regulation consists both in standardizing procedures to discover those services (e.g. through mechanisms typical of the Internet such as UDDI (UDDI, 2005)) and in specifying the set of operations that may be requested to these services (and their corresponding answers). Basically, this set of operations allows:

- Requesting information from a server. The user will be able to send a CRID, requesting descriptive metadata about it, or location information to be able to acquire it. But the set of operations will also permit the user to identify certain audiovisual attributes in the request and attach to them certain values to receive information about contents that meet those requirements.
- Sending user profile information to a server or requesting the elimination of previously submitted data. This would be about personal information or about the user's consumption history, which is aimed at helping the provider to offer customized services.

TV-Anytime foresees as well that it will be quite natural to have some heterogeneity in the capabilities of deployed services; so it also regulates a set of query operations so that customers can find out the characteristics of the service offered by a given provider and build more precise requests according to the service's features.

Finally, TV-Anytime also pays attention to the communication protocols used to carry requests and responses, which basically consist of the familiar combination of HTTP and SOAP (W3C-SOAP, 2007) for the exchange of messages in standard Web services deployed in the Internet.

Phase 2 of TV-Anytime went even a step further, recognizing the interest in exchanging personal profiles even among providers (with the necessary permission of the parties involved, of course) in order to enhance the provision of customized services to users. To this end, this second phase proceeded to standardize additional operations (and responses) that would help to initialize, modify or even eliminate the information from these profiles stored in the service providers' servers.

Chapter 8 will deal with these issues in more depth.

2.5.2 Remote Programming

The second aspect to which special attention is paid in TV-Anytime regarding the capacity to communicate bidirectionally is the remote access to terminals, that is the regulation of the mechanisms by virtue of which a user can consult and instruct a device remotely to perform the operations it was designed for.

In this case, there are three mechanisms for which TV-Anytime provides some kind of standardization, whose functionality we will present next and which will be further described in Chap. 9.

2.5.2.1 Data Exchange Format

The first contribution in this sense is rather indirect and related to the facilities provided for the encapsulation and exchange of information with entities that are not compatible with the TV-Anytime specifications. The goal in this case is to facilitate the interconnection of TV-Anytime services with others foreign to this world, to make the most of their capabilities in order to simplify their combined use by the user.

In this regard, a packaging format of TV-Anytime data (descriptive or location resolution information) is defined within the standard so that services outside TV-Anytime can send information to others that do follow these guidelines. This format contains fields to identify the content, the corresponding tables to structure its description, the *ContentReferencingTable* to attach location resolution information or even the URL of a Web service to get more information.

Additionally, and here lies the connection with remote programming, the information sent may be accompanied by instructions to specify what should be done with the data received, for example recording the contents described in such information, reminding the user of their broadcast or just recommending them to the user.

2.5.2.2 Remote Programming of a PDR

The second aspect of this set of facilities to allow the remote control of a device focused on enabling a procedure to allow the remote programming of the user's PDR. This would allow us to order recordings at any time and place, for example through the office computer or through a *smartphone*.

To this end, the TV-Anytime standard establishes a procedure through an email service, that is the user would only have to send an email to the receiver indicating which contents should be recorded. This simple procedure could even be used so that external service providers could take care of the task, ordering recordings of the programmes that they believe may be of interest to the user based on their profile and consumption history.

2.5.2.3 Remote Programming of an NDR

Finally, the most complex case considered by TV-Anytime in this section is the remote programming of an NDR (*Network Digital Recorder*), a device outside the user's home, possibly owned by a service provider, which can be used by subscribers to request recordings when it is impossible to do so in their PDR. The reasons may be very different, from a lack of space in the device to an impossibility to access the source of the content or a need for simultaneous recordings that the PDR cannot do.

The standardized procedure not only allows the remote programming of recordings (and the subsequent transfer to another device belonging to the user) but also considers the consultation or cancellation of previously submitted orders. To this end, TV-Anytime standardizes the formats of the operations to be sent in each case, including fields to identify contents and users, protocols used for the later transfer of contents and possible changes in content format.

As in the case of the standardization of access to metadata provision services described above (Sect. 2.5.1), the possible responses to each operation are also subject to standardization as well as the transport protocols for messages and certain additional operations so that customers can check the capabilities of each service, thus being sure that the requested operations can be performed by the service provider.

2.6 An Illustrative Example

To end this chapter, we are going to provide a broad outline of a service that implements a simple feature of TV-Anytime, one of the most basic described so far, showing the data elements involved and the sequence of processes that take place.

The different stages taking place during the deployment in this use case perfectly fit into a generic sequence that characterizes the life cycle of a TV-Anytime service, which is shown in Fig. 2.6.

This life cycle comprises all possible stages: the creation of the service, its publication by the operator, the viewer's search, the content selection among the

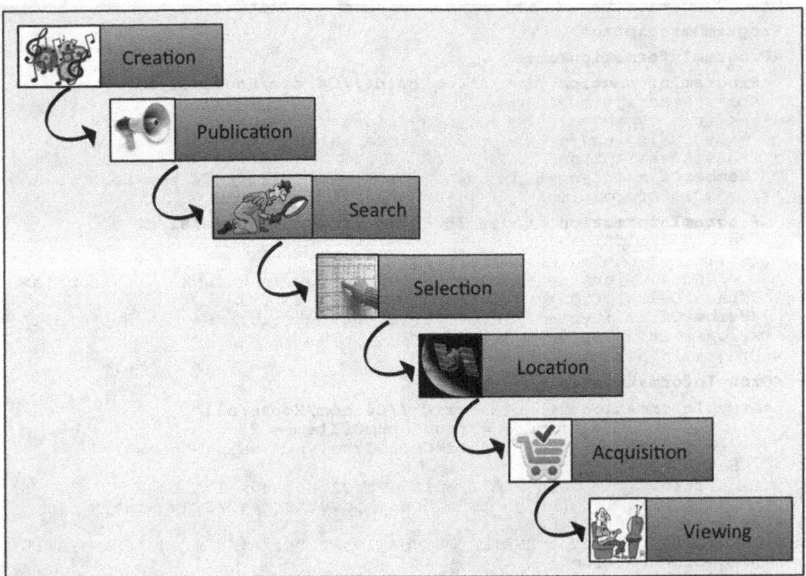

Fig. 2.6 Life cycle of a TV-Anytime service

system's recommendations, the contents' location by the PDR, the later acquisition of the content and the final reproduction by the viewer.

The example shown is relatively simple, though it is useful to illustrate how a service with these properties is implemented within a TV-Anytime environment. Its functionality basically consists in that a user can order the recording of all the episodes of a series from a simple advertisement.

As a starting point, we will assume that a content provider (in this case, channel *C4*) holds the rights to broadcast a series, such as *House M.D.*, made up of several episodes of the first season (we will suppose there are only two to limit the length of XML descriptions).

First of all, the service provider should publish the metadata that advertises the series to viewers, be it their own or received from the content creator. For example, part of this metadata could be the one shown in Listing 2.6.

The listing shows the description of the series in the *<ProgramDescription>* element (line 1). In this case, it is content description metadata, which specifies the creation of a CRID ("*crid://C4.com/House/all*") to represent the *House M.D* series as a whole and two additional CRIDs ("*crid://C4.com/House/S1/E1*" and "*crid://C4.com/House/S1/E2*") to identify each of the two episodes, respectively.

Inside the *<ProgramDescription>* root element, you can see a *<ProgramInformationTable>* element (line 2) that, in turn, contains two *<ProgramInformation>* elements (lines 3 and 10). Each of them describes an episode, giving it at the time a single CRID (lines 3 and 10) and stating its belonging to a group (the series) by means of the *<MemberOf>* elements in lines 8 and 15.

```
1 <ProgramDescription>
2  <ProgramInformationTable>
3   <ProgramInformation programId="crid://C4.com/House/S1/E1">
4    <BasicDescription>
5      <Title type="main"> Everybody lies… </Title>
6      <Synopsis length="short"> A kindergarten teacher… </Synopsis>
7    </BasicDescription>
8    <MemberOf xsi:type="EpisodeOfType" crid="crid://C4.com/House/all"/>
9   </ProgramInformation>
10  <ProgramInformation programId="crid://C4.com/House/S1/E2">
11   <BasicDescription>
12     <Title type="main"> Paternity </Title>
13     <Synopsis length="short"> A teenage boy is struck … </Synopsis>
14   </BasicDescription>
15   <MemberOf xsi:type="EpisodeOfType" crid="crid://C4.com/House/all"/>
16  </ProgramInformation>
17 </ProgramInformationTable>
18 <GroupInformationTable>
19  <GroupInformation groupId="crid://C4.com/House/all"
20                    ordered="true" numOfItems="2">
21    <GroupType xsi:type="ProgramGroupTypeType" value="show"/>
22    <BasicDescription>
23      <Title type="main"> All episodes of House </Title>
24      <Synopsis length="short"> House adventures </Synopsis>
25    </BasicDescription>
26    <MemberOf xsi:type="MemberOfType" crid="crid://C4.com/drama/all"/>
27  </GroupInformation>
28 </GroupInformationTable>
29 </ProgramDescription>
```

Listing 2.6 Descriptive metadata for the series *House*

After this, we can see a *<GroupInformationTable>* element (line 18) containing a *<GroupInformation>* element (line 19) that describes the group composed of all the episodes of the series (two, as declared in line 20) and assigns it the group CRID (line 19).

It is also possible that the operator has certain additional information about the episodes, such as specific details regarding their broadcast. In this case, we would be referring to instance description metadata, which would be structured and sent within a *<ProgramLocationTable>* element.

It could be the case, for example, of the metadata in Listing 2.7, which contains a piece of the information about the broadcast scheduled by that channel on a specific day. In particular, it only shows the fragment where the broadcast of the first episode of the series is announced.

In this listing, all information is structured around one element named *<Schedule>* (line 2), which comprises information about several programmes (each of them in a *<ScheduleEvent>* element, in line 4) to be broadcast on a specific channel ("*serviceIDRef*" attribute, in line 2) throughout a certain period of time ("*start*" and "*end*" attributes, in line 3). In this case, given that the fragment only informs about one programme, only one *<ScheduleEvent>* element appears.

The *<ScheduleEvent>* element provides some details about the broadcast of the first episode, for example the identification of the episode, in line 5; the channel and programme location within the DVB transport stream (*<ProgramURL>* element, line 6); a compilation of certain details of the copy of the programme to be

```
1 <ProgramLocationTable>
2   <Schedule serviceIDRef="Ch4"
3             start="2011-10-12T00:00:00Z" end="2011-10-12T23:59:59Z">
4     <ScheduleEvent>
5       <Program crid="crid://C4.com/House/S1/E1"/>
6       <ProgramURL>
7         dvb://1.4ee2.3f4;3ef@2011-10-12T21:59:59Z/PT01H00M
8       </ProgramURL>
9       <InstanceDescription>
10        <AVAttributes>
11          <VideoAttributes>
12            <Coding
13              href="urn:mpeg:mpeg7:cs:VisualCodingFormatCS:2001:3.1">
14                <Name lang="en"> MPEG-4 Visual Simple Profile </Name>
15            </Coding>
16            <FrameRate> 30/1.001 </FrameRate>
17          </VideoAttributes>
18        </AVAttributes>
19      </InstanceDescription>
20      <PublishedStartTime> 2011-10-12T22:00Z </PublishedStartTime>
21      <PublishedDuration> PT01H00M00S </PublishedDuration>
22      <FirstShowing value="true"/>
23    </ScheduleEvent>
24  </Schedule>
25 </ProgramLocationTable>
```

Listing 2.7 Metadata about the broadcast of the first episode

broadcast (*<InstanceDescription>* element, line 9); the episode's estimated date and time of broadcast (*<PublishedStartTime>* element, line 20); its estimated length (*<PublishedDuration>* element, line 21); or if the episode is to be broadcast for the first time (*<FirstShowing>* element, line 22).

The *<InstanceDescription>* element only contains in this case certain information about the technical attributes of the content's image (*<VideoAttributes>* element, line 11). This information could be broader, covering many more parameters of that signal, as well as audio signals, and even include information about the consumption models and prices of the content, in case it is not available for free.

This time information in no event should be used as a means to acquire the content. In order to do that, the content's CRID must be resolved to a locator using the corresponding location resolution service. The purpose of the metadata is merely informative, for example, so that the PDR can show an EPG with the information to the viewer or so that the receiver can dismiss the contents that it cannot reproduce correctly.

According to the stages of the life cycle shown in Fig. 2.6, we now assume the information reaches a user, for example, because the operator airs an advertisement about the upcoming broadcast of the series (accompanied with the metadata). Or the user may start a content search in his/her receiver by entering the character string "House M.D". In that case, the search system, upon comparing the information

```
1 <ContentReferencingTable>
2   <Result CRID="crid://C4.com/House/all" status="resolved"
3                                           complete="true" acquire="all">
4     <CRIDResult>
5        <Crid> crid://C4.com/House/S1/E1 </Crid>
6        <Crid> crid://C4.com/House/S1/E2 </Crid>
7     </CRIDResult>
8   </Result>
9   <Result CRID="crid://C4.com/House/S1/E1" status="resolved"
10                                          complete="true" acquire="all">
11    <LocationsResult>
12      <Locator>
13           dvb://1.4ee2.3f4;33f~@2011-10-12T23:00:00.00+01:00/PT01H00M
14      </Locator>
15    </LocationsResult>
16  </Result>
17  <Result CRID="crid://C4.com/House/S1/E2"
18          status="cannot yet resolve" complete="true" acquire="all"
19          reresolveDate="2011-10-07T12:00:00.00+01:00">
20  </Result>
21 </ContentReferencingTable>
```

Listing 2.8 Location resolution information

provided by the user with the available metadata, will display the information found about the series (based on the metadata put forward so far).

In any case, we will assume that the information is appealing to the user, and so he/she orders the recording of the whole series through the corresponding user interface.

The user's recording order makes the content location system to initiate a resolution process to which the general CRID of the whole series ("*crid://C4.com/House/all*") is provided as an initial input.

This resolution process will be carried out taking the information provided by the operator as the starting point. Searching the existing *RAR* registers for the "*C4.com*" authority, the receiver will find the register shown in Fig. 2.3, which indicates that, for that authority, the stream "*dvb:///1.2ffe.4e7*" must be read in order to find the resolution table mentioned in Sect. 2.2.2 (the so-called *ContentReferencingTable*).

The *ContentReferencingTable* the receiver would finally obtain at the time of reading the stream could be similar to what is shown in Listing 2.8.

The receiver's location resolution system will find, by consulting the table above, a record corresponding to the general CRID of the series (line 2) from which it will get the CRIDs of the two episodes that constitute the series (lines 5 and 6). The receiver's location resolution system will get a locator for each specific episode from each episode's CRID that it is supposed to include the necessary information to identify the channel, date, starting time and length.

Searching the CRID of the first episode within the table, we find it in the *<Result>* element in line 9. In it, we can observe that it is associated with a fully specified locator that includes the channel, date, time and length information (line 13).

On the contrary, the CRID's resolution for the second episode provides an indication that the corresponding information is unknown yet (the "*cannot yet*

```
1 <UserDescription>
2  <UsageHistory id="usage-history" allowCollection="true">
3   <mpeg7:UserIdentifier protected="true">
4     <mpeg7:Name xml:lang="en"> Peter Salmeron </mpeg7:Name>
5   </mpeg7:UserIdentifier>
6   <mpeg7:UserActionHistory id="useraction-history" protected="false">
7    <mpeg7:ObservationPeriod>
8      <mpeg7:TimePoint>2011-10-12T20:00</mpeg7:TimePoint>
9      <mpeg7:Duration>PT6H</mpeg7:Duration>
10   </mpeg7:ObservationPeriod>
11   <mpeg7:UserActionList id="ua-list"
12                         numOfInstances="1" totalDuration="PT2H30M">
13     <mpeg7:ActionType
14                    href="urn:tva:metadata:cs:ActionTypeCS:2004:1.3">
15       <mpeg7:Name> Record </mpeg7:Name>
16     </mpeg7:ActionType>
17     <mpeg7:UserAction>
18      <mpeg7:ActionTime>
19       <mpeg7:MediaTime>
20        <mpeg7:MediaTimePoint> 2011-10-02T23:00</mpeg7:MediaTimePoint>
21        <mpeg7:MediaDuration> PT1H </mpeg7:MediaDuration>
22       </mpeg7:MediaTime>
23      </mpeg7:ActionTime>
24      <mpeg7:ProgramIdentifier organization="TVAF" type="CRID">
25           crid://C4.com/House/S1/E1
26      </mpeg7:ProgramIdentifier>
27     </mpeg7:UserAction>
28   </mpeg7:UserActionList>
29  </mpeg7:UserActionHistory>
30  </UsageHistory>
31 </UserDescription>
```

Listing 2.9 Information added to the user's history

resolve" that can be observed as the value of the *status* attribute of the third *<Result>* element in lines 17 and 18). Together with that indication, the receiver is informed of a re-resolution date when it must repeat the query to obtain the desired information (line 19). At that time, the receiver will restart the resolution process of the second episode.

When the time indicated in the locator for the first episode comes, the PDR will tune in the specified channel and record the episode.

According to the settings, the PDR may be programmed to record the user's activity. In that case, it will create a description of his/her actions (record the first episode of *House M.D*) and add it to the user's profile, specifically to the section that records the user's usage history.

That description, for example, may be similar to the one in Listing 2.9. We can see there a brief history record (the *<UsageHistory>* element in line 2) of a user called Peter Salmeron (the *<UserIdentifier>* element in lines 3 and 4).

This history includes the actions performed during a certain observation period (line 7). Among these actions, there is one of the "record" type (lines 13, 14 and 15). The *<UserAction>* element in line 17 has the descriptive information of this action, including the instant (line 20) and length (line 21), as well as the identifier of the content that was the object of the recording (the CRID of the first episode of *House M.D* in line 25).

```
1 POST /tva/remote-service HTTP/1.0
2 Host: www.servprovider.com
3 Content-Type: text/xml; charset="utf-8"
4 Content-Length: nnnn
5 SOAPAction: "control_NDR"

6 <?xml version="1.0" encoding="UTF-8"?>
7   <Envelope xmlns="http://schemas.xmlsoap.org/soap/envelope/">
8     <Body>
9       <ndr:Control_NDR xmlns:ndr="urn:tva:ndr:2010"
10                       xmlns:tva="urn:tva:metadata:2010"
11                       xmlns:xsi="http://www.w3.org/2001/XMLSchema-instance"
12                       xsi:schemaLocation="urn:tva:ndr:2010 tva_ndr_9_v141.xsd">
13          <RecordRequest>
14            <SubscriptionId> 3456-4567-5677-4321 </SubscriptionId>
15            <ContentId CRID="CRID://C4.com/House/S1/E1"/>
16            <Locator> dvb://1.4ee2.3f4;33f </Locator>
17          </RecordRequest>
18        </ndr:Control_NDR>
19      </Body>
20  </Envelope>
```

Listing 2.10 HTTP message ordering a recording operation

However, in order to exemplify other types of functionalities enabled by the standard, let us suppose that, soon before the broadcast of the first episode, the user (alerted perhaps by the receiver) realizes that the antenna signal, through which he receives the broadcast channel with the programme, is gone. Faced with the difficulty, the user decides to make use of another functionality provided by a service developed within the TV-Anytime standard: request the recording of that episode to an NDR (*Network Digital Recorder*), a device belonging to an external service provider with whom he/she has previously hired such functionality.

To this end, the user only has to turn on the corresponding option in his/her receiver, which will send through the return channel the HTTP message shown in Listing 2.10 to that provider's server.

In that request, properly wrapped within a SOAP message, a *<Control_NDR>* element (line 9) can be found, enclosing the operation requested of the server. This operation is represented by the *<RecordRequest>* element (line 13), used to send the user's identification (line 14), the content to be recorded (line 15) and the channel that broadcasts this content (line 16).

After the recording, the user will be able to order his/her receiver to communicate with the NDR again and download the recorded content to the user's device.

As a final illustration of the stages that take place in the development of the service, Fig. 2.7 (taken from (ETSI TS 102 822–2, 2007)) shows a chart with the different participating entities and the time sequence followed by the information streams that they exchange.

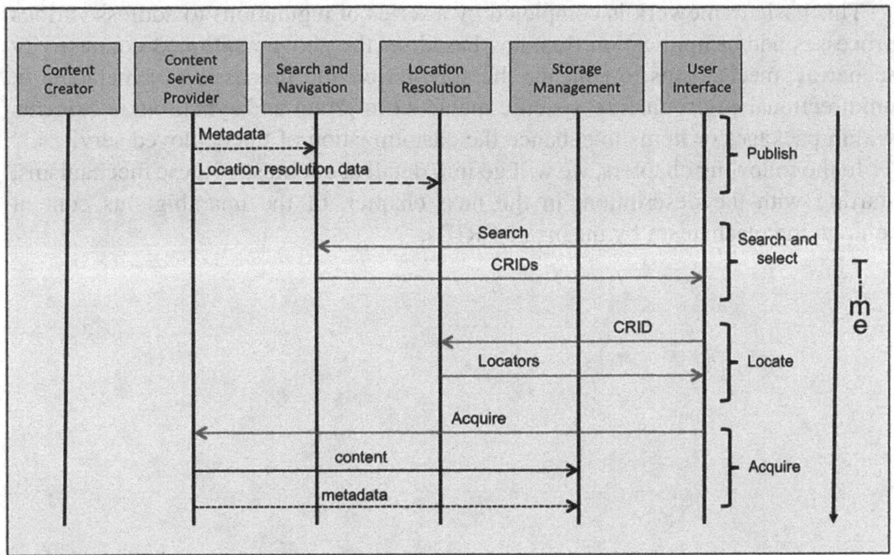

Fig. 2.7 Stages of service evolution

2.7 Summary

In this chapter, we have presented an overview of the general architecture of the TV-Anytime standard, briefly describing its capabilities and mechanisms. This has allowed us to get an overall idea of the scenario where the standard plays its role, the objectives pursued and the kind of means used to achieve them.

To that aim, we have seen that TV-Anytime is based on two main tools:

- First, an unambiguous content reference mechanism to easily identify programmes without relying on no exclusive characteristics like their title. This mechanism is also aimed at making generic allusions to contents, regardless of the specific copies of each programme. All of this is complemented with resolution mechanisms to get the location of each copy from those references.
- Second, an extensive repertoire of metadata to describe contents with great detail, characterizing and classifying them in several dimensions. Additionally, a similar mechanism to record the preferences and historical consumption of viewers opens the door to the development of matching algorithms that form the basis of a more personalized television.

For the implementation of these tools, TV-Anytime identifies, generally speaking, two broad scenarios: a unidirectional context, where the receiver can only receive information through a broadcast channel, and a fully bidirectional one, where the receiver has the ability to connect at high speed with external servers to exchange information.

This basic framework is completed by a series of regulations to address various processes and/or application domains based on the abovementioned connectivity scenarios: mechanisms to enhance the submission and processing of metadata in unidirectional environments, specific metadata to group and synchronize contents within packages or items to enhance the customization of the deployed services.

In the following chapters, we will go into detail about most of these mechanisms, starting with the description, in the next chapter, of the unambiguous content referencing mechanism by means of CRIDs.

Content Reference IDentifier (CRID) 3

3.1 Introduction

3.1.1 Referencing Contents Unambiguously

As stated in the previous chapter, the concept of CRID is an element of prime importance in the TV-Anytime universe we are describing. In order to implement services with a high added value such as those presented in Chap. 1, it is vital to be able to reference contents unambiguously, regardless of their location, that is without knowing specific broadcast information (time, date and channel) or how to obtain them through a network, for instance, by means of a streaming service or by downloading a file from an Internet server.

Evidently, the receiver must be able to resolve these unambiguous references, that is translate them into specific data that will allow it, when the time comes, to obtain the location of that content in order to acquire it (limiting the user's intervention to a hypothetical selection among similar choices).

This would make it possible for recording processes (i.e. content-acquisition processes in general) to take place without knowing that information and even without knowing beforehand the duration or nature of the content to be recorded. Several scenarios can be pictured in which this capacity becomes vital to provide advanced features such as those that the standard intends to promote:

- The user sees the advertisement of a film that will air soon. The existence of a reference for that film would allow the user to schedule its recording immediately, even if the operator is still unaware of the broadcast information (such as time, date and channel). To achieve this, the operator would simply have to assign an unambiguous reference that would be broadcast as metadata along with the advertisement. The PDR would put this reference under watch. Once the operator has decided the specific broadcast information for the film, it would make it public and this would allow the PDR to resolve the reference into specific location information and schedule the recording.

A. Gil Solla and R.G. Sotelo Bovino, *TV-Anytime*, X.media.publishing,
DOI 10.1007/978-3-642-36766-3_3,

- The user sees the advertisement of a TV series that will air soon (the date has not been determined yet) and wants the receiver to record every episode. In this case, it is even possible that the operator is unaware of the specific number of episodes to air (maybe they have not even been filmed yet), but it wishes to advertise it as soon as possible. The operator would only have to assign a generic (group) reference to the series, and the receiver would put it under watch. Once the information was available, the operator would make public the specific episode list for the series, providing unambiguous references for each of them. These references would then be under the receiver's watch. Finally, once it was known when and where the episodes air, the operator would make public the necessary information to resolve each of those references into the corresponding location information (such as time, date and channel, which may vary from episode to episode).
- The operator could be airing music videos of different genres, without the complete composition ever being known, given the fact that the selection is made on the way, day by day, while the programme lasts. In order for the user to secure the recording of videos of a given genre, the operator would only have to assign a group reference to that genre. The user would then order the receiver to record all contents that are described as belonging to that group. In this case, at no time does the operator make public a list of references or any location information; conversely, it is an ongoing dynamic process in which the receiver will be constantly monitoring the contents looking for those that belong to the group the user is interested in.

That is, the user could secure the recording of contents with little action on his part: upon seeing an advertisement for the contents, he/she would only have to indicate to the PDR that he/she wants the contents recorded. The rest of the process will be carried out with no user intervention, and he/she can just relax and let the PDR do the work.

The purpose of this chapter is, precisely, to present the way TV-Anytime defines to identify contents regardless of their location or availability, find out what the location information necessary for their due acquisition consists of and, finally, give details about the location resolution process, by means of which it is possible to find out the necessary information to acquire a given content from its reference.

3.1.2 CRID

In the TV-Anytime standard, this unambiguous reference to a given content is called CRID (*Content Reference IDentifier*), and it allows for the separation between the reference to a given content (the CRID) and the necessary information to acquire it, which is called a "locator". This separation into two information elements allows a one-to-many association relation between CRIDs and locators, that is each CRID may lead to one or more locators which will represent different copies of the same content. They may be identical copies that air on different channels and dates or cost different prices. They may also be distinct copies with different technical parameters such as format or quality.

It may also be the case that the resolution process of a CRID provides another CRID as a result (e.g. its reference in a different network, where it has an alternative identifier assigned by a different operator) or a set of CRIDs (for instance, if the original CRID represents a TV series, in which case the resolution process would result in the list of CRIDs representing each episode).

From the above it is obvious, provided that a given content can belong to many groups (each possibly defined by distinctive qualities), that many CRIDs can lead to the same content, even within the scope of the same authority that created the CRID. In other words, several CRIDs may be resolved into the same locator.

From the perspective of a TV-Anytime system, a CRID is the result of a search and selection process, in which the user ends up choosing the content, of which only a reference (the CRID) is known. Then, the resolution process starts (see Fig. 3.1), which finishes when the receiver has gathered all the necessary information to acquire the content (i.e. a locator). Therefore, the resolution process itself involves the central part of Fig. 3.1, excluding both the content search and acquisition processes.

In this figure, it can be seen that the resolution process receives a CRID as input and may result in one or many CRIDs (e.g. if the original CRID represents a content group) or one or several locators, each of which includes the necessary information to obtain a specific copy of the content.

If several CRIDs are obtained, these would be sent back to the content selection process so that one can be chosen, which would be returned to the resolution process. If several locators are returned, one of them would be chosen to acquire the content according to the service's setup criteria.

As suggested in Fig. 3.1, this location resolution process can be autonomous or involve some interaction with the user or a receiver agent, for example, to choose among alternatives or sub-elements represented by several CRIDs or locators (choosing broadcast time, choosing among different qualities or different costs, etc.).

3.1.3 References Versus Identifiers

It is important to clarify that a CRID (a reference) is not exactly a universal, unique and exclusive identifier for a given content.

A CRID is a code designed to make it easier to locate a given content, meaning it contains or leads to the necessary information for the user to acquire the content once it has been chosen. A CRID is closely related to the authority that creates it, to the resolution service provider and to the content provider in such a way that the same content may have different CRIDs depending on the field in which they are used (e.g. a different CRID for each television operator that has the rights to air the content).

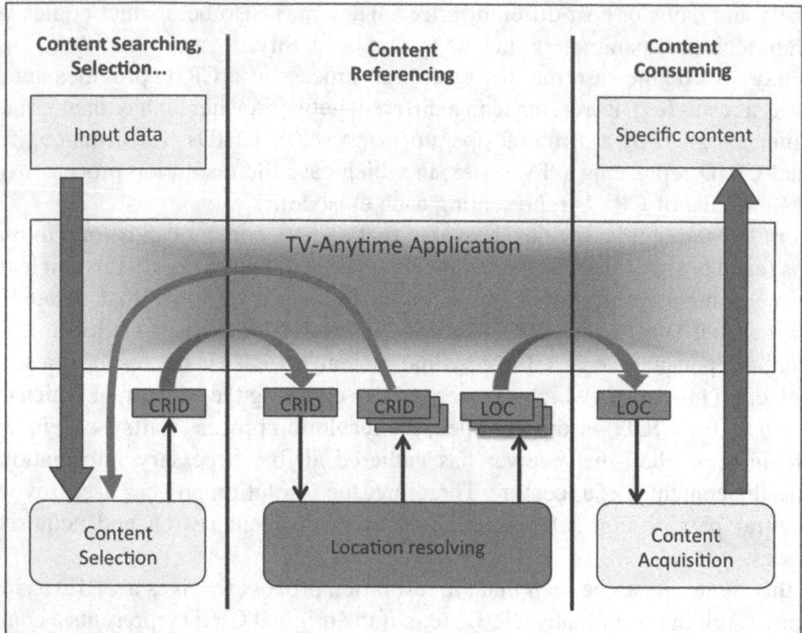

Fig. 3.1 Location resolution process

On the other hand, the identifier is a unique key which is normally assigned after the content is created so that it goes with it all the time, representing it. From this viewpoint, the identifier must be the same for a given content, regardless of the operator, aggregator or third parties involved in the commercialization. This mechanism would call for a central and global identifier resolution service aware of all the copies of the content, which would be especially difficult to agree upon and implement among all the participants in this industry.

A model based on references such as the one defined in TV-Anytime allows each entity to manage, reference and resolve the location of its contents autonomously, thus enabling the availability of the content catalogue of each operator immediately, with no business-to-business agreements.

3.1.4 Roles in the Creation and Resolution of CRIDs

As stated before, the creator of a CRID is called an *authority*, and it is the entity in charge of making sure there are no ambiguities within its resolution scope.

For all practical purposes, the authority that creates the CRID and the resolution service provider that provides the location information must be clearly distinguished. Although both tasks (CRID creation and resolution) may be performed by the same entity, they are essentially different tasks and may be carried out by different agents.

In this context, there are basically three different entities that may play a role: the content creator, the operator that aggregates the contents and distributes them and third parties that provide value-added services (e.g. a customized EPG with content recommendation). Although any of these can functionally carry out both tasks (assignment and resolution), it is true that some of the combinations are more natural and, therefore, they are expected to be more usual.

For example:

- If the content creator is the one who assigns the CRID, the resolution service is feasible and reasonable for any of the three agents. In this case, the operator and the third party would be acting as proxies for the content creator, for example, if the third party gathered information about the different operators that distribute the content.
- If it is the operator/aggregator/distributor who assigns the CRID, it can be solved naturally by the same agent and by a third party (which would be working as proxy for the operator), but it is not clear if this task may be carried out easily by the content creator.
- Conversely, if it is a third party that creates the CRID, it seems natural that this party itself resolves it. It does not seem to be appropriate for the operator to do it, and it would be very difficult for the content creator to do it.

3.2 Reference and Locator Formats

3.2.1 CRID Format

In order to secure the unambiguous identification of authorities which assign CRIDs to contents, the format of the identifier that makes reference to them is that of a string of characters according to the name system used by the Internet to identify machines instead of their IP address, the well-known *Domain Name System*, or DNS (IETF RFC 1591, 1994). According to it, valid authority names are:

www.national-geographic.com
www.telefonica.com
www.provider-z.com

From this, the complete syntax of a CRID according to what is established in the TV-Anytime standard (ETSI TS 102 822–4, 2011) is the following, where each and every part is not case sensitive:

crid://<*authority*>/<*data*>

The <*authority*> field represents the entity that created the CRID, and its format is that of a DNS name, as explained above. The <*data*> field represents a string of characters that will unambiguously identify the content within the authority scope (it is a string of characters assigned by the authority itself). For instance:

crid://www.national-geographic.com/sahara-nights
crid://www.telefonica.com/335-network-documentary
crid://www.provider-z.com/quizshow-23445-questions

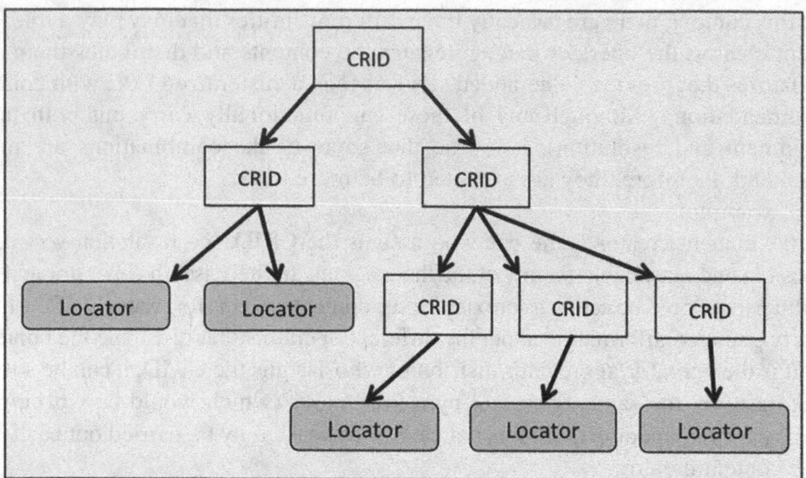

Fig. 3.2 CRID hierarchical resolution

As mentioned before, a CRID can be resolved into one or more locators or into one or more CRIDs, for example, if a CRID represents a group of contents or if an entity wants to create a CRID that makes reference to a content managed by another entity, for instance, by making reference to the CRID that the content has in that other entity.

In any event, this is a hierarchical resolution system that after many repetitions must always end in one or more content locators (Fig. 3.2).

3.2.2 Locator Format

A locator is a string of characters that contains all the necessary information for a receiver to find and acquire a given content, whether it is received through a transport stream, located in the local storage, or downloaded as a file from an Internet server or through a streaming service. For example, a DVB locator will include all the necessary parameters to identify a specific content within a transport stream: network identifier, transport stream identifier, service identifier, table identifier and/or event identifier.

Apart from the corresponding information to know how to access the content, it is also common for the locator to include information about temporal availability, which will not have time zone ambiguity, since a device can receive contents from places in different time zones.

The locator's format, as established in TV-Anytime (ETSI TS 102 822-3-4, 2011), is quite generic and simple and corresponds to:

<transport-mechanism>:*<specific-data>*

In the receiver's acquisition mechanism, it is usual for a specific system agent to be selected based on the locator. This agent is a manager for the corresponding "transport mechanism" that knows the details of the protocol to access information depending on the channel through which it is available and provides access to the content, hiding the communication complexities.

The first part of the locator's format (the identifier that describes the transport mechanism) must be a string of characters that is unique for each mechanism (transport stream, local file, HTTP Internet access, etc.), excluding the "CRID" string. The second part, on the other hand, must be unambiguous only within the scope of a given transport mechanism and will be standardized by the institution in charge of the regulation of the mechanism itself. In any case, the format of these *<specific-data>* will be unique within each mechanism. Many providers may share the same transport mechanism to provide users with their contents, and the locators must be absolutely clear about that.

If the locator includes specific information about the content's time availability, there are two options:

- Planned broadcast. Normally, the locator specifies the starting time and duration of the content.
- On-demand access. The content may be acquired within a specific time frame, and normally the locator indicates the beginning and end of this frame.

Some examples of valid locators are:

- In the case of an AVI format video ("*example.avi*") stored in the directory ("*videos*") of a server ("*www.server.com*") accessible through the "*ftp*" protocol: *ftp://www.server.com/videos/example.avi*
- In the case of an MHP object carousel within a transport stream: *mhp://65.1000.1;1.0.1 ~ 20111025T214000 + 0900*
- And in the most frequent case that we will find in this book, a DVB locator to identify contents within the transport stream of networks that follow this standard (ETSI TS 102 851, 2010): *dvb://112.4a2.5ec;2d22 ~ 20111012T220000Z—PT01H30M* which would indicate a television show (identified by the string of characters "*2d22*") that airs on a channel available on a DVB distribution network identified by the address *"112.4a2.5ec"* (network identifier "112", transport stream identifier *"4a2"* and television service identifier *"5ec"*), on OCT/12/2011 at 10 p.m. and with a duration of 90 min.

3.2.3 Instance Metadata Identifier (*IMI*)

A CRID represents all the variations of a given content, regardless of certain temporary features such as location information, cost, format or encoding details. However, there are times when it may be advisable to have a mechanism to reference a given copy, precisely because we are interested in some of its particular features (format, quality, audio encoding, etc.).

For these kind of situations, there is an element of Instance Metadata Descriptions that makes it possible to assign a different identifier for each of those variations. This identifier will be unique only in the context of a given CRID.

This identifier is called *IMI* (*Instance Metadata Identifier*), which makes it possible to unambiguously identify each of the different copies of a given content which, for example, may differ in some of the abovementioned attributes. If the content's location changes, its locator will also change, but its *IMI* should stay the same.

This allows a receiver to automatically track the specific copy that the user has selected and to acquire it, even if there are any changes in the results of the location resolution process that may create ambiguity.

The format of an *IMI* is as follows:

`imi:[<name>/]<data>`

The *<name>* field represents the entity that creates the identifier and follows the format of a DNS name. Its inclusion is optional, and if it is not there, it is because it matches the name of the authority that created the CRID this *IMI* is associated to. The *<data>* field is a string of characters that is significant for the entity represented by *<name>*.

Some examples of correct *IMI* identifiers are:

imi:citibank.es/loans
imi:www.repsol.com/oil
imi:president

Let us assume, for example, that the user has decided to acquire a given programme *P* whose CRID is *C*. We will suppose that the receiver resolves the CRID *C* resulting in two different locators *L1* and *L2*, which differ in the quality of the video image (e.g. standard definition vs. high definition):

L1 = transport:channel2 ~ 16:00
L2 = transport:channel2 ~ 18:00

The user, probably because of his/her preferences, chooses the first one and the PDR schedules the recording. When the day of broadcast is approaching, the PDR resolves the CRID *C* again (to make sure nothing has changed) and finds changes in the airing time of both; so now locators *L3* and *L4* appear:

L3 = transport:channel2 ~ 21:00
L4 = transport:channel2 ~ 23:00

The problem this poses is that the PDR, without any help, is not capable of knowing with certainty which of the new locators (*L3* or *L4*) corresponds with the one that the user scheduled to be recorded at the time (i.e. *L1*).

In order to solve this problem, each locator may be completed with the *IMI* string of characters to distinguish among the different copies of the same content. These *IMIs* will not change, even if the original locators did.

In other words, the location resolution process would give as result in the first case:

L1 = transport:channel2 ~ 16:00; imi:rtve.com/prog-sd
L2 = transport:channel2 ~ 18:00; imi:rtve.com/prog-hd

And in the second case:

L3 = transport:channel2 ~ 21:00; imi:rtve.com/prog-hd
L4 = transport:channel2 ~ 23:00; imi:rtve.com/prog-sd

Now, the PDR knows that the copy the user had chosen (*L1*) is the one that can be acquired with the new *L4* locator, since this is the one that contains the *IMI* that was also present in the original locator.

3.3 Relevant Information in the Resolution Process

The location resolution process is a procedure by which, starting from the CRID of a given content, one or several locators of that content are obtained. As described before, resolving a CRID can be a direct process, which leads immediately to one or many locators, or it may also happen that in the first place one or many intermediate CRIDs are returned, which must undergo the same procedure to finally obtain one or several locators.

This procedure, described in detail in Sect. 3.4, involves many information elements, among which we find two data tables or structures, named *Resolving Authority Record* (RAR) and *ContentReferencingTable,* respectively. Consulting them repeatedly will take us from a CRID to one or many locators that will allow us to acquire the content.

3.3.1 Resolving Authority Record

The *Resolving Authority Record* (*RAR*) table is one or many data structures that provide us, for each authority that submits CRIDs, information on the corresponding resolution service provider. Among other things, it also informs about which mechanism is used to provide information to resolve the CRIDs from each authority (an example is shown in Fig. 3.3).

Each authority must have one or many *RAR* records that indicate the PDR where it has to go to resolve the CRIDs of that particular authority.

For example, in the first record of Fig. 3.3, there is an authority called "*tve.es*", whose resolution service provider is the entity "*rtve.es*", available on the URL "*dvb://1.2eef.3f5*", which means there is resolution information[1] in the DVB transport stream identified with that URL.

Each *RAR* record must reach the PDR somehow, possibly depending on the transport mechanism, which is not standardized by TV-Anytime.

TV-Anytime specifications do not regulate either a representation and transport format for *RAR* records in unidirectional contexts. They simply describe the information fields that must be present in those records, which are the following, shown in Fig. 3.4:

- *Authority name*. The authority that created the CRID whose information appears in this record.

[1] This information is surely the second table we talked about that will be described in Sect. 3.3.2.

Field Name	RAR A	RAR B	RAR C
Authority name	tve.es	media.com	media.com
Resolution provider	rtve.es	media.com	a3tv.es
URL	dvb://1.2eef.3f5	http://media.com/lr	dvb://1.104.e5f
Version	4	2	6
Other			

Fig. 3.3 Sample RAR table

Field Name	Content
Authority name	tve.es
Resolution provider	rtve.es
Class	Secondary class
Version	4
URL	http://tva.rtve.es/locres/tve
First valid date	9:30 am October 12th 2011
Last valid date	6:00 pm October 28th 2011
Weighting	1

Fig. 3.4 Fields in a *RAR* record

- *Resolution provider*. The name of the entity that provides the resolution service for that authority.
- *Class*. This field indicates whether this provider can resolve all CRIDs for this authority (*class* = *primary*) or only some of them (*class* = *secondary*).
- *Version number*. A version number for the *RAR* record, which increases every time the record is updated.
- *URL*. The location of the site where the resolution process will take place. It can be, for instance, an Internet service (in bidirectional contexts) or a table within a transport stream (e.g. in unidirectional contexts).
- *First valid date*. The first moment when this information can be used.
- *Last valid date*. The last moment when this information can be used.
- *Weighting*. A number that will be used to assign a priority to each *RAR* record in case there are many entries for the same authority and the same location resolution service provider. Only in this case (same authority and same resolution provider) may this field be used to decide which one will be attempted first.

And Listing 3.1 shows a possible encoding for a *RAR* record in an XML structure, according to the *XML Schema* defined in the TV-Anytime standard (ETSI TS 102 822–4, 2011).

```
1 <ResolvingAuthorityRecordTable xmlns="urn:tva:ResolvingAuthority:2008">
2   <ResolvingAuthorityRecord>
3     <AuthorityName> media.es </AuthorityName>
4     <ResolutionProvider> media.es </ResolutionProvider>
5     <Class> primary </Class>
6     <VersionNumber> 1000 </VersionNumber>
7     <URL> http://www.media.es/lr </URL>
8     <FirstValidDate> 2011-08-16T00:00:00Z </FirstValidDate>
9     <LastValidDate> 2011-11-28T23:59:59Z </LastValidDate>
10    <Weighting> 1 </Weighting>
11  </ResolvingAuthorityRecord>
12  <ResolvingAuthorityRecord>
13    <AuthorityName> media.es </AuthorityName>
14    <ResolutionProvider> a3tv.es </ResolutionProvider>
15    <Class> secondary </Class>
16    <VersionNumber> 1000 </VersionNumber>
17    <URL> dvb://112.4a2.5ec </URL>
18    <FirstValidDate> 2011-07-21T00:00:00Z </FirstValidDate>
19    <LastValidDate> 2011-11-17T12:00:00Z </LastValidDate>
20    <Weighting> 3 </Weighting>
21  </ResolvingAuthorityRecord>
22 </ResolvingAuthorityRecordTable>
```

Listing 3.1 RAR table in XML format

In this listing, two entries are included to resolve the CRIDs of the "*media.es*" authority (lines 3 and 13), which possibly represents a content creator. The first one declares a resolution service of the authority itself (line 4), valid for all of its CRIDs because the *class* is characterized as *primary* (line 5) and available on the Internet URL "*http://www.media.es/lr*" (line 7). The second one indicates that an operator, entity "*a3tv.es*" (line 14), also resolves some of its CRIDs (secondary class, line 15) through the information broadcast in the transport stream "*dvb://112.4a2.5ec*" (line 17).

3.3.2 ContentReferencingTable

The second structure involved in the location resolution process is a proper resolution table which, given a content's CRID, returns one or several locators that enable us to access an instance of that content, or to one or many CRIDs that allow us to move forward in the resolution process.

Listing 3.2 shows an example of this second structure, an XML document according to the specifications of the *XML Schema* defined in the corresponding TV-Anytime document (ETSI TS 102 822–4, 2011). In it, many different sections are included (*<Result>* elements) that structure the information that describes each resolution case:

- The first one (line 2) declares how a CRID ("*crid://C4.com/House/all*"), which corresponds to a group content that encompasses several episodes of the *House M.D.* series (three in this case, to limit the length of the example), is resolved. The result of the resolution process of this kind is a *<CRIDResult>* element

```
1 <ContentReferencingTable version="1.0">
2   <Result CRID="crid://C4.com/House/all"
3           status="resolved" complete="false" acquire="all">
4     <CRIDResult>
5       <Crid>crid://C4.com/House/S1/E1</Crid>
6       <Crid>crid://C4.com/House/S1/E2</Crid>
7       <Crid>crid://C4.com/House/S1/E3</Crid>
8     </CRIDResult>
9   </Result>
10  <Result CRID="crid://C4.com/House/S1/E0"
11          status="discard CRID" complete="true" acquire="all">
12  </Result>
13  <Result CRID="crid://C4.com/House/S1/E1"
14          status="resolved" complete="true" acquire="any">
15    <LocationsResult>
16      <Locator>
17          dvb://1.4ee2.3f4;4f5~@2011-10-12T22:00:00.00+01:00/PT01H00M
18      </Locator>
19      <Locator>
20          dvb://1.4ee2.3f4;4f6~@2011-10-19T23:00:00.00+01:00/PT01H00M
21      </Locator>
22    </LocationsResult>
23  </Result>
24  <Result CRID="crid://C4.com/House/S1/E2"
25          status="resolved" complete="false" acquire="any">
26    <LocationsResult>
27      <Locator instanceMetadataId=”imi:C4.com/House/sd">
28          dvb://1.4ee2.3f4;4f5~@2011-10-19T22:00:00.00+01:00/PT01H00M
29      </Locator>
30      <Locator instanceMetadataId=”imi:C4.com/House/hd">
31          dvb://1.5a2.2bc;2d3~@2011-10-20T22:00:00.00+01:00/PT01H00M
32      </Locator>
33    </LocationsResult>
34  </Result>
35  <Result CRID="crid://C4.com/House/S1/E3" status="cannot yet resolve"
36          complete="false" acquire="all"
37          reresolveDate=”2011-10-20T00:00:00.00+01:00”>
38  </Result>
39 </ContentReferencingTable>
```

Listing 3.2 Sample *ContentReferencingTable*

(line 4) that provides three new CRIDs, each corresponding to one of the three episodes: "*crid://C4.com/House/S1/E1*", "*crid://C4.com/House/S1/E2*" and "*crid://C4.com/House/S1/E3*" (on lines 5, 6 and 7, respectively).

- The second *<Result>* element (line 10) resolves the CRID for Episode 0, possibly the pilot. Since this episode is no longer available, the result for the "*status*" attribute is a "*discard CRID*" value (line 11) that concludes the resolution process.
- The third *<Result>* element (line 13) resolves the CRID of the first episode. The result of the resolution process is two DVB locators (the content of the two *<Locator>* elements within the *<LocationsResult>* element in lines 17 and 20). The "*acquire*" attribute with "*any*" value in line 14 indicates that any of them are good, which means that the second one is a repetition aired a week later, after the second episode of the first season.

- The fourth *<Result>* element (line 24) resolves the CRID of the second episode of the first season, providing two DVB locators (lines 28 and 31) that indicate two channels (with different times) where that episode is aired. Each locator is accompanied by an *IMI* which describes it (distinguishing the standard definition version from the high definition one). The "*complete*" attribute with the "*false*" value in line 25 indicates that this CRID will be resolved in the future into more locators (probable future repetitions of the episode).
- The last *<Result>* element (line 35) gives information about the third episode. It indicates that it cannot be resolved yet ("*status*" attribute with the "*cannot yet resolve*" value on line 35), indicating a date on which the request for resolution information must be repeated (line 37).

3.4 Location Resolution Process

Once the user has selected a given content (identified by the corresponding CRID) to perform some action upon it, the receiver begins the location resolution process that shall lead to specific location information that allows access to a copy of the content.

This procedure depends mainly on the receiver's connectivity. It is possible to make a basic distinction between unidirectional networks, where the receiver can only receive information through the broadcast channel, and bidirectional networks, where there is also a return channel through which the receiver can communicate with the outside world (typically an Internet access).

With more or less variety depending on the type of connectivity in hand, there will be various means to deliver the information, each with their corresponding protocols: file system access, transport stream in DVB networks, direct Internet access, etc. The receiver, in any case, must have a set of resolution handlers, software entities that know the access details through the corresponding protocol, among which it will choose the most appropriate one for carrying out the resolution process based on the information included in the CRID.

3.4.1 Resolution in Unidirectional Networks

For receivers connected only to one broadcast channel, it is clear that the resolution information must come directly from that channel or be available somehow in an existing local storage system.

After selecting a CRID, the first thing the receiver needs to do is check the information about where to find the resolution table. For this, it must find a *RAR* record associated with the authority of the selected CRID. These *RAR* records will have reached the receiver in an indefinite form, unimportant for the TV-Anytime specification, which will depend on the specific transport mechanism of the network to which the receiver is connected. Each family of standards that regulates distribution networks (DVB, ATSC, ISDB, IPTV, etc.) will have previously defined such a procedure, which will be used by devices certified according to those standards.

If no *RAR* record corresponds to the CRID's authority, the resolution process will be over, obviously failing to achieve its goal.

Once a *RAR* record corresponding to that authority is found, the receiver will know, by referring to the *URL* field, where to access (or, in this case, where to listen) the resolution information,[2] along with the most appropriate resolution handler for the corresponding access protocol.

The information the handler will receive through that access point will consist of a message for each of the consulted CRIDs (e.g. a *<Result>* element in the *ContentReferencingTable* of Listing 3.2). That message will begin with a field called *Status*, which will be an indicator of the type of response and which could take the following values:

- *"discard CRID"*. Unable to resolve the CRID (e.g. line 11 of Listing 3.2).
- *"resolve after date<xxx>"*. The resolution information is still not available, and a retry must take place after the date <xxx> (e.g. lines 35 and 37 of Listing 3.2).
- *"CRID is resolved"*. The resolution is successful and is accompanied by information on the result, which is distributed into the fields that follow the current one:
  – *"Acquisition directive"*. It could take the values "*all*" (if all the elements that follow should be captured because they are part of the content—line 3 of Listing 3.2) or "*any*" (if it is only necessary to capture one of them, because they are alternative elements—line 14 of Listing 3.2).
  – *"List CRIDs/Locators"*. A list of results of the resolution process, whether they are new CRIDs or locators (as is the case of the *<LocationsResult>* element on line 15 of Listing 3.2).
  – *"Resolution complete"*. An indicator that can take the value "*yes*" (if the previous list contains all possible results—line 14 of Listing 3.2) or "*no*" (if more results may be provided on a later date—line 25 of Listing 3.2).
  – *"Re-resolution date"*. It is a date on which the receiver should repeat the location resolution process to get more results (line 37 of Listing 3.2). Logically, it makes sense only if the previous field's indicator was "*no*".

According to the values taken by the described fields ("*Acquisition directive*" and "*Resolution complete*"), we may find ourselves before different situations, depending on their combination:

- "*All*"–"*No*". All elements on the list must be acquired and more should be expected to come. In the event that the result is a list of CRIDs, this may indicate that the report includes all the identified episodes of a series, but that more are supposed to exist (e.g. series with no scheduled end). Logically, the receiver should allow the known results to be consumed. In contrast, if it is a list of locators, the receiver can wait to obtain them all in order to provide them to the user.

[2] This generic description does not include enhancement mechanisms that would logically exist in most systems, such as the use of cache queries on information resolved in the past.

- "*All*"–"*Yes*". All elements on the list must be acquired, after which the process is finished.
- "*Any*"–"*No*". One of the elements on the list must be acquired (or wait until more appear), after which the process is finished.
- "*Any*"–"*Yes*". One of the elements on the list must be acquired, after which the process is finished.

3.4.2 Resolution in Bidirectional Networks

In the case of bidirectional networks, where the receiver has a return channel to communicate with the outside world, it is necessary to have a protocol for the PDR to initiate a connection to communicate with one or more servers and resolve a CRID.

Although the complete description of this scenario in the documents of the TV-Anytime specification is intentionally generic, here we will focus on the case of a receiver connected to the Internet, which makes its connections through a TCP/IP network.

3.4.2.1 Discovery of the Resolution Server

The starting data is, precisely, the CRID of the selected content and, specifically, the DNS name of the authority that generated it. With this name, the PDR will query a DNS name server to find the server hosting the resolution service (you can see the sequence of stages in Fig. 3.5).

This DNS server must implement the DNS extension defined in RFC 2782 (IETF RFC 2782, 2000), originally designed so that computers connected to a network could find email servers, but it can also be used to implement the resolution of other kinds of services. Specifically, the generic format used in a consultation of this type is:

```
_Service._Protocol.Name
```

In the case of a TV-Anytime location resolution service, the standardized name of the service is "*_lres*" (which stands for *location resolution*), and the format of a consultation that asks about the resolution server that corresponds to a CRID of a given authority would be:

```
_lres._tcp.<authority>
```

The result of this consultation would be the name of the machine (and the TCP port) where the location resolution service is provided, which would later be translated into an IP address (as shown in Fig. 3.5).

3.4.2.2 Request Format

Once the receiver has the address of the location resolution server, the format of the consultation to that server is based on the usual requests of the HTTP protocol, using a *GET* request. The generic form of that request would be:

http://server/path-to-server-script?[key=value]&[key=value]&...

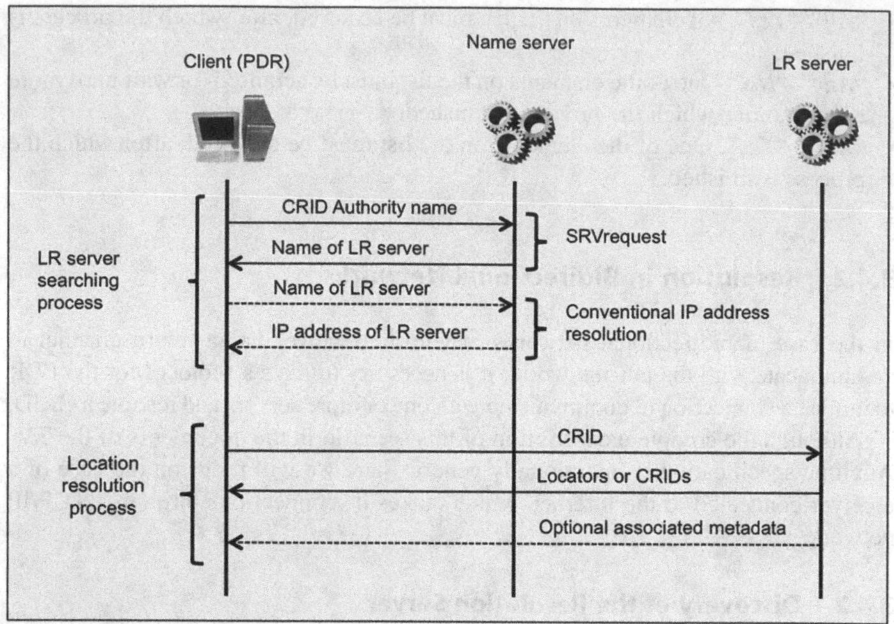

Fig. 3.5 TCP/IP-based CRID resolution

The possible values of the parameters (the *key* fields) are:

- *Key="CRID"*. The value would be the string that identifies the CRID we are asking about. It could be repeated several times if we ask about several CRIDs in one consultation.
- *Key="SubmittedCRID"*. The value could be 1 if we want the server to retrieve the metadata it has on that CRID (e.g. a *ProgramInformationTable*) or 0 if we only want the locator and not the metadata associated to the CRID.
- *Key="Result"*. The value could be 1 if we want the server to retrieve the metadata it has on that result, whether they are CRIDs or locators, or 0 if we do not want such metadata.

The only mandatory key is the first one ("CRID") that can be repeated several times. The others can only appear once, applying to all CRIDs inquired. In case a key does not appear, it would mean that its value is 0.

3.4.2.3 Server Response

The response of the location server could be any of the following three:

- The final result of the location resolution process, consisting of the *ContentReferencingTable*. If we have requested metadata and it is available on that server, it will also provide us the *GroupInformationTable* and/or *ProgramInformationTable* structures (if the result is about CRIDs) or the *ProgramLocationTable* (if they are locators).

- A *RAR* record, where the address of another server to query is specified in the *URL* field.
- An HTTP redirection response, with the address of another server to query.

3.5 Summary

In this chapter, the content referencing mechanism defined by TV-Anytime has been presented, so that receivers can identify unambiguously any content in a generic way, regardless of the specific copy they may access later (even though it is possible to reference a concrete copy through the *IMI* tag). As stated, this mechanism offers a great flexibility to applications that provide functionalities to users, so that they can easily provide new value-added services that nowadays are not available or require an expensive and proprietary infrastructure.

Together with the information structures involved (*RAR* records and *ContentReferencingTable*), the resolution procedures that make it possible to convert references into location information, both in unidirectional contexts and in fully interconnected devices, have been presented.

In the next chapter, we will present the main element defined in the TV-Anytime documents to facilitate the implementation of the standardizing framework, that is the metadata structures available to describe contents and users, allowing for their smart classification, comparison and selection.

Metadata 4

4.1 Introduction

4.1.1 Objectives of Metadata

In this chapter, we will study in depth the most important element in the framework defined by the TV-Anytime standard. Although the CRID assignment and resolution infrastructure described in the previous chapter is an essential tool to implement processes that will allow the user to acquire and consume contents, it is also true that these processes will not be triggered until the user effectively wants to consume those contents, that is it all starts when the user wants to enjoy a content and decides to select it among the ones that are available.

This is precisely the main task of metadata: making contents visible to the user, describing their characteristics so that any programmes which may be attractive to the user do not go unnoticed. Therefore, metadata is, essentially, a lure to attract users towards contents (hence the English term "attractors"), so that consumers can easily detect the features of contents which generally are attractive to them, favouring their consumption.

In addition, if it is important to have the right descriptive information to attract consumers, this requirement becomes even more essential to make it possible for those contents to be processed by smart applications. The software that implements the advanced services we are discussing needs plenty of sources of information, particularly formal and structured ones, in order to make the right decisions in the interests of users. It is necessary for the available information to reflect the content's characteristics in the most detailed and reliable way possible so as to be able to make effective comparisons that reveal the similarities and relations that exist between the broadcast contents and the users' profiles. The profile must include the preferences, the socio-demographic data or the characteristics of the devices in which the contents are to be reproduced but also the programmes that the user has said he/she liked in the past (direct feedback) or simply those that he/she has recorded and fully or partially consumed (indirect feedback).

A. Gil Solla and R.G. Sotelo Bovino, *TV-Anytime*, X.media.publishing,
DOI 10.1007/978-3-642-36766-3_4, © Springer-Verlag Berlin Heidelberg 2013

Therefore, not only tools to describe the contents in depth are required but also the right instruments to capture the user's profile and keep it up to date, as regards his/her taste, preferences or socio-demographic characteristics, as well as what concerns his/her historical consumption records, that is the explicit or implicit ratings of programmes made in the past. This information about users is essential to be able to develop intelligent services that choose and customize contents applying personalization criteria.

It is interesting to note that the detailed information we are talking about need not only include those immutable aspects of contents (e.g. its starring actor, the time in which the plot unfolds or the genre to which it belongs) but also the specific information of every concrete copy that is distributed. We are referring to the typically technical characteristics, such as image format, video or audio quality, details of the encoding used, or the requirements for its reproduction, not to mention the price. Taking these aspects into account at the time of assessing how appropriate a given content is for a specific user is fundamental to guarantee that the viewer will always enjoy the most pleasant experience possible.

The concept of group receives special attention in TV-Anytime, since there are many contents that are normally grouped according to multiple criteria. Thus, a group can bring together various contents, and content can belong to several groups (possibly each based on a different criterion). Likewise, a group can belong to and/or contain other groups. This information can only be accurately found out from the resolution process, since the CRID format does not allow for guessing the nature of the referenced object.

The description of what TV-Anytime defines regarding all of this (including some other things it adopts from existing standards) will take up the following sections.

4.1.2 The Metadata Life Cycle

The process of creation and aggregation of metadata can take place throughout various stages, from the creation of a given content to its delivery to the user. Even this does not need to be the final stage of the process, given that the user may contribute to characterize those contents with his/her opinions or ratings, which is happening more and more frequently, especially on the Internet. All that is needed is to provide users with the right tools so that their contributions are added to the existing metadata following the right format.

This metadata accumulation process can involve many organizations in the different stages, from the creation of content until its delivery to the user, going through the different stages of content aggregation and distribution. It is clear, then, that it is important to define a common and homogeneous framework for the different contributions to be able to integrate easily and coherently, thus guaranteeing the interoperability of all participants' softwares.

In Fig. 4.1, we can see a general outline of the content and metadata flows, showing a distribution in three layers of the different processes involved: creation,

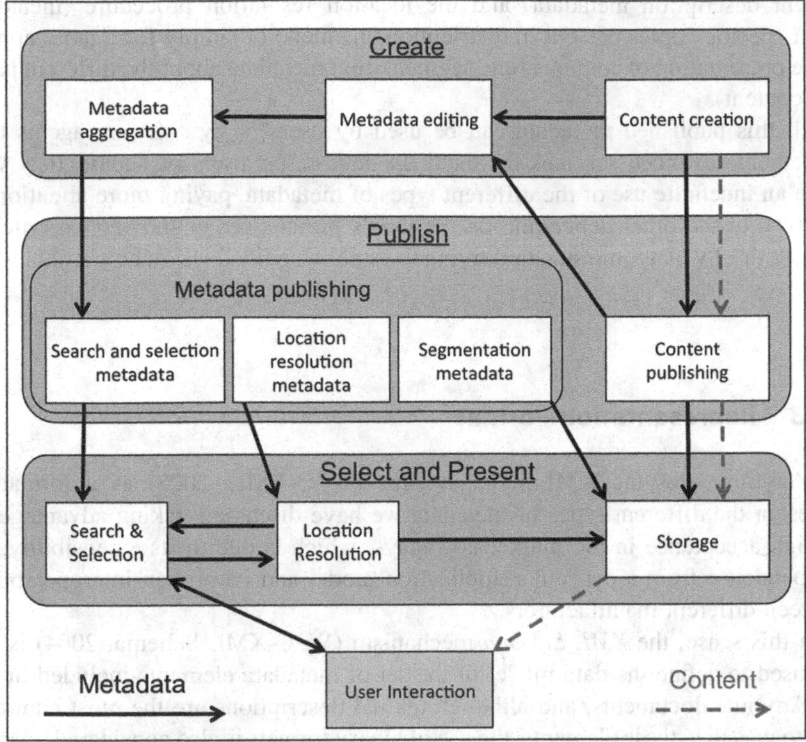

Fig. 4.1 Content and metadata flow

publication and selection by users. We can see there the simple and direct path that contents usually follow in comparison with the richer and more diverse evolution of metadata, which is constantly augmented by new aggregations, often resulting from feedback processes.

In the content creation phase, it is possible that plenty of metadata is generated about it, although it is usual for it to be in a format which is not elaborate enough to be submitted to the user. This usually requires a subsequent editing phase in which the aggregation of metadata belonging to other creators or operators also takes place. It is usual as well for metadata to be expanded in the content publication process, especially regarding the specific characteristics of the copy being distributed, such as audio and video signal technical details, or information concerning the schedule of the broadcast. In most cases, post-processing is also necessary in the editing stage.

Afterwards, this metadata must be made public (e.g. hosted on an Internet server or broadcast as Service Information inside a transport stream of a digital television network) to feed the search and selection processes (that is the case, for instance, of content description metadata) and the location resolution procedure (metadata about specific copies present in distribution channels) or simply for a more appropriate presentation of contents (e.g. segmentation metadata about the different parts of a content).

All this published metadata can be used by users or by software agents that implement advanced services for them. In both cases, users or agents, they will make an indefinite use of the different types of metadata, paying more attention to one type or the other depending on the user's preferences or the service criteria, without the TV-Anytime standard trying to establish guidelines on how it should be used.

4.1.3 Representation Format

TV-Anytime uses the XML metalanguage (W3C-XML, 2008) as a format to represent the different types of metadata we have discussed, taking advantage of its high acceptance in the market nowadays, which is due to its extensibility, its independence from a particular application model and its proven interoperability between different manufacturers.

In this sense, the *XML Schema* mechanism (W3C-XML Schema, 2004) is the one used to define the data model of the set of metadata elements included in the TV-Anytime documents, and although textual descriptions are the most common way to visualize these elements, the use of binary formats is also considered, mainly in view of improving its efficiency, as analysed in Chap. 7.

As for the details of the specific XML language through which metadata is structured, TV-Anytime adopts the DDL (*Description Definition Language*) (ISO/IEC 15938–2 (2001) created in the MPEG-7 standard for this purpose. This language, which is also defined through an *XML Schema*, provides the syntax, structure and vocabulary (including default values) of most of the descriptions considered in TV-Anytime, as well as multiple data types appropriate for the characterization of audiovisual contents and user profiles.

Thus, TV-Anytime descriptions use multiple descriptive elements which come from different namespaces (following XML terminology). The most frequently used among them during TV-Anytime Phase 1 are:

- *tva (xmlns:tva = "urn:tva:metadata:2010")* ➔ for those elements defined in structures (*Description Schemes*) specially created in the TV-Anytime standard, highlighting in particular the external structures that function as information containers
- *mpeg7 (xmlns:mpeg7 = "urn:tva:mpeg7:2008")* ➔ for structures used to describe contents, users and auxiliary data types adopted from the MPEG-7 standard

New namespaces were added during Phase 2, among which we may find:

- *tva2 (xmlns:tva2 = "urn:tva:metadata:extended:2010")* ➔ for the new data structures defined in this phase

- *mpeg21 (xmlns:mpeg21 = "urn:tva:mpeg21:2010")* ➔ to reference some data types originally from the MPEG-21 standard, particularly related to the areas of content packaging and identification of the intended audience for a given content

4.1.4 Types of Metadata

The main core of the repertoire of descriptive metadata defined by TV-Anytime was already introduced in Phase 1, and it covered the characterization of the necessary elements to implement the services depicted in Chap. 1. This means it included all the necessary elements to create services to be deployed in a mainly unidirectional basic broadcasting environment.

This initial metadata was structured in four sections:

Content description metadata: It is meant to describe the unchanging characteristics of contents (title, actors, creation date, etc.), regardless of the details of the specific copies that may be accessed.

Instance description metadata: It is meant to be used in the description of the particular characteristics of a specific copy of the content (image format, encoding, quality, acquisition and consumption models, availability, etc.).

Consumer description metadata: Its aim is to facilitate the description of the profile which characterizes a user: personal preferences, socio-demographic data and even the consumption history of audiovisual products, along with the most significant things that he/she did in relation to them (playback, record, rate, etc.).

Segmentation metadata: It is used to describe the different parts a given content can be divided into, allowing for the identification of certain points which are particularly relevant (e.g. goals in a football match).

Throughout Sect. 4.2, we will analyse in depth which contents' properties we can describe with each type of this metadata, and we will see several specific examples of many of the available elements. Later, in Sect. 4.3, we will describe how the different structures presented come together in a single TV-Anytime document.

Apart from descriptive metadata, Phase 1 also considers a kind of metadata whose aim is to standardize the access to third-party metadata provision services through bidirectional networks. This will be discussed in Chap. 8.

Other than extending some specific aspects of the metadata defined in Phase 1, Phase 2 created new tools to deal with the more ambitious contexts, in many cases purely bidirectional, identified in Chap. 1. One of the main objectives of these extensions is to go beyond the mere description of contents to be able to provide indications of how to consume each of the contents. Chapters 5 and 6 will be devoted to these extensions, covering the facilities provided by TV-Anytime to implement mechanisms such as the following:

- *Packaging*. It consists of facilitating the packaging of several contents meant to be consumed as a group and possibly in a synchronized way.
- *Targeting*. It provides many tools to be able to identify the most appropriate audience for a given content, that is the users who might find it interesting.

- *Interstitials.* It facilitates the identification of the most appropriate advertisements for a given user at a given time and provides mechanisms to replace them in real time.
- *Coupons.* It introduces a new framework of promotional discounts associated with contents to motivate their consumption.

In addition, as we will see in Chaps. 8 and 9, Phase 2 also includes another type of non-descriptive metadata, aimed at facilitating communication processes through bidirectional networks. For example:

- A group of facilities to go in depth into the metadata exchange through bidirectional networks, especially to favour user profiles' portability and sharing
- A format to facilitate the simple exchange of metadata between different applications when any of them are not compatible with TV-Anytime
- A mechanism to allow for the remote access and setup of TV-Anytime devices that implement the smart services we are dealing with (ordering searches and recordings, accessing contents, modifying profiles, etc.)

4.1.5 Classification Schemes

Classification Schemes are a fundamental element in TV-Anytime. This tool is an instrument to define groups of controlled terminology, that is limited sets of terms which represent the possible values of some elements or attributes used to describe contents.

The classification schemes defined by TV-Anytime (based on the original idea of MPEG-7, from which some classification is sometimes adopted as a starting point) offer a simple way to identify some of the content's characteristics within a limited namespace. This use of a predetermined namespace to assign values to elements and attributes allows us to easily classify and compare those characteristics, which easily translates into a simple comparison of contents themselves.

In (ETSI TS 102 822-3-1, 2011) for Phase 1 and (ETSI TS 102 822-3-3, 2011) for Phase 2, multiple classifications are presented through which a content can be characterized following diverse criteria, such as genre, format, intended audience and alerts it can trigger, or even the role a particular character plays within the content (actor, director, scriptwriter, etc.).

In essence, it is about a multidimensional classification, given that each content can be classified into each and every one of the defined classifications, that is it can be characterized in each and every existing dimension, each of them representing a particular criterion which characterizes the content from a different perspective. In many cases, each of these dimensions does not provide information relevant enough to assess the content. It is the combination of multiple dimensions that generally provides an added value to the description of a given content.

The format used to unambiguously identify each term follows the pattern set forth in the MPEG-7 standard, where each identifier is formed of different parts, joined by the ":" symbol. These parts are as follows:

- A common prefix, which shows that an identifier belongs to the classifications field:

  urn:tva:metadata:cs

- An unambiguous identifier for the actual classification, which may be followed by the year when the referenced revision took place. For example, for the content genre classification which corresponds to the year 2010, it would be:

  ContentCS:2010

- A last part which identifies (usually with a number) the selected term within the defined set, generally listed following a hierarchical structure. For example, within SPORTS (*3.2*), we can find cycling (*3.2.2*), and within that sport, we can find indoor cycling (*3.2.2.3*).
  Therefore, the complete identifier for indoor cycling would be:

  urn:tva:metadata:cs:ContentCS:2010:3.2.2.3

In Sect. 4.5, we will present in depth the different classifications defined in TV-Anytime (or adopted from MPEG-7), although throughout the next two sections a lot of these identifiers will appear within the examples that illustrate each metadata type or element.

4.2 Phase 1 Metadata

In this section, we will go into detail about the descriptive objectives for each of the four abovementioned subcategories of Phase 1 metadata and the main data types they offer to materialize those descriptions.

The different metadata we will now present are organized into several information tables (elements of an XML language defined by *XML Schemas* (W3C-XML Schema, 2004)), which in the end will be organized into a unified document within a root element called *TVAMain*.

We will present various examples throughout this section with the only aim of illustrating some of the existing possibilities, which in no case are thorough descriptions that include all the optional structures defined in the standard which, due to its extension, is beyond the scope of this book.

4.2.1 Generic Content Description Metadata

The metadata that describes contents consists of descriptions of the contents' properties which remain unchanged regardless of how the content is published or broadcast, for example the title, genre and synopsis. Therefore, it is common for most of the metadata to be generated by the content's creator before the publication process.

The elements which fall into this category can be classified into different sections that we review below:

Basic types: Many auxiliary descriptive elements are included within this subsection, some created in TV-Anytime and others imported from the MPEG-7

```
1 <BasicDescription>
2   <Title type="main"> Everybody lies</Title>
3   <Synopsis> A kindergarten teacher collapses in her classroom ... </Synopsis>
4   <Keyword> House </Keyword>
5   <Keyword> Hospital </Keyword>
6   <Genre href="urn:tva:metadata:cs:FormatCS:2010:2.2.1" type="main"/>
7   <Language type="original"> en </Language>
8   <RelatedMaterial>
9     <HowRelated href='urn:tva:metadata:cs:HowRelatedCS:2010:10'>
10      <Name> For more information </Name>
11    </HowRelated>
12    <MediaLocator>
13      <mpeg7:MediaUri> http://www.fox.com/house </mpeg7:MediaUri>
14    </MediaLocator>
15  </RelatedMaterial>
16  <CreditsList>
17    <CreditsItem role="urn:mpeg:mpeg7:cs:RoleCS:2010:ACTOR">
18      <PersonNameIDRef ref="AC145"/>
19    </CreditsItem>
20  </CreditsList>
21 </BasicDescription>
```

Listing 4.1 Example of the *<BasicDescription>* element

standard, which are used as the basis to compose other more complex elements that will be presented in the following pages.

We can find among them some relatively simple types to express unique identifiers or references to them, CRIDs, time instants or frames, prices, references to classifications, people or organizations, etc. and some more complex ones which describe some information related to a content, list of awards, credits, etc.

Content description: They are a set of elements to articulate the basic description of a given content, encompassing properties such as genre, synopsis, keywords, credits, prices and subtitles. Most of these characteristics are grouped in an element called *<BasicDescription>*, which represents the key tool to describe a given content. We can see a simple example in Listing 4.1, where an episode of the *House* series is described.

The description in Listing 4.1 includes the title (line 2), a summary (line 3), some keywords (lines 4 and 5), a classification of the content according to its format (line 6), the original language (line 7), a reference to extra informative material from a Web page (line 8) and a list of credits (line 16), which contains a reference to an actor (a unique identifier that references an item from another part of the metadata—a table of credits—where there is a detailed description of that person, which can be reused with the mere mention of its reference).

Description of audio and video components: The elements used to specify certain properties of the audiovisual signals of the content are grouped in this category. These properties can be of unchanging character (mono or stereo, colour or B/W), or they may have different values in alternative copies of the content, in

```
1 <AVAttributes>
2 <FileFormat href="urn:mpeg:mpeg7:cs:FileFormatCS:2001:3">
3    <Name xml:lang="en"> mpeg </Name>
4 </FileFormat>
5 <System href="urn:mpeg:mpeg7:cs:SystemCS:2001:1">
6    <Name xml:lang="en"> PAL </Name>
7 </System>
8 <AudioAttributes>
9   <Coding href="urn:mpeg:mpeg7:cs:AudioCodingFormatCS:2001:1">
10      <Name xml:lang="en"> AC3 </Name>
11   </Coding>
12   <NumOfChannels> 2 </NumOfChannels>
13   <AudioLanguage purpose='urn:tva:metadata:cs:AudioPurposeCS:2005:1'>EN</AudioLanguage>
14   <BitsPerSample> 8 </BitsPerSample>
15 </AudioAttributes>
16 <VideoAttributes>
17   <Coding href="urn:mpeg:mpeg7:cs:VisualCodingFormatCS:2001:3.1">
18      <Name xml:lang="en"> MPEG-4 Visual Simple Profile </Name>
19   </Coding>
20   <Scan> Progressive </Scan>
21   <AspectRatio> 16:9 </AspectRatio>
22   <Color> blackAndWhite </Color>
23   <FrameRate> 30/1.001 </FrameRate>
24 </VideoAttributes>
25 </AVAttributes>
```

Listing 4.2 Example of the *<AVAttributes>* element

which case their presence in this section would denote the values of the original copy (available languages, format, *bitrate*, etc.).

All this information is structured in an element called *<AVAttributes>*, of which we can see an example in Listing 4.2. In this listing, we can see an initial section with generic properties (such as the *<FileFormat>* element in line 2) followed by two blocks which describe the attributes of the audio signal (*<AudioAttributes>* element in line 8) and the video signal (*<VideoAttributes>* element in line 16).

This element can also appear in the metadata to describe instances or specific copies of a given content (we will see this in Sect. 4.2.2), in which case it would refer to the specific characteristics of that copy and it would prevail over the contents of this section.

Information about a programme: The two structures we have just defined (*<BasicDescription>* and *<AVAttributes>*) are grouped through a new element called *<ProgramInformation>*, which is extended with new fields, for example the *<MemberOf>* element to reflect a content's belonging to more general entities (groups, more abstract categories, etc.).

The different instances of this *<ProgramInformation>* element are finally grouped into a programme information table, called *ProgramInformationTable*. An example of this table is shown in Listing 4.3, which includes a single element of the *<ProgramInformation>* type (line 2) with information about a programme.

As we can see in the listing, the information about this programme consists of a *<BasicDescription>* element (line 3), an *<OtherIdentifier>* element to include

```
1 <ProgramInformationTable>
2   <ProgramInformation programId="crid://C4.com/House/S1/E1" lang="en">
3     <BasicDescription>
4         CONTENT EXAMPLE IN LISTING 4.1
5     </BasicDescription>
6     <OtherIdentifier>
7       urn:mpeg:mpeg21:diid:isan:39ed-91b8-33c6-5eba-cc88-e-5235-9a3cf
8     </OtherIdentifier>
9     <MemberOf crid = "crid://C4.com/House/all" index = "1" xsi:type ="EpisodeOfType"/>
10  </ProgramInformation>
11 </ProgramInformationTable>
```

Listing 4.3 Example of a *ProgramInformationTable*

```
1 <GroupInformationTable>
2   <GroupInformation groupId="crid://C4.com/House/all">
3     <GroupType xsi:type="ProgramGroupTypeType" value="series"/>
4     <BasicDescription>
5       <Title type="main"> All the episodes in the House series </Title>
6       <Synopsis> House is a very special doctor </Synopsis>
7       <Keyword> House </Keyword><Keyword> Hospital </Keyword>
8       <Genre href="urn:tva:metadata:cs:FormatCS:2007:2.2.1" type="main"/>
9     </BasicDescription>
10    <MemberOf xsi:type="MemberOfType" crid="crid://C4.com/comedies/all"/>
11  </GroupInformation>
12 </GroupInformationTable>
```

Listing 4.4 Example of a *GroupInformationTable*

another identifier for the programme expressed in an alternative format (line 6) and a *<MemberOf>* element to define its belonging to a series (line 9).

Group information: Several elements to declare programme groups are included within this category. In particular, a new element called *<GroupInformation>* is used to define and characterize a new group, and a table called *GroupInformationTable* is created to contain the declarations of one or more groups.

In Listing 4.4, we can see an example of the *GroupInformationTable* in which a single group is defined (line 2), that is the *House* series. This group is characterized through the *<BasicDescription>* element (line 4), to which the *<MemberOf>* element is added (line 10) to declare its belonging to a broader group: comedies.

Review information: Finally, the last type of information included in this category to characterize a given content is constituted by available reviews published in the media or signed by experts in the area it may be subject to.

The *<Review>* element is introduced to bring together the information from the reviews of a given content. Multiple instances of this element can be included in a table called *ProgramReviewTable*.

In the example shown in Listing 4.5, we can see a review of the first episode of the first season of the *House* series (identified by the "*programId*" attribute in

```
1 <ProgramReviewTable>
2  <Review programId="CRID://C4.com/House/S1/E1">
3   <mpeg7:Rating>
4     <mpeg7:RatingValue> 7 </mpeg7:RatingValue>
5     <mpeg7:RatingScheme best="10" worst="1" style="higherBetter"/>
6   </mpeg7:Rating>
7   <FreeTextReview>
8       Entertaining detective story in our beloved Princeton Plainsboro
9   </FreeTextReview>
10  <mpeg7:Reviewer xsi:type="mpeg7:PersonType">
11    <mpeg7:Name>
12      <mpeg7:FamilyName> Nice </mpeg7:FamilyName>
13      <mpeg7:GivenName> Philip </mpeg7:GivenName>
14    </mpeg7:Name>
15  </mpeg7:Reviewer>
16 </Review>
17 </ProgramReviewTable>
```

Listing 4.5 Example of a *ProgramReviewTable*

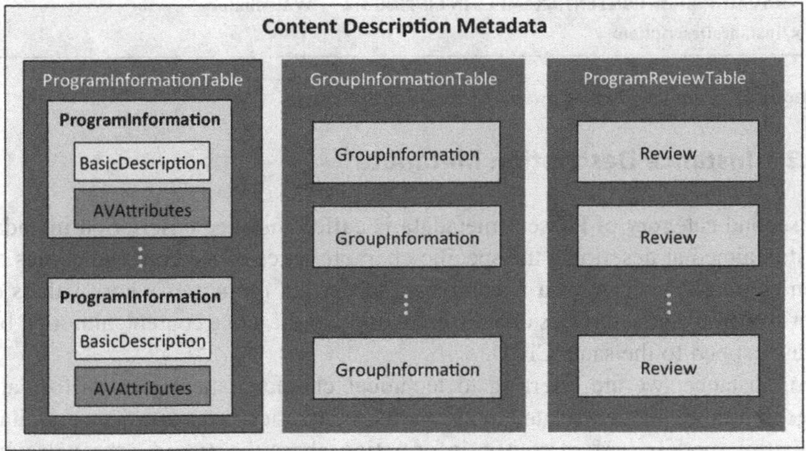

Fig. 4.2 Content description metadata

line 2). The review was made by Philip Nice (*<Reviewer>* element in line 10), the cited content being given a 7 out of 10 rating in the review (*<Rating>* element in line 3), and described the plot of the episode as "entertaining detective story" in a free comment (*<FreeTextReview>* element in line 7).

In conclusion, the main structures of this metadata category, as summarized in Fig. 4.2, are the XML elements that store:

- Tables of information about programmes, in a *<ProgramInformationTable>* element
- Tables of information about groups, inside a *<GroupInformationTable>* element
- Tables of information about reviews, inside a *<ProgramReviewTable>* element

```
1 <InstanceDescription>
2   <Title type="main"> Everybody lies </Title>
3   <Synopsis> A kindergarten teacher collapses in her classroom... </Synopsis>
4   <Genre href="urn:tva:metadata:cs:FormatCS:2010:2.2.1" type="main"/>
5   <PurchaseList>
6       <PurchaseItem start="2011-04-01T00:00:00" end="2011-08-31T00:00:00">
7          <Price currency="EUR"> 3 </Price>
8          <Purchase>
9             <PurchaseType  href="urn:tva:metadata:cs:PurchaseTypeCS:2004:playForPeriod"/>
10            <QuantityUnit href="urn:tva:metadata:cs:UnitTypeCS:2004:month"/>
11            <QuantityRange max="1"/>
12         </Purchase>
13         <Purchase>
14            <PurchaseType  href="urn:tva:metadata:cs:PurchaseTypeCS:2004:playCounts"/>
15            <QuantityUnit href="urn:tva:metadata:cs:UnitTypeCS:2004:plays"/>
16            <QuantityRange max="5"/>
17         </Purchase>
18         <PricingServerURL> http://C4.com/prices </PricingServerURL>
19      </PurchaseItem>
20  </PurchaseList>
21  <CaptionLanguage closed='true'> EN-UK </CaptionLanguage>
22  <AVAttributes> CONTENT EXAMPLE IN LISTING 4.2 </AVAttributes>
23 </InstanceDescription>
```

Listing 4.6 Example of the *<InstanceDescription>* element

4.2.2 Instance Description Metadata

The second category of Phase 1 metadata is called instance description metadata, and it is aimed at describing the specific characteristics of the concrete copies of a given content. This metadata is composed of certain properties whose values can differ from the characteristics of a different copy of the same content, although both copies respond to the same CRID.

For instance, we are referring to technical characteristics, such as format or image definition, matters related to its commercialization, such as price or available acquisition models, and, of course, information about the provider through which we can acquire the copy. Thus, it is common for this information to be generated by the content's provider during the publication process.

The metadata corresponding to this category can also be classified into different sections:

Instance description: The elements to describe the characteristics of a specific instance of a given content are included in this section. Most of these characteristics may differ between copies. Many of these elements replicate their homonyms of the *<BasicDescription>* element from the content metadata description subsection and have precedence over them.

As shown in the example in Listing 4.6, it also includes technical information about the audiovisual signals of the specific copy we are studying, through the *<AVAttributes>* element (line 22), which is more likely to appear in this section than in the previous one and over which it has priority in any case.

```
1 <Schedule serviceIDRef='Cha4' start='2011-10-12T00:00:00Z' end='2011-10-12T23:59:59Z'>
2   <ScheduleEvent>
3     <Program crid='crid://C4.com/House/S1/E1'/>
4     <ProgramURL>
5         dvb://233a.4000.4700;abec@2011-10-12T22:00:00Z/PT01H00M
6     </ProgramURL>
7     <InstanceDescription> CONTENT EXAMPLE IN LISTING 4.6 <InstanceDescription>
8     <PublishedStartTime> 2011-10-12T22:00:00Z </PublishedStartTime>
9     <PublishedDuration> PT01H00M00S </PublishedDuration>
10  </ScheduleEvent>
11 </Schedule>
```

Listing 4.7 Example of the *<Schedule>* element

Finally, it is also necessary to emphasize the existence of a *<PurchaseList>* element (line 5) to gather relevant information about the price (*<Price>* element in line 7) and the ways to acquire the content, which in this case are two: monthly purchase (line 8) or a purchase to reproduce it five times (line 13). All of this is grouped into an element called *<InstanceDescription>*, the root element in the example in Listing 4.6.

Instance location: The previous information (the *<InstanceDescription>* element) along with the content's CRID, a URL where it is possible to acquire it and a field to specify a possible *IMI* compose an abstract type called *ProgramLocation*. This abstract type is extended in several ways to express the different methods to locate a programme, that is place it in a distribution mechanism accompanied by its schedule or access conditions.

There are four possible elements stemming from the *ProgramLocation* abstract type (which inform us of the ways to access the content, cost, availability, etc.), which are called *<ScheduleEvent>*, *<BroadcastEvent>*, *<OnDemandProgram>* and *<PushDownload>*, respectively.

- *ScheduleEvent*: It is used to declare programme instances that are broadcast through a television service, at a specific date and time. A set of them forms a *Schedule*, which represents a piece of EPG of a specific channel, identified within the metadata of the *<Schedule>* element. That is, a *Schedule* has a channel associated to it, whereas a *ScheduledEvent* is independent from any channel.

  In the example shown in Listing 4.7, we can see a simple *Schedule* for channel *Cha4* (line 1) composed of a single event (a single *ScheduleEvent*), the first episode of the first season of *House* (line 3).

  This event is broadcast on a given service of a transport stream, on a given date and time (DVB locator in lines 4 and 5), with additional information on its description (line 7) and publication period (lines 8 and 9).
- *BroadcastEvent*: Stemming from the *<ScheduleEvent>* type, the *<BroadcastEvent>* element is used to reference a specific event, described as an extension of a *ScheduleEvent* and associating it with a service without a need to form a *Schedule* for it.

```
1 <BroadcastEvent serviceIDRef="Cha4">
2    <Program crid="crid:// C4.com/House/S1/E1"/>
3    <ProgramURL> dvb://1.4ee2.3f5/ </ProgramURL>
4    <InstanceMetadataId> imi:hd </InstanceMetadataId>
5    <InstanceDescription> CONTENT EXAMPLE IN LISTING 4.6 <InstanceDescription>
6    <PublishedStartTime> 2011-10-12T22:00:00</PublishedStartTime>
7    <PublishedDuration> PT01H </PublishedDuration>
8    <Live value="false"/>
9    <Repeat value="true"/>
10   <FirstShowing value="false"/>
11   <LastShowing value="false"/>
12   <Free value="false"/>
13 </BroadcastEvent>
```

Listing 4.8 Example of the *<BroadcastEvent>* element

```
1 <OnDemandProgram>
2    <Program crid="crid://C4.com/House/S1/E15"/>
3    <InstanceDescription> CONTENT EXAMPLE IN LISTING 4.6 <InstanceDescription>
4    <PublishedDuration> P60M </PublishedDuration>
5    <StartOfAvailability> 2011-10-10T00:00:00.00+01:00 </StartOfAvailability>
6    <EndOfAvailability> 2011-10-31T23:59:59.00+01:00 </EndOfAvailability>
7    <FirstAvailability value="true"/>
8    <LastAvailability value="false"/>
9    <ImmediateViewing value="true"/>
10 </OnDemandProgram>
```

Listing 4.9 Example of the *<OnDemandProgram>* element

We can see a simple example of a *<BroadcastEvent>* in Listing 4.8, where the association with the service is made in line 1. In lines 8 through 12, many fields are shown where the abovementioned extensions about the *<ScheduleEvent>* element are materialized (the *<Live>*, *<Repeat>*, *<FirstShowing>*, *<LastShowing>* and *<Free>* elements, which make reference to broadcasting characteristics that do not need further explanation because of their names).

- *OnDemandProgram*: In this case, what is referenced through the *<OnDemandProgram>* element is an instance of a programme available on demand, on the user's initiative.
  We can see a simple example in Listing 4.9, where we have highlighted the elements that define the period during which the content can be downloaded (lines 5 and 6), certain indications on whether this is the first or the last time the content is available (lines 7 and 8) or the *<ImmediateViewing>* element (line 9), whose "*true*" value in the attribute forbids recording the content.
- *PushDownload*: Lastly, we have the case of the *<PushDownload>* element used to identify contents which are downloaded to the receiver on the service provider's initiative, without the user requesting them.

```
<ProgramLocationTable>
  <Schedule serviceIDRef='Cha4' start='2011-10-12T00:00:00Z' end='2011-10-12T23:59:59Z'>
      CONTENT EXAMPLE IN LISTING 4.7
  </Schedule>
  <BroadcastEvent serviceIDRef="Cha4">
      CONTENT EXAMPLE IN LISTING 4.8
  </BroadcastEvent>
  <OnDemandProgram>
      CONTENT EXAMPLE IN LISTING 4.9
  </OnDemandProgram>
</ProgramLocationTable>
```

Listing 4.10 Example of a *ProgramLocationTable*

Finally, the different structures stemming from the *ProgramLocation* abstract type (the *<ScheduleEvent>*, *<BroadcastEvent>*, *<OnDemandProgram>* and *<PushDownload>* elements), which describe the access to one or more instances in many ways, can be grouped into a table called *ProgramLocationTable* (which we can see in Listing 4.10) that groups information about different programme instances the user has access to.

Information about a television service: Finally, one last component of instance description metadata is an element that declares all the descriptive information about a television service. This description is materialized in an element named *<ServiceInformation>* which groups a set of data such as the service's name, owner, description, the genre of the contents usually broadcast by it and the default language of its programmes.

The different *<ServiceInformation>* elements that describe each of the television services the user receives are finally grouped into a table called *ServiceInformationTable*.

We can see an example of this table in Listing 4.11, which contains two *<ServiceInformation>* elements. A simple description of channel *C4* starts in line 2, which only details its name and owner (lines 3 and 4). A more extensive description of channel *TeleSport* starts in line 6, which includes its description (line 9), the genre of its contents (line 10), its default language (line 11) or a reference to a Web page with more information (*<RelatedMaterial>* element starting in line 12).

Therefore, the main structures of this metadata category (instance description) are the *ProgramLocationTable* and the *ServiceInformationTable* (Fig. 4.3).

4.2.3 Consumer Description Metadata

As we have been emphasizing from the first chapter, one of the main objectives of TV-Anytime is to establish a standardizing framework to facilitate the provision of smart audiovisual services that offer features the user finds interesting. This requires necessarily an in depth knowledge about the user, having his audiovisual

```
<ServiceInformationTable>
  <ServiceInformation serviceId="Ch4">
    <Name length="short"> C4 </Name>
    <Owner> Media3 </Owner>
  </ServiceInformation>
  <ServiceInformation serviceId="tve-tdp">
    <Name length="medium"> TeleSport</Name>
    <Owner> RTVE </Owner>
    <ServiceDescription length="short"> Sports channel</ServiceDescription>
    <ServiceGenre type="main"  href='urn:tva:metadata:cs:ContentCS:2010:3.2'/>
    <ServiceLanguage> ES </ServiceLanguage>
    <RelatedMaterial>
      <HowRelated href='urn:tva:metadata:cs:HowRelatedCS:2010:10'>
        <Name> For more information </Name>
      </HowRelated>
      <MediaLocator>
        <mpeg7:MediaUri>http://www.rtve.es/telesport</mpeg7:MediaUri>
      </MediaLocator>
    </RelatedMaterial>
  </ServiceInformation>
</ServiceInformationTable>
```

Listing 4.11 Example of a *ServiceInformationTable*

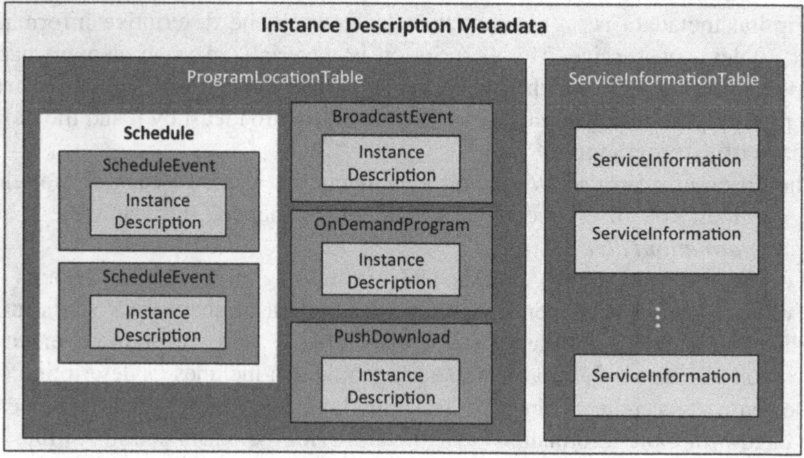

Fig. 4.3 Instance description metadata

preferences and personal characteristics in mind and building different smart comparisons of each service from that information.

This is why TV-Anytime pays special attention to the metadata necessary to elaborate an appropriate profile for every user. This metadata about the consumer covers both exhaustive records of the user's actions in the past (which include his/her content consumption history along with the ratings submitted, if any) and descriptions of his/her audiovisual preferences, in addition to the socio-demographic

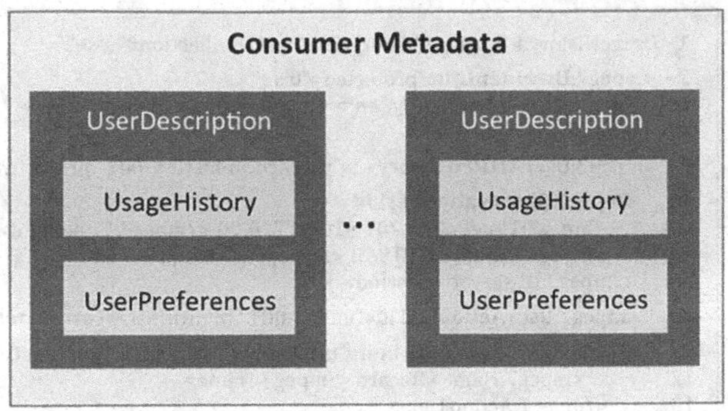

Fig. 4.4 User description metadata

data which can influence the interest the user can have in a programme (e.g. if it is about the area he/she lives in or his/her profession).

Most of the elements used in this category are extensions of information structures previously defined in the MPEG-7 standard and adopted by TV-Anytime as the starting point for subsequent refinement (or in some cases "as is", without any alterations).

The final result is an element called *<UserDescription>* for each of the users we want to gather information about. This element contains the two elements which result from the following two subsections: *<UsageHistory>*, to store the users' previous action history, and *<UserPreferences>*, to store his/her preferences and socio-demographic information (Fig. 4.4).

4.2.3.1 Consumption History

Consumption history allows for the user's actions in a given time frame to be gathered (recordings, queries, playbacks, purchases, etc.). The analysis thereof, especially of the explicit ratings the user could have made of some contents, allows for the automatic generation of preferences resulting directly from his/her behaviour (all of this with the user's consent, of course), enabling the construction of customized guides or recommendations, the commercialization of viewers' profiles or the creation of new contents with greater chances of success.

The distinct elements to capture the user's actions, the lists with action sets and their history finally derive in an element called *<UsageHistory>* which gathers the history of the actions for a given user (we can see an example of this structure in Listing 4.12).

We can see in the listing that a fragment of a user's interaction history is presented (identified by the *<UserIdentifier>* element in line 2). The history (*<UserActionHistory>* element, starting in line 5) begins by describing the recorded period (*<ObservationPeriod>* element in line 6) and later goes on with lists of similar observed actions (each type of list in a *<UserActionList>* element, as in line 10). The type of action in a list is defined by the *<ActionType>* element (line 11) and every time an action happens by a *<UserAction>* element (line 14), which in turn is made up of the time instant when it took place and its duration

```
1 <UsageHistory id="usage-history-001" allowCollection="true">
2   <mpeg7:UserIdentifier protected="true">
3     <mpeg7:Name xml:lang="en"> Charles White </mpeg7:Name>
4   </mpeg7:UserIdentifier>
5   <mpeg7:UserActionHistory id="useraction-history-001" protected="false">
6     <mpeg7:ObservationPeriod>
7       <mpeg7:TimePoint> 2011-10-11T18:00 </mpeg7:TimePoint>
8       <mpeg7:Duration> PT96H </mpeg7:Duration>
9     </mpeg7:ObservationPeriod>
10    <mpeg7:UserActionList id="ua-list-001" numOfInstances="1" totalDuration="PT2H30M">
11      <mpeg7:ActionType href="urn:tva:metadata:cs:ActionTypeCS:2004:1.3">
12        <mpeg7:Name> Record </mpeg7:Name>
13      </mpeg7:ActionType>
14      <mpeg7:UserAction>
15        <mpeg7:ActionTime>
16          <mpeg7:MediaTime>
17            <mpeg7:MediaTimePoint> 2011-10-12T22:00:00 </mpeg7:MediaTimePoint>
18            <mpeg7:MediaDuration> PT1H </mpeg7:MediaDuration>
19          </mpeg7:MediaTime>
20        </mpeg7:ActionTime>
21        <mpeg7:ProgramIdentifier organization="TVAF" type="CRID">
22          crid://C4.com/House/S1/E1
23        </mpeg7:ProgramIdentifier>
24      </mpeg7:UserAction>
25    </mpeg7:UserActionList>
26  </mpeg7:UserActionHistory>
27 </UsageHistory>
```

Listing 4.12 Example of the *<UsageHistory>* element

(*<ActionTime>* in line 15), and the identification of the programme which was the subject of the action (*<ProgramIdentifier>* element in line 21).

Although this containing element (*<UsageHistory>*) has been defined in TV-Anytime, we can see in Listing 4.12 from the prefixes in the namespaces that almost all its content belongs to the sphere of MPEG-7.

4.2.3.2 User Preferences

The tools used by TV-Anytime in order to annotate the explicit preferences that a user declares are entirely adopted from the MPEG-7 standard. Because of the structures defined in it, it is possible to compare the users' preferences and habits with the characteristics of the programmes which are now or will be in the near future available to facilitate the development of content customization services, to propose them to a particular user or a group of users who want (or have) to enjoy contents in company.

Apart from reflecting the explicit preferences provided by a user, the information gathered in these structures could have been automatically generated from the user's consumption history. Likewise, users themselves can prevent the service software from changing the information automatically, so that nothing can be changed without the user's permission, or establish which preferences should be private, so that they are not considered by customization services.

The different types of information used for this task finally come together in a structure called *<UserPreferences>*, which stores the preferences of a user (or user group). In addition, this structure allows us to assign a different importance to each preference and establish conditions that will determine their validity (mainly indications on the time and place these preferences apply to) through the *<PreferenceCondition>* element.

Apart from the user identifier the preferences belong to, the *<UserPreferences>* element can include two structures:

BrowsingPreferences: It stores preferences on how the content is consumed by the user, giving indications on how the user prefers the non-linear navigation of contents.

FilteringAndSearchPreferences: It contains preferences of the characteristics of contents a user likes (or dislikes). These characteristics can be of three types:

- *ClassificationPreferences*: To establish the user's preferences depending on the classifications a given content can have (by genre, format, language, etc.)
- *CreationPreferences*: To establish the user's preferences depending on the properties of a given content (favourite actor, historical time, keywords, etc.)
- *SourcePreferences*: To establish the user's preferences depending on the content's origin (television channel, producer, etc.)

In Listing 4.13, we can see an example where some of these characteristics are included. Apart from the user's identifier to which these preferences belong (line 2), we can observe three *<FilteringAndSearchPreferences>* elements which inform us of three of the user's favourite characteristics.

The first (line 5), of a *<ClassificationPreferences>* type, contains a clause to specify that the user likes news programmes (line 8) whose original language is French (line 7). In addition, this clause is accompanied by a condition that governs the application of this rule (line 10) and which consists of the user being in a specific place, which in this case is Paris (line 12).

The second (line 17), of a *<ClassificationPreferences>* type as well, specifies that the user likes action drama movies (line 19) which have received a review (line 20) by expert Francis Gale (line 26) in which he ranked them at least as an 8 out of 10 (line 21).

Lastly, the third *<FilteringAndSearchPrefences>* element (line 34), of a *<CreationPreferences>* type, establishes that this user likes programmes in which Antonio Banderas (line 39) participates as an actor (line 37).

4.2.4 Segmentation Metadata

The last big metadata category introduced in TV-Anytime Phase 1, segmentation metadata, allows us to define, consult and manipulate time instants or intervals (called segments) of a given content. Using this information, a hypothetical application could easily restructure the content, offering selective or non-linear consumption (highlighted instances of the programme, headings for each section, etc.), or it could allow and help the user carry out the task himself/herself, to customize its content.

```
<UserPreferences>
 <mpeg7:UserIdentifier protected="true">
   <mpeg7:Name xml:lang="en"> Marc Caster </mpeg7:Name>
 </mpeg7:UserIdentifier>
 <mpeg7:FilteringAndSearchPreferences>
   <mpeg7:ClassificationPreferences preferenceValue="10">
     <mpeg7:Language> fr </mpeg7:Language>
     <mpeg7:Genre href="urn:tva:metadata:cs:ContentCS:2010:3.1.1"/>
   </mpeg7:ClassificationPreferences>
   <mpeg7:PreferenceCondition>
     <mpeg7:Place>
       <mpeg7:Name xml:lang="en"> Paris </mpeg7:Name>
       <mpeg7:Region> France </mpeg7:Region>
     </mpeg7:Place>
   </mpeg7:PreferenceCondition>
 </mpeg7:FilteringAndSearchPreferences>
 <mpeg7:FilteringAndSearchPreferences>
   <mpeg7:ClassificationPreferences preferenceValue="12">
     <mpeg7:Genre href="urn:tva:metadata:ContentCS:20010:3.4.6"/>
     <mpeg7:Review>
       <mpeg7:Rating>
         <mpeg7:RatingValue> 8 </mpeg7:RatingValue>
         <mpeg7:RatingScheme best="10" worst="1" style="higherBetter"/>
       </mpeg7:Rating>
       <mpeg7:Reviewer xsi:type="mpeg7:PersonType">
         <mpeg7:Name>
           <mpeg7:FamilyName> Gale </mpeg7:FamilyName>
           <mpeg7:GivenName> Francis </mpeg7:GivenName>
         </mpeg7:Name>
       </mpeg7:Reviewer>
     </mpeg7:Review>
   </mpeg7:ClassificationPreferences>
 </mpeg7:FilteringAndSearchPreferences>
 <mpeg7:FilteringAndSearchPreferences>
   <mpeg7:CreationPreferences>
     <mpeg7:Creator preferenceValue="100">
       <mpeg7:Role href="urn:mpeg:mpeg7:cs:RoleCS:2001:ACTOR"/>
       <mpeg7:Agent xsi:type="mpeg7:PersonType">
         <mpeg7:Name>
           <mpeg7:GivenName> Antonio </mpeg7:GivenName>
           <mpeg7:FamilyName> Banderas </mpeg7:FamilyName>
         </mpeg7:Name>
       </mpeg7:Agent>
     </mpeg7:Creator>
   </mpeg7:CreationPreferences>
 <mpeg7:FilteringAndSearchPreferences>
</UserPreferences>
```

Listing 4.13 Example of the *<UserPreferences>* element

The basic information structure that characterizes the properties of a segment is an element called *<Description>*, which at the same time contains other elements to specify generic properties of the segment, such as title, synopsis, genre, keywords and credits.

Along with this type, TV-Anytime defines (basing itself on other data types adopted from MPEG-7) certain additional elements in order to specify time

```
<SegmentInformationTable>
  <SegmentList>
    <SegmentInformation segmentId="Segment-Id1">
      <ProgramRef crid="crid://a3tv.com/futbol/Madrid-Barcelona"/>
      <Description>
          <Title xml:lang="en"> First goal </Title>
          <Synopsis xml:lang="en"> First goal by Barcelona, scored by Iniesta </Synopsis>
      </Description>
      <SegmentLocator>
          <MediaRelIncrTimePoint  mediaTimeUnit="PT1N25F"> 10291 </MediaRelIncrTimePoint>
          < MediaIncrDuration  mediaTimeUnit="PT1N25F"> 15470 </MediaIncrDuration>
      </SegmentLocator>
    </SegmentInformation>
    <SegmentInformation segmentId="Segment-Id2">
      <ProgramRef crid="crid://a3tv.com/futbol/Madrid-Barcelona"/>
      <Description>
          <Title xml:lang="en"> Second goal </Title>
          <Synopsis xml:lang="en"> Madrid ties, goal by Ronaldo </Synopsis>
      </Description>
      <SegmentLocator>
          <MediaRelIncrTimePoint mediaTimeUnit="PT1N25F"> 22291 </MediaRelIncrTimePoint>
          < MediaIncrDuration mediaTimeUnit="PT1N25F"> 26470 </ MediaIncrDuration>
      </SegmentLocator>
    </SegmentInformation>
  </SegmentList>
  <SegmentGroupList>
      <SegmentGroupInformation groupId="Group-Id1">
          <ProgramRef crid=" crid://a3tv.com/futbol/Madrid-Barcelona"/>
          <GroupType xsi:type="SegmentGroupTypeType" value="highlights/goals"/>
          <Description>
              <Title xml:lang="en"> Highlights of the game</Title>
              <Synopsis xml:lang="en"> Goals of the match </Synopsis>
          </Description>
          <Segments refList = "Segment-Id1  Segment-Id2"/>
      </SegmentGroupInformation>
  </SegmentGroupList>
</SegmentInformationTable>
```

Listing 4.14 Example of a *SegmentInformationTable*

references (*<TimeBaseReference>* element) and programme instants or intervals from those references (*<SegmentLocator>* element).

All this information is integrated into a parent element called *<SegmentInformation>* which stores the reference to the original content, the segment's characteristics, and the necessary information to delimit the instant when the segment starts and its duration.

In addition to this basic type, TV-Anytime defines another element called *<SegmentGroupInformation>*, which allows us to group different segments which share a given characteristic (e.g. goals in a football match) or which are temporarily grouped with a specific objective. This element specifies a group of references to segments that make up this group (even including other groups if such was the case).

The set of all these segments and segment groups forms a type called *SegmentInformationTable*, which stores all the relevant information of a set of segments and

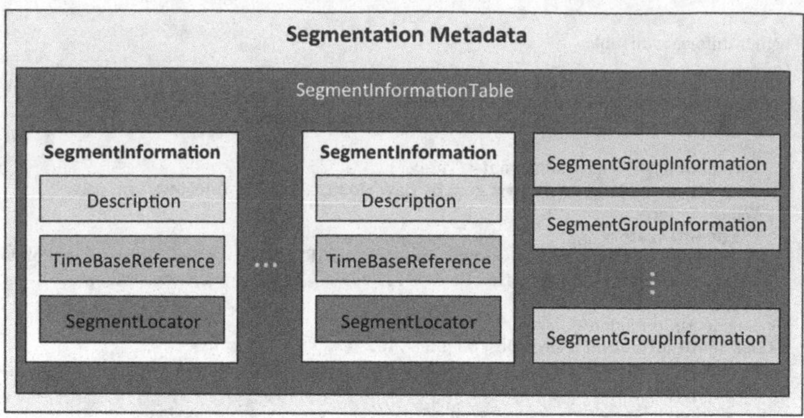

Fig. 4.5 Segmentation metadata

segment groups which correspond to many programmes. In Listing 4.14 we can see an example of the *SegmentInformationTable* structure type.

In this listing we can identify several segments (two) of a football match between Real Madrid and Barcelona, and later, a group formed by those two segments is defined.

The first segment (the *<SegmentInformation>* element in line 3) describes a video fragment of the original content (identified by the CRID in line 4). An identifier is assigned to the segment in line 3 (*Segment-Id1*). This fragment includes the first goal of the match (as declared in the title, line 6, and comment, line 7). The limits of this fragment are identified by the time reference described through the *<SegmentLocator>* element in line 9, where a time instant is added within the content and the segment's duration.

The same description takes place for the second goal of the match through the *<SegmentInformation>* element in line 14. In this case, the segment receives the *Segment-Id2* identifier (in line 14).

Lastly, a group of segments is defined in line 27 (the two segments which correspond to the two goals). The segments which compose the group are referenced through their corresponding identifiers (line 34).

In conclusion, the metadata which results from this category is contained in its entirety in a table called *SegmentInformationTable*, composed of various *<SegmentInformation>* and *<SegmentGroupInformation>* elements, as summarized in Fig. 4.5.

4.3 Global Structure of Metadata

Now that we have analysed the different metadata categories defined in Phase 1 of TV-Anytime, we will explain how they combine to form a unique element which contains the others.

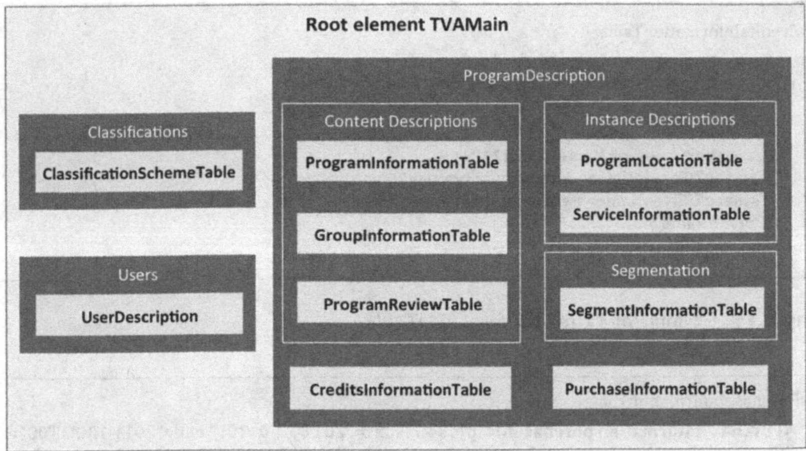

Fig. 4.6 Global structure of metadata

The root element we talk about, which structures a whole group of TV-Anytime metadata stored into a document, is called *<TVAMain>*. This element gathers all the metadata described so far and contains three main sub-elements (depicted in Fig. 4.6):

ClassificationSchemeTable: This is a table which stores the different classification schemes used in the description of the subsequent contents (as mentioned in Sect. 4.1.5 and which will be studied in depth in Sect. 4.5). It is because of these schemes that it is possible to characterize contents (genre, format, intended audience, etc.), people (role in the content) or events (actions upon a given content) easily for their effective comparison in the processes carried out by the implemented services.

UserDescription: This is the element presented in Sect. 4.2.3, which stores all the relevant information on the preferences of one or more users along with the historical record of their content consumption.

ProgramDescription: This is an element which stores many tables that describe a set of programmes, namely:

- The content description metadata tables we have seen in Sect. 4.2.1 (i.e. the *ProgramInformationTable*, the *GroupInformationTable* and the *ProgramReviewTable*).
- The *ProgramLocationTable* and *ServiceInformationTable* tables, that is the tables which contain the instance description metadata seen in Sect. 4.2.2.
- The *SegmentInformationTable*, seen in Sect. 4.2.4, which informs about the content segments identified in this document.
- The *CreditsInformationTable*, which was not presented before. This table lists, describes and associates a unique identifier to the people or organizations relevant for the programmes described in this document so that, in the future, they can be referenced in a simple way, without the need to repeat their entire description every time they appear. It is classified as a content description metadata table, and it can be seen in a simple example in

```
1 <CreditsInformationTable>
2   <PersonName personNameId="ac156">
3     <mpeg7:FamilyName> Banderas </mpeg7:FamilyName>
4     <mpeg7:GivenName> Antonio </mpeg7:GivenName>
5   </PersonName >
6   <PersonName personNameId="di71">
7     <mpeg7:FamilyName> Almodovar </mpeg7:FamilyName>
8     <mpeg7:GivenName> Pedro </mpeg7:GivenName>
9   </PersonName >
10 </CreditsInformationTable >
```

Listing 4.15 Example of a *CreditsInformationTable*

```
1 <PurchaseInformationTable>
2   <PurchaseInformation purchaseId="pid345" start="2011-10-01T00" end="2011-10-31T00">
3     <Price currency="EUR"> 5 </Price>
4     <Purchase>
5       <PurchaseType href="urn:tva:metadata:cs:PurchaseTypeCS:2004:playForPeriod"/>
6       <QuantityUnit href="urn:tva:metadata:cs:UnitTypeCS:2004:month"/>
7       <QuantityRange max="1"/>
8     </Purchase>
9     <Purchase>
10      <PurchaseType href="urn:tva:metadata:cs:PurchaseTypeCS:2004:playCounts"/>
11      <QuantityUnit href="urn:tva:metadata:cs:UnitTypeCS:2004:plays"/>
12      <QuantityRange max="5"/>
13    </Purchase>
14    <PricingServerURL>http://C4.com/prices/</PricingServerURL>
15  </PurchaseInformation>
16 </PurchaseInformationTable>
```

Listing 4.16 Example of a *PurchaseInformationTable*

Listing 4.15, where lines 2 and 6 show identifiers for Antonio Banderas and Pedro Almodovar. These identifiers can be used as unique references to these people in the remaining structures of this document.

- The *PurchaseInformationTable*, which has not yet been presented either, includes certain relevant information when it comes to buying some of the contents described in this document. The table shows purchase models, which can be applied to all contents declared in the rest of the document. It can be classified either as a content description or instance description metadata table.

In Listing 4.16 we can see a simple example which contains a unique *<PurchaseInformation>* element (to which an identifier is assigned in line 2), whose price is €5 (the *<Price>* element in line 3). This element shows an acquisition model which contemplates two possibilities: to reproduce it unlimitedly for 1 month (*<Purchase>* element in line 4) or for an unlimited time period but only five times (*<Purchase>* element in line 9). Any content which wants to

```
<TVAMain xmlns="urn:tva:metadata:2007"  xmlns:mpeg7="urn:tva:mpeg7:schema:2005"
    xmlns:xsi=http://www.w3.org/2001/XMLSchema-instance
    xsi:schemaLocation= "urn:tva:metadata:2007 schemas/tva_metadata_3-1_v141.xsd"
    version="03"  xml:lang="en"  publicationTime="2011-10-10T00:00:00.00+01:00">
  <CopyrightNotice>...</CopyrightNotice>
  <ProgramDescription>
    <ProgramInformationTable> CONTENTS OF LISTING 4.3 </ProgramInformationTable>
    <GroupInformationTable> CONTENTS OF LISTING 4.4 </GroupInformationTable>
    <ProgramLocationTable> CONTENTS OF LISTING 4.10 </ProgramLocationTable>
    <ServiceInformationTable> CONTENTS OF LISTING 4.11 </ServiceInformationTable>
    <CreditsInformationTable> CONTENTS OF LISTING 4.15 </CreditsInformationTable>
    <ProgramReviewTable> CONTENTS OF LISTING 4.5 </ProgramReviewTable>
    <SegmentInformationTable> CONTENTS OF LISTING 4.14 </SegmentInformationTable>
    <PurchaseInformationTable> CONTENTS OF LISTING 4.16 </PurchaseInformationTable>
  </ProgramDescription>
  <UserDescription>
    <UserPreferences> CONTENTS OF LISTING 4.13 </UserPreferences>
    <UsageHistory> CONTENTS OF LISTING 4.12 </UsageHistory>
  </UserDescription>
</TVAMain>
```

Listing 4.17 Structure of a TV-Anytime document

identify itself with this commercialization model only has to make reference to the identifier declared in line 2.

Lastly, we can see an example of an XML document which contains the structure of a *<TVAMain>* element in Listing 4.17, including all the information presented so far in Phase 1.

4.4 Extensions of TV-Anytime Phase 2

4.4.1 New Content Types

The first relevant extension of Phase 2 is related to the need to contemplate the integration of new content types that are not common in the television environment, with characteristics whose interests and implications depend, in many cases, on the consumption context.

That is why TV-Anytime Phase 2 starts with a reformulation of the structures defined at the time (see Sect. 4.2.1) to specify the content's attributes, establishing a distinction between those which are unchanging and those which depend on the context of use.

The first, named *ContentAttributes* (Fig. 4.7), are structured as new, slightly modified versions of the *AudioAttributes* and *VideoAttributes* structures already introduced in Phase 1 (see Listing 4.2 in Sect. 4.2.1), and a new type, named *StillImageContentAttributes*, to characterize the properties of static images.

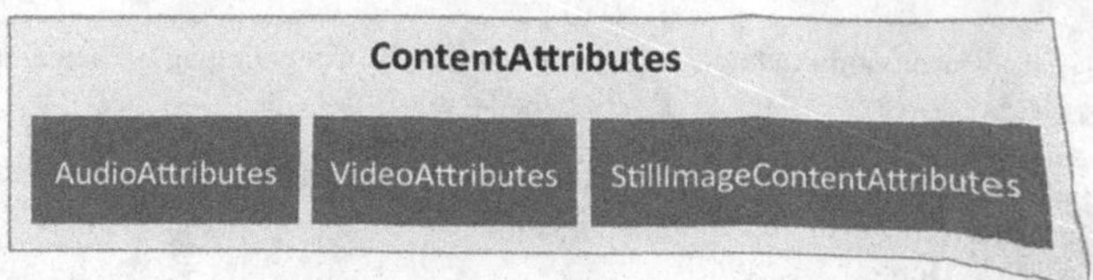

Fig. 4.7 *ContentAttributes* structure

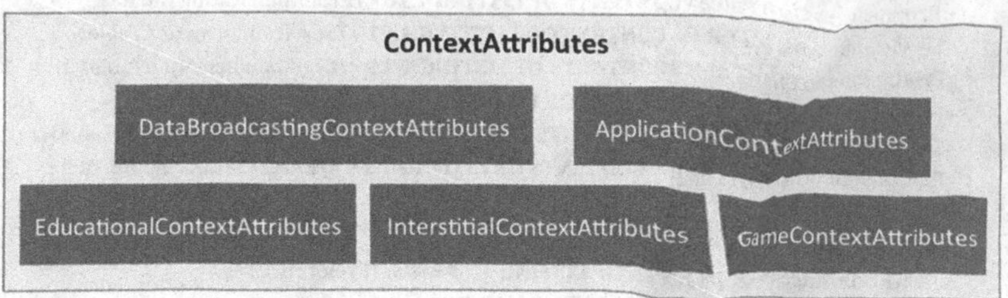

Fig. 4.8 *ContextAttributes* structure

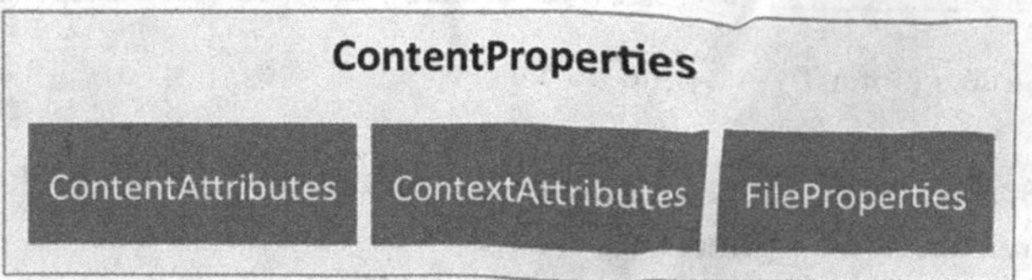

Fig. 4.9 *ContentProperties* structure

The second type of attributes, named *ContextAttributes*, describe the characteristics of the contents that depend partly on the context and the circumstances in which each content is consumed. In regard to this, TV-Anytime defines a series of contexts (*DataBroadcasting*, *Interstitial*, *Educational*, *Application* and *Game*) and declares several properties for each of them (Fig. 4.8).

For example, given a video, in the *Educational* context it is possible to characterize it with properties to specify who the intended user is (e.g. student or teacher) and the type of educational material it represents (experiment, exam, etc.). These properties clearly cannot be applied to that video in a different context. For example, if the same video is used as an asset for a commercial advertisement in an *Interstitial* context, there could be other properties of interest, such as the name of the brand it is advertising or if it is part of a broader commercial campaign.

The final result, a structure named *ContentProperties* (Fig. 4.9), is the result of the combination of the two aforementioned types, to which a new structure is added (*FileProperties*) to reflect the properties of the file which contains the content.

4.4.2 New Phase 2 Metadata

Phase 2 of TV-Anytime introduces many very ambitious functionalities to facilitate the development of value-added services especially designed for bidirectional environments in which the receiver is fully connected to the outside through a network like the Internet. It is because of the importance of these new characteristics that we will devote separate chapters to their description and analysis.

On the one hand, we are talking about new descriptive metadata tools to gather the characteristics of new types of audiovisual metadata with a different sign:

Packaging. It is a set of rules and procedures to describe the structure and composition of a group of contents (and the relations between them), which are thought of and grouped to be consumed jointly in a coordinated way. This will be described in Chap. 6.

Targeting. It regulates specific information which allows us to identify and decide on the appropriateness between contents and users, based on the users' profiles. This will be described in Chap. 5.

Interstitials. It defines a framework that allows for the automatic substitution of advertisements when a given content is played, based on diverse criteria, and is especially oriented towards the customization of advertisements. This will be described in Chap. 5.

Coupons. It establishes a framework to attach price information, and discount or gift coupons, to audiovisual contents or the products offered in advertisements. This is described in Chap. 5.

On the other hand, this second phase also includes metadata (or goes in depth into aspects started in Phase 1) to standardize the characteristics of the access to possible services deployed in bidirectional networks, when the PDR has access to the outside:

Metadata provision services and exchange of profiles: It establishes the necessary metadata to discover the services, know their characteristics and make queries, standardizing both the possible operations and their responses. It is described in Chap. 8.

Data exchange format: It establishes a data format to exchange information between TV-Anytime and non-TV-Anytime devices, mainly for the latter to be able to send information to the former, along with indications of what should be done with it. It is described in Chap. 9.

Remote programming: It defines various mechanisms to access a TV-Anytime device remotely, whether it is in the user's home (a PDR) or in a service provider's facilities (an NDR) with the objective of making queries or ordering operations. It is described in Chap. 9.

4.4.3 Extensions to Structures Defined in Phase 1

The second phase of TV-Anytime carries out an extension of multiple data structures defined in Phase 1 to integrate some aspects of these new capabilities; this is largely due to the new important functionalities we just mentioned. Among these new structures, the most important are as follows:

- The *<PurchaseItem>* element (see Listing 4.6), aimed at describing relevant information to acquire a content, is extended with various elements meant to attach promotional coupons to the contents in order to encourage their consumption.
- The basic description of a given content is extended (see *<BasicDescription>* element in Listing 4.1) with new elements and attributes to include many characteristics, such as the new content types, content packages and targeting information presented above.
- The description of a content's instance is also extended (see *<InstanceDescription>* element in Listing 4.6) to gather the new way of characterizing the content's properties described in Sect. 4.4.1 (*ContentProperties*).
- The description of a segment is extended (see *<SegmentDescription>* element in Listing 4.14) with a new element to attach promotional coupons to a given content's segment to encourage its consumption.
- The description of material related to a content is extended (see *<RelatedMaterial>* element in Listing 4.1) to gather the new way of characterizing the content's properties described in Sect. 4.4.1 (*ContentProperties*).
- The *<UserDescription>* structure is extended (see Fig. 4.4), from including users' descriptions and consumption history, with new elements coming from the *Targeting* section (described in detail in Chap. 5).

  The users' biographical and accessibility information is added among other things, in addition to descriptions of the consumption environment they are in: information on the capabilities of their receivers, the network they are connected to, their location, time and even weather conditions.

  The result of this combination is materialized in a structure called *<ExtendedUserDescription>*, which is highly enriched to participate in customization processes.

Finally, Phase 2 of TV-Anytime extends the root element of TV-Anytime Phase 1 documents (*<TVAMain>*) in order to integrate all these extensions and structure them into a unique document, extending it with the different tables defined to structure the new aforementioned capabilities: the *PackageTable*, the *TargetInformationTable*, the *InterstitialCampaignTable*, the *CouponTable* and the *InterstitialTargetingTable*. The result is a new, top-level element now called *<ExtendedTVAMain>*, which will be used as root for a TV-Anytime document when any of the new Phase 2 characteristics we have introduced are present.

4.5 Classifications

4.5.1 Objectives

As anticipated in Sect. 4.1.5, the *Classification Schemes* are tools created in MPEG-7 and adopted and extended in the documents of the TV-Anytime standard to define various groups of controlled terminology, or finite vocabularies, which offer a collection of alternatives to specify the values of certain characteristics of the content (genre, format, intended audience, etc.) or the characters that take part in it.

Each of these characteristics can be seen as a dimension in which the content is located through the selection of one of the possible values of that classification. The result is a multidimensional content classification, which describes a programme by assigning it one or many values in each dimension. This allows us to establish an objective classification of each content and, more importantly, to compare contents with each other depending on their characteristics from an intrinsically mathematical perspective.

In Annex A of (ETSI TS 102 822-3-1, 2011) for Phase 1 and Annex A of (ETSI TS 102 822-3-3, 2011) for Phase 2, TV-Anytime defines a collection of classifications and declares a set of terms in each of them. Each term, generally numeric, is associated with a specific value (out of those included in the classification) that a characteristic of the content can take.

Generally, these controlled terminology sets are hierarchically structured, which facilitates their comparison or the spread of qualities from the more generic layers to the more specific ones. This hierarchical organization provides greater accuracy and flexibility in the description of each aspect and in the comparison between the corresponding attributes of many contents, given that the similarity between them does not need to be discrete: it can be measured according to the proximity between them in the hierarchical tree.

In addition, even though the standard provides predefined sets of terms, the extension, modification or substitution of these vocabularies is possible for the implementers to attend to special requisites, such as certain regional restrictions.

4.5.2 Classification Types

The classifications defined in the TV-Anytime specifications are the ones we will present next, with the identifiers and current version numbers indicated between brackets, always logically preceded by the "*urn:tva:metadata:cs:*" prefix, as presented in Sect. 4.1.5.

The classification schemes defined in Phase 1, which represent the core set, are as follows:

ActionType (ActionTypeCS:2010). This classification organizes the actions that the user can take on a content (record, playback, rate, etc.), which can be monitored by the receiver and analysed by a service's software to get to know the user's behaviour and automatically extract his/her preferences.

HowRelated (HowRelatedCS:2010). It declares a group of possible relations between contents (episodes of a series, documentary trailer, making of a movie, etc.) or between a given content and an external source of information that describes or complements it (e.g. a Web page).

TVARole (TVARoleCS:2010). It establishes a group of possible roles that people who are involved in the making of a given content (participant, photography director, costume designer, etc.) can play. It is an extension of another pre-existing classification from MPEG-7, called *Role* (*urn:mpeg:mpeg7:cs:RoleCS:2010*), that already gathered a classification with fundamental roles (reporter, actor, musician, producer, etc.).

Intention (IntentionCS:2005). It identifies a series of possibilities which describe the operator's intention for broadcasting this programme (entertainment, information, education, etc.).

IntendedAudience (IntendedAudienceCS:2010). It provides terms to describe the audience the content is aimed at. It is composed of multiple hierarchies which allow us to catalogue the intended audience of a programme according to different criteria: gender, age, socioeconomic profile, language, etc.

Format (FormatCS:2010). It allows for the classification of programmes according to their format (magazine, show, artistic representation, etc.), that is depending on how the programme is structured, regardless of the topics dealt with in it.

Content (ContentCS:2010). This classification, perhaps the most important of them all, has a vocabulary set organized in extensive hierarchies, which can be used to describe the nature or topic of a given content (sports, religion, drama, etc.).

ContentCommercial (ContentCommercialCS:2005). It contains terms to describe the subject matter of an advertisement (food products, furniture, transportation, etc.).

Origination (OriginationCS:2005). It contains terms to describe a given content's origin (taped in a live studio, cinema-distributed movie, user made, etc.).

ContentAlert (ContentAlertCS:2005). It offers the means to identify alerts about the content which the viewer should receive (strong language, violence, strong erotic content, etc.).

MediaType (MediaTypeCS:2010). It offers terms to describe what kind of audiovisual elements compose the content (audio and video, multimedia application, graphics, etc.).

Atmosphere (AtmosphereCS:2005). It contains terms to describe the psychological or emotional characteristics of the environment in which a given content is developed (fast moving, distressing, depressing, etc.).

AudioPurpose (AudioPurposeCS:2007). It includes terms to identify the purpose of the programme's audio (director's cut, support for handicapped users, abridged versions, etc.).

PurchaseType (PurchaseTypeCS:2004). It allows for the description of the content purchase type: may be reproduced indefinitely, for a period of time or a limited number of times.

UnitType (UnitTypeCS:2007). It defines a set of terms to refine the purchase type identified in the previous classification, for example specifying the different measurement units a given content might have been bought for (years, months, weeks, days, etc.).

DerivationReasonType (DerivationReasonCS:2007). It establishes a vocabulary to identify the criteria according to which a given content was derived from an original one (edited to eliminate sex or violent scenes, to reduce the duration, etc.).

CaptionCodingFormat (CaptionCodingFormatCS:2007). It offers terms to identify the format used in the subtitle encoding (WST, DVB, etc.).

It is advisable for some of these classifications (e.g. *Format, Origination* or *MediaType*) to provide only one term associated to each content (which is known as *instancing* the classification for the content). For others (such as *Intention, Content* or *IntendedAudience*), multiple *instantiations* are completely reasonable, and even appropriate, to correctly express the nature of the content in that aspect (any movie, although catalogued within a genre, usually has aspects of the plot which can be identified with a different genre, such as a war movie which includes sentimental relations between the main characters). If each instance's weight was not the same, there are mechanisms to make the importance of some *instantiations* over others explicit.

On the other hand, Phase 2 defines new classifications, all with the "*urn:tva:metadata:extended:cs*" prefix, such as the following:

Accessibility (AccessibilityCS:2005). It defines a specific vocabulary to catalogue a user's accessibility characteristics (unable to use the remote control, only voice interaction, etc.).

ContentType (ContentTypeCS:2005). It provides a set of terms to specify the information types present in a given content or content package (video, application, game, etc.).

CPUType (CPUTypeCS:2005). It declares a set of terms to specify the user's receiver CPU type (8080, K-6, Motorola, etc.).

EducationalUse (EducationalUseCS:2005). It offers a set of terms to specify what the expected use of a given educational content is (lecture, experiment, exam, etc.)

FamilyMember (FamilyMemberCS:2005). It provides a collection of terms to specify what the relationship is between a given member of the family and the user (wife, son, father-in-law, etc.).

GamePerspective (GamePerspectiveCS:2005). It establishes a vocabulary to describe what the perspective of a player about a game is, for example if the scene is seen in the first person (what the main character's eyes see is shown) or in the third person (it is possible to see the player in the image shown).

IntendedEducationalUser (IntendedEducationalUserCS:2005). It allows us to choose a term to state what the expected role of the user is in relation to an educational content (teacher, student, etc.).

Middleware (MiddlewareCS:2005). It provides a set of terms to specify the type of *middleware* (to execute applications) that the user's receiver has (MHP, OCAP, OpenTV, etc.).

OperatingSystem (OperatingSystemCS:2007). It defines a set of terms to specify the operating system type the user's receiver has (Windows XP, Linux, Mac OS X, etc.).

OtherSystemSoftware (OtherSystemSoftwareCS:2005). It provides a set of terms to specify certain system software the user's receiver has, other than the *middleware* and the virtual machine (DirectX8.1, Windows Media Player, MySQL, etc.).

PlaceType (PlaceTypeCS:2005). It establishes a set of terms to be able to specify the type of location the user is at when the content is consumed (home, airport, office, school, etc.).

SpatialRelation (SpatialRelationCS:2005). It provides a set of terms to specify certain spatial relations between the different components of a content package (whose description will be seen in the next chapter), for example above, below, on, and to the right.

TemporalRelation (TemporalRelationCS:2005). It provides a set of terms to specify certain temporal relations between the components of a content package (whose description will be seen in the next chapter), for example precedence relations, overlapping and continuation.

TerminalType (TerminalTypeCS:2005). It provides a set of terms to specify the user's terminal type classification (PDA, mobile phone, television, etc.).

VirtualMachine (VirtualMachineCS:2005). It establishes a set of terms to specify the type of virtual machine the user's receiver has (J2ME, J2SE, KVM, etc.).

WeatherType (WeatherTypeCS:2005). It provides a set of terms to specify the weather conditions the user is experiencing at the time (rain, heat, fog, etc.).

4.5.3 Example

For the effort developed in this task by the TV-Anytime forum to be seen clearly, we will sketch an example of the most extensive classification among the above: the *Content* classification, which offers terms to describe the genre a given content belongs to.

This classification presents an initial level with nine subcategories which are assigned the terms "3.0", "3.1"... "3.9". The nine categories in this initial stage are shown in Fig. 4.10.

The term "3.3" does not appear because it belongs to a historical term which was later eliminated or merged with another category. This elimination of terms due to obsolescence does not imply the renumbering of the others, and the absent values should not be used to add private extensions (the corresponding entries normally called "PROPRIETARY" are already offered in the root of each classification for this purpose, such as "3.0" in this case).

Within each of these main categories of content genres, the standard establishes successive subcategories, with more of fewer granularities, to identify the different subgenres of each area. For example, up to 18 subcategories are defined for category "3.4" (*FICTION/DRAMA*), which are shown in Fig. 4.11.

Fig. 4.10 Level one of *ContentCS* classification

Code	Value
3.0	PROPRIETARY
3.1	NON-FICTION/INFORMATION
3.2	SPORTS
3.4	FICTION/DRAMA
3.5	AMUSEMENT/ENTERTAINMENT
3.6	MUSIC
3.7	INTERACTIVE GAMES
3.8	LEISURE/HOBBY/LIFESTYLE
3.9	ADULT

Fig. 4.11 Level two of *ContentCS* classification

Code	Value
3.4.1	General Light Drama
3.4.2	Soap
3.4.3	Romance
3.4.4	Legal Melodrama
3.4.5	Medical Melodrama
3.4.6	Action
3.4.7	Fantasy/Fairy Tale
3.4.8	Erotica
3.4.9	Drama based on real events
3.4.10	Musical
3.4.13	Classical Drama
3.4.14	Period Drama
3.4.15	Contemporary Drama
3.4.16	Religious
3.4.17	Poems/Stories
3.4.18	Biography
3.4.19	Psychological Drama
3.4.20	Political Drama

And, once again, for each of these subcategories, the standard identifies a new subset of subcategories that allow us to detail even more the genre we wish to assign the content to. For instance, for category "3.4.6" (*Action*), up to 13 new subcategories are identified, listed in Fig. 4.12.

Therefore, a specific content could be classified into a genre assigning it one of the presented terms, making use (or not) of all the refining capacities provided by the hierarchy of the above categories. For example, a movie can have an attribute

Fig. 4.12 Level three of *ContentCS* classification

Code	Value
3.4.6.1	Adventures
3.4.6.2	Disaster
3.4.6.3	Mystery
3.4.6.4	Detective/Police
3.4.6.5	Historical/Epic
3.4.6.6	Horror
3.4.6.7	Science Fiction
3.4.6.8	War
3.4.6.9	Western
3.4.6.10	Thriller
3.4.6.11	Sports
3.4.6.12	Martial Arts
3.4.6.13	Epic

"*href*" in its "*Genre*" field, whose value can classify it as belonging to a given genre, such as:

- *urn:tva:metadata:cs:ContentCS:2007:3.4* ➔ Drama
- *urn:tva:metadata:cs:ContentCS:2007:3.4.6* ➔ Action drama
- *urn:tva:metadata:cs:ContentCS:2007:3.4.6.8* ➔ War movie

The logical approach would obviously be to classify it into the category which describes it in the greatest detail, meaning "3.4.6.8". Additionally, nothing prevents us from classifying this content into other categories of this same classification (*Content*), given that it can be very normal for a content to have more or less relation with several genres (e.g. a love story within a war movie, or a biographical movie about a sports star).

Listing 4.18 shows a specific example corresponding to the various classifications that can be made of the movie *Terminator* (line 3).

The description of this movie tells us that:

- Regarding the *Intention* classification, the movie is intended for "*entertainment*" (*1.1, Entertainment*), indicated in line 4.
- Regarding its format, the category that fits it best is the "*fictional portrayal of life*" (*2.2.1, Fictional portrayal of life*), indicated in line 5.
- Its genre is clearly "*science fiction*" (*3.4.6.7, Science fiction*), indicated in line 6.
- As for its intended audience, it is assigned the term "*adults*" (4.2.2, *Age:Adults*), indicated in line 7, even though many studies would also say it is a type of movie that "*men*" like (*4.6.1, Gender:Male*), indicated in line 8.
- Regarding its origin, it is classified as a "*cinema movie*" (5.7, *Cinema*), indicated in line 9.
- And, finally, as regards its environment, we can say it fits within the "*fast moving*" adjective (8.17, *Fast moving*), indicated in line 10.

```
<ProgramInformation programId="crid://tele5.com/movies/terminator">
 <BasicDescription>
   <Title> Terminator </Title>
   <Genre href="urn:tva:metadata:cs:IntentionCS:2005:1.1"/>
   <Genre href="urn:tva:metadata:cs:FormatCS:2005:2.2.1"/>
   <Genre href="urn:tva:metadata:cs:ContentCS:2005:3.4.6.7 "/>
   <Genre href="urn:tva:metadata:cs:IntendedAudienceCS:2005:4.2.2"/>
   <Genre href="urn:tva:metadata:cs:IntendedAudienceCS:2005:4.6.1"/>
   <Genre href="urn:tva:metadata:cs:OriginationCS:2005:5.7"/>
   <Genre href="urn:tva:metadata:cs: AtmosphereCS:2005:8.17"/>
 </BasicDescription>
</ProgramInformation>
```

Listing 4.18 Example of content classification

4.6 Summary

This chapter has presented the main contribution of TV-Anytime to promote the deployment of value-added audiovisual services—the available metadata structures to describe contents. Throughout the previous sections, a review was made of the main axis along which the different metadata types introduced in TV-Anytime Phase 1 are organized: the description of generic contents; the description of specific instances; the detailed analysis of user profiles, including their consumption history; and the definition of segmentation information to identify specific points within the contents. Following this, the global organization of metadata tables that structure and interrelate all these descriptions was presented.

After that, we outlined the main extensions introduced in Phase 2 to these structures, mainly to support packaging and personalization processes on which we will expound in the coming chapters.

In addition, we have presented the basic lines of the classification scheme mechanism to facilitate the cataloguing and comparison of content characteristics through the declaration of defined and restricted vocabularies to assign values to their properties.

In the next chapter, we will begin to present the main extensions that were defined in TV-Anytime Phase 2. Specifically, Chap. 5 will be devoted to targeting. We will present the mechanisms to direct specific contents according to user qualities or the user's usage environment, as well as the substitution of advertisements and the issuance of discount coupons taking certain viewer characteristics into consideration.

5 Targeting and Advertising

5.1 Introduction

As stated before, TV-Anytime makes a decisive bet on the fact that the future of television will come true through new advanced features organized around the PDR (or implemented by smart televisions similar to it). Thus, Phase 2 of the standard conceives devices able to connect to the Internet through broadband and to other consumer electronic devices, including the possibility to gather, store and exchange information about users. This scenario certainly makes it easier for a great variety of new interaction possibilities and services to be available to the user.

Given that TV-Anytime aspires to last and to make a new generation of audiovisual services possible, one of the main objectives is to standardize certain infrastructure elements to facilitate the development of the services that can be imagined based on the new reality it foresees. As the television industry is mostly based on advertising investments, it is extremely important that these new services provide tools for television to maintain its role in society in view of the emergence of new devices and media that demand the user's attention, avoiding (or minimizing) possible advertiser migrations to other means of entertainment such as streaming or social networks.

This chapter deals with some mechanisms that will allow a more effective commercialization as well as others that make it possible to target contents to specific viewers or to the equipments in which they consume the contents. We are talking about, for instance, targeting advertising according to a geographical area or according to the profile or needs of each viewer.

Many of the key business models considered in TV-Anytime Phase 2 make reference to these capacities, involving the viewer and the broadcaster but also other players such as advertisers and service providers. Many of these foreseen functionalities have been mentioned in Sect. 1.3.2. For example, we could think of some terminal-related features, such as the guarantees for the consumer regarding that any content he/she looks for and acquires can be played in his/her device; otherwise, it would not make sense to get it. Other new functionalities refer to

A. Gil Solla and R.G. Sotelo Bovino, *TV-Anytime*, X.media.publishing,
DOI 10.1007/978-3-642-36766-3_5,

advertising, as, for example, an advertiser should be certain of meeting the standards and the regional and national advertising regulations of the place where an advertisement is to be broadcast, opportunely aided by the capacity of the receiver to replace spots dynamically. An advertiser could also pay extra to the broadcaster if it could guarantee that its commercial message will be targeted at consumers especially interested in products similar to the one it offers. It could also be possible to envisage the replacement of the advertisement according to various conditions such as the periods during which a certain product will be offered, changing it according to whether it is on a promotional date or not. All these technological possibilities open up with innovative ways to target advertisements and contents aimed at consumers and to offer them new chances of buying or getting discounts while they are watching television.

The previous features are only some of the functionalities enabled by the three tools that are presented in this chapter and that will be described briefly below:

- *Targeting*—It is TV-Anytime specific information that allows the distribution of content that is important for a specific user based on his/her consumer profile, usage history and preferences, as well as the characteristics of the device he/she uses. This information contains both specific terms expressly defined in TV-Anytime as well as others incorporated from the MPEG-7 standard. As mentioned in Chap. 1, this mechanism is fully described in Part 3-3 (ETSI TS 102 822-3-3).
- *Interstitials*—It is a framework provided by TV-Anytime to replace advertisements at the moment of playback, deciding it according to specific criteria such as the viewer's profile, the place of playback and the times that it has been played, or even trying to prevent advertisements of certain competing products from being broadcast one after the other. Its description is in Part 3-4 of the standard (ETSI TS 102 822-3-4).
- *Coupons*—It is an instrument standardized by TV-Anytime to attach information about prices and discounts offered for other products to audiovisual contents, thus enabling a new sales or advertising method. Part 3-3 of the standard (ETSI TS 102 822-3-3) details its operation.

5.2 Targeting

5.2.1 Introduction

According to what TV-Anytime has foreseen, the PDR or an external server should have at its disposal a great deal of information about users (as long as the required permissions are duly granted). There may be different kinds of information: from biographical information to some characteristics of the used equipment and from preferences and usage history to environmental conditions the user is in and even the description of particular disabilities that the viewer may have.

The broadcaster, the PDR itself or another entity is therefore suited to make up a viewer's profile. Knowing the profile information and by making a correlation between users and contents based on the metadata that describes them, it is possible for the provider (or equipment) to target the contents that are offered or sent to viewers, choosing them among those that are considered to be more interested in the contents. *Targeting* consists precisely of articulating the knowledge of the consumer through their user profile, by comparing it to content descriptions, in order to automatically provide the viewer with those contents he/she might find relevant.

There are two kinds of *targeting*, according to who initiates the process. In the so-called Push Targeting, it is the television operator who broadcasts contents with associated metadata (or orders their recording) according to the user's preferences, usage history, environmental information and the other variables taken into account. Meanwhile, in *Pull Targeting* it is an intelligent agent in the PDR who uses the user's preferences and other attributes to capture, play and record the content selectively.

We will move on to introduce the *targeting* information, which can be divided into user-related information and environmental information. We will see that in both cases there are large amounts of information that can potentially be transmitted and there is a wide classification.

5.2.2 User Information

There are two kinds of new user information, biographical and accessibility information, which are described in the next two sections.

5.2.2.1 Biographical Information

The so-called biographical information obviously gathers the consumer or viewer's personal data. Structured around an element called *<BiographicInformation>*, this section adds information such as the user's name, sex and date of birth. It is possible to state the actual age, the age range they fall into or the age group they belong to. It can describe which languages (native, secondary and others) the user can speak and write. Finally, it can include information about the consumer's family members.

Listing 5.1 shows an example with the biographical information of viewer Jane Gunter, born April 10, 1914. She is, therefore, 98 years old. She speaks both English and Spanish (lines 7 and 8) and lives with her daughter, son-in-law and two grandchildren (lines 11–17 making reference to *FamilyMember* classification).

As one could imagine, this detailed information allows the operator (or third parties) to classify the users into a specific stereotype and, based on that, identify which television shows, films and even commercials are more likely to awaken their interest, thus being those most likely to be recommended.

5.2.2.2 Accessibility Information

In addition to the merely biographical information, it is also possible to include a different kind of especially relevant information about the user: accessibility. This information, structured through an *<AccessibilityInformation>*element, describes some of the disabilities the consumer may have (hearing, visual or other).

```
<tva2:BioGraphicInformation>
  <mpeg7:Name>
      <mpeg7:GivenName> Jane </mpeg7:GivenName>
      <mpeg7:FamilyName> Gunter </mpeg7:FamilyName>
  </mpeg7:Name>
  <tva2:Gender> Female </tva2:Gender>
  <tva2:Language type="mainSpoken"> es </tva2:Language>
  <tva2:Language type="secondarySpoken"> en </tva2:Language>
  <mpeg7:Age> 98 </mpeg7:Age>
  <mpeg7:BirthDate> 10/04/1914 </mpeg7:BirthDate>
  <tva2:OtherFamilyMember
        href="urn:tva:metadata:cs:FamilyMemberCS:2005:23">
         Daughter
  </tva2:OtherFamilyMember>
  <tva2:OtherFamilyMember href="..."> Son-in-law </tva2:OtherFamilyMember>
  <tva2:OtherFamilyMember href="...">Grand-daughter</tva2:OtherFamilyMember>
  <tva2:OtherFamilyMember href="..."> Grandson </tva2:OtherFamilyMember>
</tva2:BioGraphicInformation>
```

Listing 5.1 Biographical information

This accessibility information is ultimately used to indicate whether the user has some kind of access disability, for instance if he/she is deaf in the left ear or blind. This information would allow making more appropriate choices regarding the variations of a given content among the available alternatives. For instance, an audio channel with content description could be offered if the user is blind or subtitles to read if the user is deaf or contents with gestural language overprint.

Once again, in order to specify this accessibility information, the TV-Anytime standard uses metadata from other standards—in this particular case, from part 7 of MPEG-21 (ISO/IEC 21000–7, 2006).

In order to describe the hearing disability, the standardized metadata makes it possible to define an audiogram for each ear, indicating how it responds to each of the several frequencies, from 125 to 8,000 Hz, although some are optional. The response in each frequency is expressed in dB representing the shift of the hearing threshold. Listing 5.2 shows precisely an example of this description.

Between lines 3 and 10, the right ear audiogram can be seen and between lines 11 and 18, the left ear audiogram. As shown, the frequencies 250, 500, 1,000, 2,000, 4,000 and 8,000 Hz appear for both ears (the only mandatory ones to describe the audiogram), but it would be possible to include additional optional intermediate frequencies. In the case of the viewer in the example, the right ear behaves normally. The left ear, on the other hand, shows loss of hearing. This information allows an agent in the receiver to equalize the audio output to improve the user's hearing experience.

The metadata available to describe visual impairments is even more extensive. It allows informing whether the user is blind in the left eye, right eye or both. It also

```
<tva2:AccessibilityInformation>
  <mpeg21:AuditoryImpairment>
    <dia:RightEar>
       <dia:Freq250Hz> 0.1 </dia:Freq250Hz>
       <dia:Freq500Hz> 1.2 </dia:Freq500Hz>
       <dia:Freq1000Hz> -0.5 </dia:Freq1000Hz>
       <dia:Freq2000Hz> -2.2 </dia:Freq2000Hz>
       <dia:Freq4000Hz> 0.6 </dia:Freq4000Hz>
       <dia:Freq8000Hz> 4.4 </dia:Freq8000Hz>
    </dia:RightEar>
    <dia:LeftEar>
       <dia:Freq250Hz> 8.8 </dia:Freq250Hz>
       <dia:Freq500Hz> 3.0 </dia:Freq500Hz>
       <dia:Freq1000Hz> 2.0 </dia:Freq1000Hz>
       <dia:Freq2000Hz> 4.2 </dia:Freq2000Hz>
       <dia:Freq4000Hz> 9.2 </dia:Freq4000Hz>
       <dia:Freq8000Hz> 10.0 </dia:Freq8000Hz>
    </dia:LeftEar>
  </mpeg21:AuditoryImpairment>
</tva2:AccessibilityInformation>
```

Listing 5.2 Audio accessibility information

contains elements to reflect a higher level of detail, such as informing about low vision symptoms—like inability to see clearly—lack of contrast, need of light or loss of vision in the middle or periphery of the field of view. Even mild issues such as difficulties to perceive colour can be indicated, establishing whether it is a complete inability or if it is an inability to see red, green or blue.

In the example of Listing 5.3, it can be observed that the user is blind in the left eye (as indicated in line 3). In addition, lines 4 and 5 indicate loss of peripheral vision of medium intensity.

Therefore, if different versions of the same content are available, this user would be offered those which do not require the ability to see with both eyes (e.g. 3D signals that require stereoscopic vision). The fact that his/her good eye—the right eye—has the abovementioned deficit would also be taken into account. If there are two versions of the same interactive digital television application, one that is graphically rich, with more sophisticated but smaller buttons, and another with bigger graphics, the system would choose the latter for the user, given that the first one could jeopardize the user's ability to use the application.

Finally, Listing 5.4 shows how to indicate a user who is unable to use the remote control. In this case, to interact with an interactive digital television application, he/she should do it using his/her voice, if the PDR supports it. Otherwise, the user should stand up and go to the PDR to introduce commands through the buttons in front of it. Therefore, if the PDR does not respond to voice commands, the required interactive actions should be minimized for this user.

```
<tva2:AccessibilityInformation>
  <mpeg21:VisualImpairment>
    <dia:Blindness eyeSide="left" />
    <dia:LowVisionSymptoms>
      <dia:PeripheralVisionLoss TextualDegree="Medium" />
    </dia:LowVisionSymptoms>
  </mpeg21:VisualImpairment>
</tva2:AccessibilityInformation>
```

Listing 5.3 Visual accessibility information

```
<tva2:AccessibilityInformation>
  <tva2:OtherAccessibilityCharacteristics
   href=""urn:tva:metadata:extended:cs:AccessibilityCS:2005:UnableToUseRemote"/>
     <Name xml:lang="en"> Unable to use remote control </Name>
  </tva2:OtherAccessibilityCharacteristics>
</tva2:AccessibilityInformation>
```

Listing 5.4 Additional accessibility information

5.2.2.3 Combining User Information

The two metadata elements introduced in the previous sections are combined by a parent element called *<UserInformation>*, which describes a specific user. Many instances of this element may be grouped into a user description table called *UserInformationTable* (Fig. 5.1).

5.2.3 Environmental Description Information

In order to gather the information that describes the environment in which the user will consume the content, TV-Anytime considers the following three elements.

5.2.3.1 Terminal Information

It is extremely important to know the characteristics of the terminal that the user will use to play and visualize the content, since this allows the system to assess the appropriateness of a certain instance of a given content to be consumed in that device, even ruling out some of them for being incompatible. If a given content has different distribution models or different options are available (such as different screen resolutions), this knowledge would make it possible to select the most appropriate for the user's terminal.

Sometimes, the limitations will be determined by the hardware itself. For example, let us take a digital tablet with an 800×480 screen resolution that can only play video files up to that definition. In this case, TV-Anytime services should

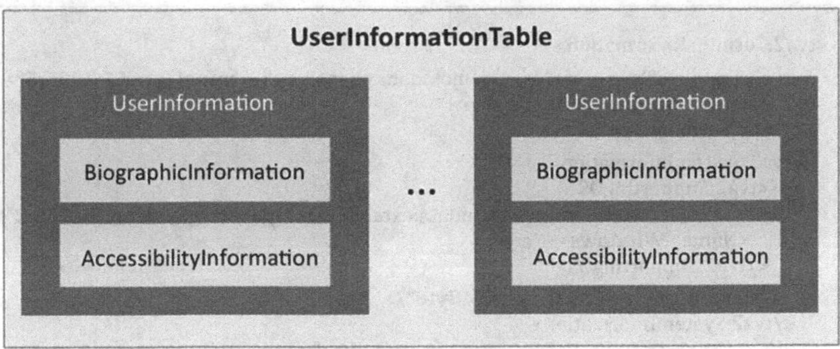

Fig. 5.1 UserInformationTable

reject downloading material indicated as being of higher definition than the specified one, since it would be useless to offer it.

In other cases, the hardware's capabilities will not necessarily be a limitation, since it could play higher definitions, but it will do it in an unnatural way. To explain this, we will use the same tablet example used above, with an 800 × 480 screen resolution, but this time it can play high-definition content (1920 × 1080) by means of a "codec" update. If two versions of the same content are available in 800 × 480 and 1920 × 1080 resolutions, evidently the first one will take up less space for the same encoding quality, and it will be possible to download it in less time occupying less bandwidth. It may even be cheaper. Clearly, it is worth checking the hardware's capabilities to send to it the most appropriate version of contents.

The same could be said of television sets commercially known as "HD Ready", which can play 1920 × 1080 high-definition content, even if their "native resolution", that is the number of pixels that form the screen, is 1366 × 768.

Broadly speaking, it is possible to depict in this category many of the characteristics of the user's terminal, structured by a *<TerminalInformation>* element:

- The manufacturer
- The operating system and *middleware* used
- The virtual machines executed in the terminal
- The RAM memory and storage capacities available
- The ability to reproduce audio and video encoded in different formats, according to the available codecs
- CPU type and speed
- The ability to interact with the user regarding how he/she enters information

Listing 5.5 shows an example of the use of terminal information. It can be seen in the XML sample that:

- The user's terminal is a cell phone (lines 2–4)
- The terminal's operating system is a version of Windows (lines 6–9)
- The terminal has 512 MB of RAM memory (line 10)
- The terminal can manage AVI files (lines 12–16)

```
<tva2:TerminalInformation>
  <tva2:TerminalType href="urn:tva:metadata:phase2:cs:TerminalTypeCS:2005:5">
      <Name> Mobile Phone </Name>
  </tva2:TerminalType>
  <tva2:SystemInformation>
      <tva2:SupportingOS
                  href="urn:tva:metadata:extended:cs:OperatingSystemCS:2005:2">
        <Name> Windows</Name>
      </tva2:SupportingOS>
       <tva2:RAM size="512" unit="MByte"/>
   </tva2:SystemInformation>
   <tva2:DecoderInformation  xsi:type="mpeg21:VideoCapabilitiesType">
       <mpeg21:Format  href="urn:mpeg:mpeg7:cs:VisualFileFormatCS:2001:7">
            <mpeg7:Name> AVI </mpeg7:Name>
       </mpeg21:Format>
   </tva2:DecoderInformation>
</tva2:TerminalInformation>
```

Listing 5.5 Example of terminal information

According to these characteristics, relatively important decisions will be made regarding content selection. For example, whoever decides that a given content should be sent (be it the terminal when it comes to *Pull Targeting* or the operator in the case of *Push Targeting*), the software that makes the decision should not select non-AVI contents, to avoid the risk that they cannot be played in the terminal.

5.2.3.2 Network Information

For *targeting* purposes, that is for the selection and delivery of programmes that are relevant for a user, it is also important to know the network in which the contents are transported. To achieve this, by means of a <*NetworkInformation*> element, a description is issued of the network the user's TV-Anytime terminal is connected to.

The possible network types are also described in part 7 of the MPEG-21 standard and include characteristics such as:

- Maximum network capacity
- Minimum guaranteed capacity
- Maximum allowed packet size
- Whether or not it has error correction
- Error rate at the packet level and bit level

Listing 5.6 shows an example of a network in which an average capacity of 2 Mbps is available and which has a 5 % bit error rate.

According to these characteristics, it is clear that the processes that assess the suitability of a given content for this user will rule out delivering HD streaming

```
<tva2:NetworkInformation>
    <mpeg21:NetworkCharacteristic >
        <dia:AvailableBandwidth average="2000000" />
        <dia:Error packetLossRate="0.05" />
    <mpeg21:NetworkCharacteristic >
</tva2:NetworkInformation>
```

Listing 5.6 Example of network information

contents, given that the network's bandwidth is probably not enough for an adequate playback.

5.2.3.3 Natural Environment Information

Finally, TV-Anytime also understands that, in order to make an appropriate *targeting*, it may be important to have information about the physical or natural environment in which the playback takes place. Characteristics such as humidity and temperature or weather conditions may affect the viewer's mood to watch different kinds of films or even affect his/her interest towards different kinds of advertisements (we will go back to this in Sect. 5.3).

For example, if it is raining, it may be more appropriate or valuable to see rain-related advertisements. This way, the viewer could be offered waterproof clothes or, if he/she is not at home, he/she could be provided car rental services with drivers or taxis.

As the name suggests, this information describes the natural environment in which the user will consume the contents. To this end, an element called *<NaturalEnvironmentInformation>* is defined, which gathers all the available environment data:

- Maximum, minimum and current temperature
- Maximum, minimum and current humidity
- What the physical location is like
- Time of day
- Weather conditions

Finally, Listing 5.7 shows the use of natural environment information on a rainy (lines 2–4) and cold (lines 5–8) day.

5.2.3.4 Combining Natural Environment Information

Different instances of the *<TerminalInformation>* element are finally grouped to form a table called *TerminalInformationTable*. The same happens with the other two elements, thus creating the corresponding *NetworkInformationTable* and *NaturalEnvironmentInformationTable*.

In turn, these tables can be grouped into a *<UsageEnvironment>* element which gathers all the environmental information.

This element (*<UsageEnvironment>*) and the user description table (*UserInformationTable*) described above are used to extend the *<UserDescription>*

```
<tva2:NaturalEnvironmentInformation>
  <tva2:Weather href="urn:tva:metadata:Phase2:cs:WeatherTypeCS:2005:6">
    <Name> Rainy </Name>
  </tva2:Weather>
  <tva:Temperature unit="Celsius">
     <tva:MinTemperature> 5 </tva:MinTemperature>
     <tva:MaxTemperature> 10 </tva:MaxTemperature>
   </tva:Temperature>
</tva2:NaturalEnvironmentInformation>
```

Listing 5.7 Example of natural environment information

element presented in Sect. 4.2.3, and this results in an element called *<ExtendedUserDescription>*, which expands the user information standardized in Phase 1.

5.2.4 Combining Targeting Information

The metadata elements described in the above sections are combined into a parent element that structures them all. This element, called *<TargetingInformation>*, is made up of the previously defined *<UserInformation>*, *<TerminalInformation>*, *<NetworkInformation>* and *<NaturalEnvironmentInformation>* elements (Fig. 5.2), among others, and it gathers all the relevant information about a user in order to estimate which contents would be more appropriate to offer him/her.

Different instances of this element (*<TargetingInformation>*) could be grouped to form a *TargetingInformationTable.*

5.3 Interstitials

5.3.1 Motivation

One of the main novelties included in TV-Anytime Phase 2 is a consistent technological framework to work with advertisements (typically known as *spots*, or *interstitials* in British English). The ample technological capacity of new PDRs introduces clear opportunities for the main funding element in the television industry, advertising, to be more effective and for new premium commercialization models to be possible, particularly in relation to targeting.

So far, this chapter has dealt with mechanisms defined by TV-Anytime to accurately identify or describe the user and his/her playback environment, making it easier to customize the contents to be offered to the user. By including now in our framework both advertisements and whole commercial breaks, new possibilities open up to use the PDR's functionalities to add value to publicity in television.

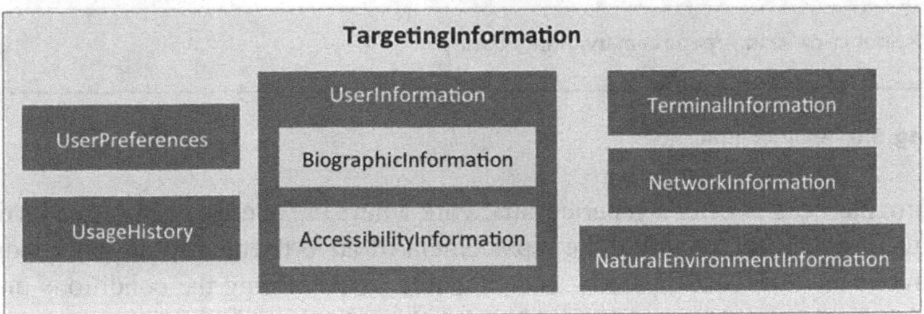

Fig. 5.2 TargetingInformation

These innovations are aimed at, for instance, the use of advanced concepts such as the ability to replace an advertisement in real time based on certain criteria that are previously defined by the content provider and dynamically evaluated by the software of the receiver.

The usefulness and relevance of this possibility cannot be questioned. It would logically allow showing a consumer preferably product advertisements that he/she has, implicitly or explicitly, recently shown some kind of interest for. Not only would it be an incentive for the user not to change channels and, therefore, consume the advertisement, but this information could also be sold at a higher price by the television operator given its alleged higher effectiveness. On the contrary, the characteristics declared in a user profile can result in an automatic block of certain products, such as hamburger advertisements for a viewer who has stated that he/she is a strict vegetarian.

However, there are also other types of circumstances not related to a concrete user. It may be interesting, as we mentioned, to change a *spot* or a whole commercial break according to the weather (a rainy summer day does not seem to be the most appropriate time to advertise sun lotion) or maybe according to the date, with Christmas and the days leading to it probably being the most characteristic example of selective promotions. It is even reasonable to think that for operators covering wide areas, it is interesting to filter their advertisements according to the viewers' geographical area (it may happen that certain products are not offered in some regions and, at the same time, the same advertiser offers other products there).

These possibilities benefit both the viewer and the advertiser since it does not waste its advertising investment in viewers who will most likely not consume its products, thus resulting in better audience segmentation. But it also benefits the operator given the fact that it can offer new services to advertisers, improving its offer through effectiveness, while also better fulfilling its mission of informing customers through better targeted advertisements.

TV-Anytime specifications contain numerous sections with references to advertising and new business models directly related to it, although the main contribution is in Part 3-4. The creators of TV-Anytime have not tried to define all the possible ways in which a broadcaster can wish to control its advertisement system by specifying the functionalities foreseen for the advertising *spots*. On the contrary,

```
1 <Spot crid="crid://pepe.com.uy/Blue_Foam"/>
```

Listing 5.8 *Spot* identification

the aim has been to offer a generic framework where the operator can define its own means of operation to control the replacement of advertisements—in other words, to favour the television operator to be capable of describing the conditions under which an advertisement must be replaced and what must take its place.

5.3.2 Spots and Pods

It is well known that the typical advertisement or single commercial unit on television is called a "*spot*" or "*interstitial*", and these terms are retained in the TV-Anytime framework. Furthermore, a "*pod*" or "*Interstitial break*"[1] is a commercial segment, that is the period of time in which the broadcaster interrupts the broadcast of a programme to show advertisements.

A *spot*, as a single audiovisual content, will be identified in the TV-Anytime context like any other content, that is using a CRID, as discussed in Chap. 3. Thus, for instance, a *spot* for "*Blue_Foam*" shaving foam could be identified as it is in Listing 5.8. The CRID's statement corresponding to the *spot* can be found in line 1.

However, within the TV-Anytime specification, the definition of elements to represent a *pod* and its contents is not considered. According to its arguments, this is something that corresponds to the standards that regulate the different distribution platforms (DVB, ATSC, ARIB, etc.). The only issue that concerns TV-Anytime is the definition of the mechanisms to specify the possible replacement of *spots* within *pods*. The starting point is that *pods* are duly identified within their scope, so they can be referenced when expressing the rules and conditions that govern replacement processes.

In order to replace *spots* and *pods*, it is necessary to define data structures to be able to express advertisement and break replacements, as well as the conditions for the changes. The topic will be further discussed in the following sections.

5.3.3 Replacement Rules

One of the first steps to take in the construction of a framework that allows the dynamic replacement of advertisements consists of expressing the conditions that govern these replacements. These conditions will involve circumstances related to

[1] Just like before, the second term is mostly used in Great Britain.

the user, geographical area, date, etc., which must be evaluated in real time to make decisions.

The main axis to articulate this mechanism is the concept of predicate, materialized in a *<Predicate>* element, which represents logical expressions that are evaluated as true or false. Through them it is possible, for example, to request the comparison of the values of certain variables with a constant and make decisions based on whether they are the same, one includes the other, etc. These expressions involve methods that obtain values related to the content, the user, the date, etc. (through a *<RuleMethod>* element); parameters to characterize these methods (with the *<MethodParameter>* element); and constants that methods are compared with (by means of the *<ConstantValue>* element).

Furthermore, various *<Predicate>* elements can be combined by means of the *<PredicateBag>* element, which includes an indication of the type of combination (OR or AND, whose meaning does not require further explanations).

Finally, various *<Predicate>* or *<PredicateBag>* elements are structured through a *<rule>* element, which represents a rule whose positive or negative evaluation may be used to condition a replacement. In other words, the rules represented by the *<rule>* element will be what may later be referenced to govern the possible replacement of a *spot* or a *pod*.

The example in Listing 5.9 shows how two rules, identified as "*WorldCup_2010*" and "*Children*", are defined. The first, defined in lines 2 and 13, is true for the dates when the World Cup was played, between June 11 and July 11, 2010. Thus, the current date (value returned by the *<RuleMethod>* element of the *SystemDateTime* type) must be less than the ending date (*<Predicate>* element in line 4) and greater than the starting date (*<Predicate>* element in line 8) of the World Cup. Both conditions must be true, which is indicated in the *<PredicateBag>* element.

On the other hand, the "*Children*" rule (lines 14–19) states that, in order to be true, the age of the user (collected by the *<RuleMethod>* element of the *ParentalControl* type in line 16) must be less than 15.

5.3.4 Conditioned Replacements

Once the way to represent the rules that will govern replacements has been determined, we shall see how these rules are associated with the replacement of advertisements. This process takes place through one or many *<Condition>* elements, each of them representing a condition. If there are many *<Condition>* elements, it is enough for one to be true, that is they combine by means of an *OR* operation.

Each *<Condition>* element may carry an attribute named "*require*", whose value will be the name of one or many rules (separated by spaces) out of those defined in the previous section. All the rules declared must be true for the condition specified by that *<Condition>* element to be true, that is they combine by means of an AND operation.

```
<RulesTable>
  <rule rule_id="WorldCup_2010">
    <PredicateBag type="AND">
      <Predicate test="less_than">
        <RuleMethod methodName="urn:pepe:Interstitials:SystemDateTime"/>
        <ConstantValue value="2010-07-12T00:00:00Z"/>
      </Predicate>
      <Predicate test="greater_than">
        <RuleMethod methodName="urn:pepe:Interstitials:SystemDateTime"/>
        <ConstantValue value="2010-06-11T00:00:00Z" />
      </Predicate>
    </PredicateBag>
  </rule>
  <rule rule_id="Children">
    <Predicate test="less_than">
      <RuleMethod methodName="urn:pepe:Interstitials:ParentalControl"/>
      <ConstantValue value="15"/>
    </Predicate>
  </rule>
</RulesTable>
```

Listing 5.9 Rules that govern replacements

```
1 <Condition require="Children" />
2 <Condition require="WorldCup_2010" except="Children" />
3 <Condition except=" WorldCup_2010 Children" />
```

Listing 5.10 Examples of conditions

The *<Condition>* element may also have an "*except*" attribute besides the "*require*" attribute. In this case, for the condition specified by this *<Condition>* element to be true, all the rules declared need to be false.

Imagine two versions of the same "*Blue_Foam*" shaving foam advertisement. While the first is generic (its CRID is the one in Listing 5.8), the second stars football player Cristiano Ronaldo (in this case, its corresponding CRID is "*crid://pepe.com.uy/Blue_Foam_CR*"), and it is meant to be broadcast for the duration of World Cup 2010. Since the advertisement is clearly not interesting for children, we will add to our board another advertisement which will be more relevant for them: the *PlayStation* console (this time, its CRID will be "*crid://pepe.com.uy/PlayStation*").

Listing 5.10 shows three conditions. Each of them represents the rules that have to be verified to decide the broadcast of the most appropriate advertisement.

If the only rule involved in the condition in line 1 is true, then the "PlayStation" advertisement must be broadcast. In order for the condition in line 2 to be true, the

```
<SpotSubstitution>
   < ReplacementSpot>
      < Condition require="Children"/>
      < Spot crid="crid://pepe.com.uy/PlayStation"/>
   </ ReplacementSpot >
   < ReplacementSpot >
      < Condition require="WorldCup_2010" except="Children"/>
      < Spot crid="crid://pepe.com.uy/Blue_Foam_CR"/>
   </ ReplacementSpot >
   < ReplacementSpot >
      < Condition except=" WorldCup _2010 Children"/>
      < Spot crid="crid://pepe.com.uy/Blue_Foam "/>
   </ ReplacementSpot >
</ SpotSubstitution>
```

Listing 5.11 *Spot* replacement

"*WorldCup_2010*" rule needs to be true and the "*Children*" rule needs to be false. In that case, the "*Blue_Foam_CR*" advertisement must be broadcast. Finally, both conditions ("*WorldCup_2010*" and "*Children*") need to be false to make the third condition true, which would lead to the broadcast of the generic "*Blue_Foam*" advertisement.

Should the receiver have to replace the current advertisement, the metadata fragment that should be used to drive its behaviour would be the one featured in Listing 5.11, where a parent *<SpotSubstitution>* element includes a *<ReplacementSpot>* element for each of the elements mentioned before.

As stated before, it is also possible to plan the replacement of an entire commercial break. This is the case in Listing 5.12, where we see an example in which if the following *pod* to be broadcast is called "*oldPOD*", the receiver must change its content (two spots only) according to the "*Children*" and "*WorldCup_2010*" rules above.

The parent element (*<InterstitialBreak>*) contains two elements: an *<InterstitialBreakSelectionRule>* (line 2) to decide if the metadata fragment is applicable to the current *pod* and a *<PodSubstitution>* (line 8) to declare the result of the replacement, if it takes place.

The *<InterstitialBreakSelectionRule>* element simply compares (the "*equals*" attribute in line 3) the identifier of the current *pod* (returned by the *targetPodID* method in line 5) with the "*oldPOD*" string (line 4).

Within the *<PodSubstitution>* element, we find a *<ReplacementPod>* element for each of the situations declared in the rules: the viewer being a child (line 10) or not (line 15). Two appropriate advertisements are chosen in each case.

Moreover, a cascade replacement can take place taking into account several conditions, maybe even replacing a whole commercial break or one or many spots within the pod. The change in a commercial break can also be made through the replacement of many individual spots.

```
1 <InterstitialBreak>
2     <InterstitialBreakSelectionRule>
3       <Predicate test="equals">
4         <ConstantValue value="oldPOD"/>
5         <RuleMethod methodName="urn:pepe:Interstitials:targetPodID"/>
6       </Predicate>
7     </InterstitialBreakSelectionRule>
8     <PodSubstitution>
9       <ReplacementPod>
10        <Condition require="Infantil"/>
11        <Spot crid="crid://pepe.com.uy/PlayStation"/>
12        <Spot crid="crid://pepe.com.uy/NiceBike"/>
13      </ReplacementPod >
14      <ReplacementPod>
15        <Condition except="Infantil"/>
16        <Spot crid="crid://pepe.com.uy/Blue_Foam"/>
17        <Spot crid="crid://pepe.com.uy/Car_iPlus"/>
18      </ReplacementPod>
19  </PodSubstitution>
20 <InterstitialBreak>
```

Listing 5.12 *Pod* replacement

Listing 5.13 shows an example of this change. We have added a *<SpotSubstitution>* element (line 20) to the previous listing (lines 1–19) to indicate new changes in the result of the last selection. In this case, if the "*Blue_Foam*" *spot* was selected, there needs to be an analysis of whether we are within the period of the World Cup, in which case the spot changes to "*Blue_Foam_CR*".

5.3.5 Recording Cache

At this point, the reader must have realized that to achieve a reasonable effectiveness in the dynamic replacement of interstitials in commercial breaks, it is essential to have these spots in the local storage.

Indeed, if the objective was to select an advertisement among two or three choices, we could trust the possibility that they would be sent in parallel with an acceptable increase in bandwidth consumption and that the receiver would have them at its disposal by accessing the right transport stream. However, if the aim is to achieve a high level of adequacy for most users, we are forced to offer at any given time a much wider range of advertisements, whose simultaneous broadcast in real time does not seem feasible.

Therefore, it is necessary to have a mechanism for the PDR to have at its disposal the contents that will eventually replace others at the right time. This mechanism will consist of a spot recording cache that will store in the local storage those interstitials that have higher possibilities of being selected for viewing, according to

```
<InterstitialBreak>
   <InterstitialBreakSelectionRule>
     <Predicate test="equals">
        <ConstantValue value="oldPOD"/>
        <RuleMethod methodName="urn:pepe:Interstitials:targetPodID"/>
     </Predicate>
   </InterstitialBreakSelectionRule>
   <PodSubstitution>
     <ReplacementPod>
        <Condition require="Children"/>
        <Spot crid="crid://pepe.com.uy/PlayStation"/>
        <Spot crid="crid://pepe.com.uy/NiceBike"/>
     </ReplacementPod >
     <ReplacementPod>
       <Condition except=" Children"/>
       <Spot crid="crid://pepe.com.uy/Blue_Foam"/>
       <Spot crid="crid://pepe.com.uy/Car_iPlus"/>
     </ReplacementPod>
  </PodSubstitution>
  <SpotSubstitution>
   <SpotSelectionRule>
      <Predicate test="equals">
        <ConstantValue value="crid://pepe.com.uy/Blue_Foam"/>
        <RuleMethod methodName="urn:pepe:Interstitials:SpotID"/>
      </Predicate>
   </SpotSelectionRule>
     < ReplacementSpot>
     < Condition require="WorldCup_2010"/>
     < Spot crid=" crid://pepe.com.uy/Blue_Foam_CR "/>
     </ ReplacementSpot >
  <SpotSubstitution>
 <InterstitialBreak>
```

Listing 5.13 Cascade replacement

the rules programmed in the receiver about the user's preferences, his consumption history or socio-demographic information.

The contents more likely to participate in replacements could be broadcast cyclically in parallel transport streams, according to the frequency that the operator deems appropriate (even making use of those free slots when the operator's schedule is less busy), or directly broadcast to each PDR through the return channel, possibly during periods of low network demand (e.g. at night).

In general terms, the storage of a set of spots would fill up any storage capacity in the PDR sooner or later. Therefore, it is also necessary to establish mechanisms to be able to specify when an advertisement expires and can be deleted from the cache. It is even possible to order its replacement for other reasons, such as low effectiveness of the advertising campaign or any kind of social issue related to the content.

```
1 <RecordingCache>
2    <Request>
3       <Item>
4          < Condition require="WorldCup_2010"/>
5          < Spot crid="crid://pepe.com.uy/Blue_Foam_CR"/>
6       </Item>
7       <Item>
8          < Condition require="Children"/>
9          < Spot crid="crid://pepe.com.uy/PlayStation"/>
10      </Item>
11   </Request>
12   <Expire>
13        < Condition except=" WorldCup _2010"/>
14        < Spot crid="crid://pepe.com.uy/Blue_Foam_CR"/>
15   </Expire>
16 <RecordingCache>
```

Listing 5.14 Example of the use of a recording cache

In order to determine the mechanisms through which operators can give instructions to PDRs about how to manage this recording cache, TV-Anytime defines a set of elements through which operators can specify which spots have to be captured, under which circumstances and when they can be deleted.

Listing 5.14 shows an example of this specification capacity structured around a *<RecordingCache>* element (line 1). Basically, the element may contain two sub-elements: a *<Request>* element to order the capture and storage of spots and an *<Expire>* element to indicate that some have expired and can be deleted. It is possible to attach the conditions that govern these operations in both cases.

An example of the first element (lines 2–11) has two blocks (each delimited by *<Item>* elements), where it is stated that two spots should be fetched: if the "*WorldCup_2010*" condition is true, then the PDR should record the Cristiano Ronaldo shaving foam spot whereas if the "*Children*" condition is true, then it is the "PlayStation" interstitial which should be constantly ready.

In the second case (lines 12–15), the operator indicates that if the "WorldCup_2010" condition is not met anymore, it does not make sense to continue storing the "*Blue_Foam_CR*" advertisement since it will not be broadcast, and so it can be deleted from the local storage.

5.4 Coupons

The strategy of offering discount coupons constitutes a successful promotion technique commonly used in other spheres such as large stores and supermarkets. These coupons may offer a discount, whether in absolute terms or a percentage over the product's price, or two units for the price of one, or buy three and get one free.

With the intention of reproducing the strategy, coupons are another possibility introduced by TV-Anytime Phase 2 to boost the commercialization of contents and associated products, offering a competitive advantage for service providers that use them. The framework for declaring coupons and their descriptive metadata will provide operators with the right tools to associate special price and promotional gift offers to certain contents. Thus, coupons are a way to provide electronic value that may be used to complement or replace money when purchasing contents.

Therefore, it is possible to imagine a wide array of interesting new business models which become feasible from the combination of the coupon's functionality and the customized selection and targeting tools described in Sect. 5.2 (*Targeting*).

Among the metadata provided by TV-Anytime to create the coupon framework, it is important to mention first the necessary metadata to announce the existence of the coupon itself. Also, the description of the coupon must be provided to the user, indicating its value, the discount method, the discount object or a text explanation. On the other hand, coupon metadata can also describe characteristics about those meant to be used in the purchase of non-TV-Anytime content.

Therefore, coupon metadata includes a series of characteristics that allow it to describe:

- A unique identifier for the coupon
- An issuing authority that guarantees its authenticity
- The object promoted by the coupon, which may be a programme, a content genre or even a whole television service
- The price and discount information of a given content (a new price, a discount in absolute terms or a discount percentage)
- The required number of coupons to have access to the promotion
- Certain targeting information about the type of users the coupon would be aimed at, to whom it could be offered in a personalized way
- The beginning and end of the promotion
- The type of acquisition (whether immediate or related to the prior purchase of a given content)
- If the user's approval is required for its validity
- A description of the promotion to be shown to the user to inform them
- A URL for the user to check the status and history of their coupons

The first example illustrated in Listing 5.15 describes a coupon that is valid over Christmas, from December 21 to 31 (lines 1 and 2), and which does not require a prior condition (indicated with the *"immediate"* value and the *"acquisitionMode"* attribute in line 3).

Lines 4–8 show that it is a promotion for certain fiction contents, a category movies tend to be classified into. Line 10 shows that the promotion consists of a 25 % discount. Line 12 adds the URL of a website to find out additional information, while line 14 includes a brief text description of the promotion, whose only aim is to be presented to the viewers.

Various *<CouponDescription>* elements, such as the one shown in Listing 5.15, may be grouped into a new table named *CouponTable*, which belongs to the range of content description metadata (category 1 of the ones shown in Fig. 2.4). The

```
<tva2:CouponDescription start="2011-12-21T00:00:00-05:00"
                        end="2011-12-31T23:59:59-05:00"
                   couponId="Movie-25off" acquisitionMode="immediate">
    <tva2:ContentTarget>
        <tva2:Genre href="urn:tva:metadata:cs:ContentCS:2010:3.4" type="main">
          <Name lang="en"> FICTION/DRAMA </Name>
      </tva2:Genre>
    </tva2:ContentTarget>
    <tva2:CouponValue>
        <tva2:ReductionPercentage> 25 </tva2:ReductionPercentage>
    </tva2:CouponValue>
    <tva2:CouponURL> http://www.latienda.com.uy </tva2:CouponURL>
    <tva2:CouponText xml:lang="es">
        Enjoy movies this Christmass with 25% off
    </tva2:CouponText>
</tva2:CouponDescription>
```

Listing 5.15 Example of discount coupon

coupons declared in those tables can be later referenced from the metadata that describes the content purchase models and prices.

Lastly, Listing 5.16 includes a broader example which shows that there exists a movie called "*Source Code*" (line 6), whose price is 3 € (line 12) as long as the user has the "*Movie-25off*" coupon described in Listing 5.15 (*<RequiredCoupon>* element in line 13).

Likewise, the purchase of this content rewards the user with a coupon identified as "*Football-3x2*" (*<RewardCoupon>* element, between lines 14 and 18). With this coupon, described in lines 26–36, the user gets an offer of three for the price of two in the purchase of football matches.

5.5 Summary

In this chapter, we have introduced new tools included in Phase 2 of TV-Anytime that provide a wide support in the way for a more personalized television: basic descriptive tools to capture specific details of each user, a framework for dynamic advertising management and a mechanism to promote contents.

By means of the tools grouped under the term *targeting*, it is possible to undertake a personalized targeting of contents according to the users' demographic data, their possible disabilities, the equipment used to play the content or the environment in which that consumption occurs. The information in these categories allows the identification of contents that may be appealing to them or those that should be avoided because of their inappropriate technical characteristics.

```
<TVAMain>
 <ProgramDescription>
   <ProgramInformationTable>
     <ProgramInformation programId="crid://www.tvcable.com.uy/source_code">
       <BasicDescription xsi:type="tva2:ExtendedContentDescriptionType">
         <Title xml:lang="en-us" type="main"> Source Code </Title>
         <Synopsis xml:lang="en" length="short">
            Action film centered on a soldier who wakes up in the body of...
         </Synopsis>
         <PurchaseList>
            <PurchaseItem xsi:type="tva2:ExtendedPurchaseItemType">
              <Price currency="EUR"> 3 </Price>
              <tva2:RequiredCoupon  couponId="Movie-25off "/>
              <tva2:RewardCoupon>
                <tva2:CouponRef>
                  <tva2:CouponIdRef> Football-3x2 </tva2:CouponIdRef>
                </tva2:CouponRef>
              </tva2:RewardCoupon>
            </PurchaseItem>
          </PurchaseList>
       </BasicDescription>
     </ProgramInformation>
   </ProgramInformationTable>
 </ProgramDescription>
 <tva2:CouponTable>
   <tva2:CouponDescription requiredNumber="2" couponId=" Football-3x2">
     <tva2:CouponValue>
       <tva2:ReductionPercentage> 100 </tva2:ReductionPercentage>
     </tva2:CouponValue>
     <tva2:ContentTarget>
       <tva2:Genre href="urn:tva:metadata:cs:ContentCS:2010:3.2.3.12" />
         <Name lang="en"> Football (Soccer) </Name>
       </tva2:Genre>
     </tva2:ContentTarget>
     <tva2:CouponText xml:lang="es"> 3x2 football</tva2:CouponText>
   </tva2:CouponDescription>
 </tva2:CouponTable>
</TVAMain>
```

Listing 5.16 Example of coupon use

The *Interstitials* framework allows for the dynamic replacement of advertisements, perhaps conditioned by the *targeting* information. Thus, the operator can instruct the receiver to play either spot based on the date, the information about the user (e.g. his age), the technical characteristics of the equipment used or the history of interstitials offered in the past.

And, finally, a framework is provided to define and use discount coupons to promote the consumption of contents in a personalized way, based on the aforementioned targeting information and the historical consumption of each user.

The next chapter will be about the content packaging mechanism (*Packaging*) to enable a synchronized and coordinated content reproduction and, in this way, to get richer and gratifying consumer experiences.

Packaging 6

6.1 Introduction

6.1.1 New Business Model

One of the main characteristics of modern consumer electronic devices is their growing connectivity, in the variety of networks and technologies as well as in their speed. This is why the user's daily experience when watching television increasingly transcends the mere fact of passively enjoying contents and frequently involves a simultaneous (and sometimes coordinated) access to the Internet. In fact, when writing these lines, the latest technological debate on this topic is centred on the potential of *second screens* (digital tablets or mobiles) as an interactive complement to enrich the television experience, providing an additional channel not only to expand information but also to act as a vehicle for the audience's participation in the evolution of programmes. Given the current competition level and the speed innovations are introduced with, it is clear that for the television industry it is at least important (if not essential) to offer an experience that goes beyond the traditional "watching" television.

TV-Anytime is born with the intention of giving this industry the mechanisms to do so. It also gives the advantage of offering a standardized path, which accelerates the dissemination and acceptance of technological improvements. In fact, regarding this last aspect, some television operators have started criticizing the policies of Smart TV manufacturers, who are in a desperate race to promote their proprietary application model, incompatible with each other. As already stated in many forums, this can only lead to a disastrous fragmentation of the market, while the use of these advances in favour of integration in the entire chain of audiovisual production is wasted.

Therefore, the promotion of new standards for content creators, broadcast operators and equipment manufacturers allows to continue trusting in a better device interoperability in the future, which will undoubtedly lead to a better user experience.

A. Gil Solla and R.G. Sotelo Bovino, *TV-Anytime*, X.media.publishing,
DOI 10.1007/978-3-642-36766-3_6, © Springer-Verlag Berlin Heidelberg 2013

In the first chapter of this book, precisely in Sect. 1.3.2, we claimed that TV-Anytime Phase 2 had the objective of boosting new business models focused on the existence of high-quality bidirectional connectivity. In this chapter, we will present the framework that would allow making one of the most ambitious come true, that is the one that enables a consumer to receive or order the acquisition of interactive packages, formed by multiple elements: traditional audiovisual contents, interactive applications, data, text, graphs, games, hyperlinks to other contents, etc. Although these elements can be enjoyed separately, what characterizes this particular context is the existence of some kind of consumption coordination, the guidance by the package itself (i.e. its creator) for the best way of enjoying them, and the fact that this way may depend on the receiver's capacities or the user's own characteristics.

6.1.2 Packages and Their New Functionalities

As stated before, TV-Anytime Phase 2 sketches a scenario in which the PDR has a broadband Internet access, which enables many possibilities of interaction. Beyond video and audio—the traditional components of a television programme—nowadays, there is a great amount of information on the Internet that is interesting for users and which is encoded in alternative formats. It is clear that being able to access these new kinds of contents through television is especially interesting for the projection and growth of this medium.

This enhanced connectivity—together with hardware having greater capabilities—makes it possible for this resource to manage games, websites, music files, graphs or data, as well as execute applications, all in a coordinated way.

The abovementioned components could be reproduced both individually and together with other components they are related to. This new capacity makes it possible for the user to be offered richer and more intensive experiences regarding the consumption of combined contents than what was foreseen in Phase 1. The richness given by TV-Anytime Phase 2 resides in the fact that the aggregated contents, although they can have several origins or formats, may be executed together as part of a unique and comprehensive experience.

Therefore, the way for a new range of audiovisual productions is paved, whose nature goes beyond the traditional programme only composed by audio and video. We can imagine, for instance, the case of a user playing a game on his/her PDR, after having downloaded it to the device from the Internet, and using television as a visualization device or to capture gestures through its camera. An educational programme aimed at young children may include an application conveniently referenced by the presenter of the programme for the child to be trained on the topic that is being taught, something like an interactive training to learn the colours or basic geometric shapes. An audiovisual geography course aimed at older children could come with an educational game in which the child can practise what he/she has learned, guessing in a world map the location of the geographic places he/she has studied about. A football match can come with an application which shows, when the viewer decides so by means of an action such as pressing the red button, online statistics, for instance how many metres a certain player has covered with his movements. Or a window could suddenly open to auction the jersey of a certain player or the ball of the game. Similarly, a programme featuring two political leaders debating about a certain topic of social interest could send text or illustrative graphs about the topic at the same time the video is being played, but without overprinting the image, aimed only at the viewer who wishes to learn more about a certain aspect.

This new feature, which in TV-Anytime is called *Packaging*, allows us to group video, audio, games, text, fixed images or even applications destined to be reproduced together in a coordinated way, with the objective of giving the consumer a harmonizing experience. The name comes from the possibility of grouping together different contents to form a single entity, manageable in an atomic way, regarding its acquisition as well as its reproduction.

The components of this package will be executed or reproduced according to a certain sequence or order established by the creator of the package, which will be conveniently reflected in the metadata that describes the package. This synchronization of contents is not only time related, deciding which element comes after another one or if some will be simultaneous, but it may also be materialized in a coordinated spatial location on the screen. However, to provide more flexibility, this multidimensional synchronization is not fixed in any case, and so the creator of the package can include the possibility of making changes according to decisions made by the viewer, the results of the execution of different components or criteria derived from current circumstances or the user's preferences.

Giving more educational examples, we can think of a course composed of many audiovisual classes, each of which ends with a task or test that the student must pass to access the next stage. In case he/she does not provide the right answer or achieve the minimum score, he could be forced to take the lesson again or go through a new one that explains the topic in more detail. With this succession of topics, we are assured that once the student reaches the end of the course, he/she has successfully learned each and every one of the didactic units.

An additional characteristic of packages is that they can group several versions of the same content created in different ways, to be reproduced or executed according to certain characteristics present in the usage environment or associated to the user that plays it. The former are related to the device, the PDR/television set, used to reproduce the package. It could refer to two versions of the content with different qualities, for example standard definition and high definition, and, according to the capacity of the device, one or the other will be reproduced. The second kind of variation refers to user preferences. It could be a package that includes audio in many languages, and while playing it, the more appropriate is (automatically) selected.

```
1 <tva2:Descriptor>
2   <tva2:ObjectDescription>
3     <tva2:ContentDescription>
4       <Title> First goal in the Copa América 2011 final</Title>
5     </tva2:ContentDescription>
6   </tva2:ObjectDescription>
7 </tva2:Descriptor>
```

Listing 6.1 Simple example of a *<Descriptor>* element

6.2 Package Description

6.2.1 Introduction

So far we have discussed packages in general, without giving a precise definition. It is natural to assume that they consist of smaller elements, which play different hierarchical roles in their own internal dynamic. To effectively define what is meant by a content package and thus being able to relate it with what we know so far about TV-Anytime, we must define other previous concepts such as *Component* or *Item*. We will address this issue below. These concepts were originated in the MPEG-21 standard, specifically in the section entitled *Digital Item Declaration* (DID), which is responsible for the way of declaring everything about digital items (digital representations of real multimedia objects).

But, first, we will introduce an auxiliary element, the *<Descriptor>*, used crossways in all the examples in this chapter and whose purpose is to associate descriptive information to an element, whether it is a *Component*, an *Item*, a *Package* or other additional elements that will be presented in the following pages.

This descriptive information may be of various kinds, for example a basic description of a given content as defined in Phase 1 (you can see an example in Listing 4.1), a *ContentProperties* structure with the extensions of Phase 2 (Fig. 4.9) or the *targeting* information presented in the previous chapter (Fig. 5.2). For instance, in Listing 6.1 it can be seen what may be the simplest case to show, in which a mere description of a given content's title (line 4) is provided.

A more complete case is shown in Listing 6.2, where some *targeting* information is provided which describes a user's device through the *<TerminalInformation>* element (line 5). Specifically, this information includes two features of that device: it supports the execution of F*lash* animations (lines 7–10) and it has at least 1 GB of RAM memory (line 11).

As we will discuss later, this information can be used by the creator of a package to specify the requirements to be met by a receiver to correctly reproduce some parts of the package. In light of this information, the reproduction of a package will take place in one way or another depending on the characteristics of the user's device.

```
<tva2:Descriptor>
  <tva2:ObjectDescription>
    <tva2:ContentDescription>
      <tva2:TargetingInformation>
        <tva2:TerminalInformation>
          <tva2:SystemInformation>
            <tva2:OtherSystemSW
             href="urn:tva:metadata:extended:cs:OtherSystemSoftwareCS:2005:2.6">
                <Name xml:lang="en"> flash </Name>
            </tva2:OtherSystemSW>
            <tva2:RAM size="1" unit="GByte"/>
          </tva2:SystemInformation>
        </tva2:TerminalInformation>
      </tva2:TargetingInformation>
    </tva2:ContentDescription>
  </tva2:ObjectDescription>
</tva2:Descriptor>
```

Listing 6.2 Broader example of the *<Descriptor>* element

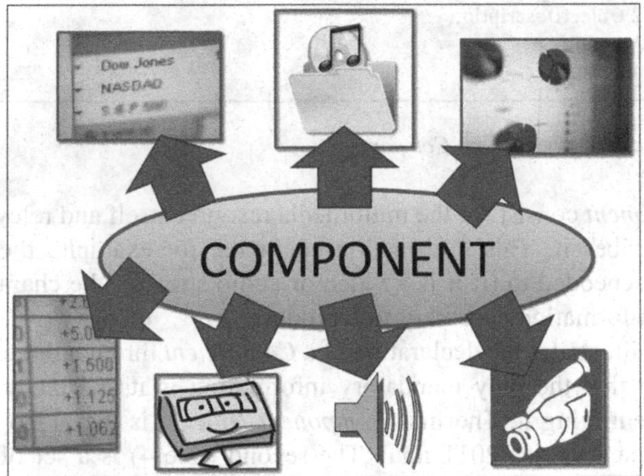

Fig. 6.1 Examples of *Components*

6.2.2 *Component*

The *Component* is the simplest entity to be obtained by the viewer or user from the audiovisual system. For example, it could be a video or audio resource (file or stream) (Fig. 6.1).

Each of the text files or graphs we referred to in the example of the political debate constitutes a *Component*, as well as the application that executes the test to be passed by the student that we saw in another example.

```
1 <tva2:Component>
2    <tva2:Resource crid="CRID://football.ar/Video_FINAL_COPA_AMERICA_2011"/>
3 </tva2:Component>
4 <tva2:Component>
5    <tva2:Descriptor>
6      CONTENT EXAMPLE IN LISTING 6.2
7    </tva2:Descriptor>
8    <tva2:Resource crid="CRID://football.ar/Stats_Forlan_CA_2011_flash"/>
9 </tva2:Component>
10 <tva2:Component>
11    <tva2:Resource crid="CRID://football.ar/Previous_Goals_CA_2011"/>
12    <tva2:Descriptor>
13      <tva2:ObjectDescription>
14        <tva2:ContentDescription>
15          <tva2:ContentProperties>
16            <tva2:ContentAttributes xsi:type="tva2:AudioAttributesType">
17              <tva2:Coding href="AAC"/>
18              <tva2:NumOfChannels> 1 </tva2:NumOfChannels>
19              <tva2:AudioLanguage> en </tva2:AudioLanguage>
20            </tva2:ContentAttributes>
21          </tva2:ContentProperties>
22        </tva2:ContentDescription>
23      </tva2:ObjectDescription>
24    </tva2:Descriptor>
25 </tva2:Component>
```

Listing 6.3 Declaration of several *Components*

The *Component* consists of the multimedia resource itself and relevant information that describes it. This information could be, for example, the bit rate the *Component* is encoded to (if it is a video or audio stream), the character set used or the codec information necessary to reproduce it.

Listing 6.3 illustrates the declaration of a *Component* through three examples, in which we see that the only mandatory information is its CRID, with the clear purpose of identifying it. The first *Component* (line 1) is the video of a football game, the Copa America 2011 final. The second (line 4) is a set of graphs with statistics on the performance of a player up to that game. We can see that it is accompanied by a *Descriptor*, the one shown in Listing 6.2, which indicates that in order to reproduce these statistics, the user's device must support Flash and have at least 1 GB of RAM memory. The last *Component* (line 10) is a video with the goals scored during the tournament by each of the finalist teams. In this last case, the *Component* is accompanied by a descriptor (line 12) that characterizes it, indicating that the audio of this video is monochannel (line 18), in English (line 19) and encoded in AAC (line 17).

The declaration of a *Component* also allows the identification of different instants in the same audiovisual resource, as shown in Listing 6.4, to facilitate a direct access to them. It defines the *Component* corresponding to the Copa America

```
1 <tva2:Component>
2     <tva2:Resource crid="CRID://football.ar/Video_FINAL_COPA_AMERICA_2011"/>
3     <tva2:Anchor>
4         <tva2:Condition require="First_Goal"/>
5         <tva2:Descriptor>
6             <tva2:ObjectDescription>
7                 <tva2:Description> The final's first goal </tva2:Description>
8             </tva2:ObjectDescription>
9         </tva2:Descriptor>
10        <tva2:TemporalLocation>
11            <TimePoint> T00:11:03 </TimePoint>
12        </tva2:TemporalLocation>
13    </tva2:Anchor>
14    <tva2:Anchor>
15        <tva2:Condition require="Second_Goal"/>
16        <tva2:TemporalLocation>
17            <TimePoint> T00:42:00 </TimePoint>
18        </tva2:TemporalLocation>
19    </tva2:Anchor>
20    <tva2:Anchor>
21        <tva2:Condition require="Third_Goal"/>
22        <tva2:TemporalLocation>
23            <TimePoint> T01:44:00 </TimePoint>
24        </tva2:TemporalLocation>
25    </tva2:Anchor>
26 </tva2:Component>
```

Listing 6.4 Access to different instants in a *Component's* video

2011 final, providing, as before, its CRID (line 2) but also declaring three temporal points, each associated to a different condition (used as presented in the previous chapter). They are called "*First_Goal*" (line 4), "*Second_Goal*" (line 15) and "*Third_Goal*" (line 21) and represent the corresponding instants when the corresponding goals were scored.

6.2.3 *Item*

An *Item* is a consumable element, that is an entity that is offered to the user as a complete unit to be reproduced in the PDR. It constitutes an autonomous multimedia experience that could be, for example, a video or audio clip, which might have versions in different formats, each of which would be a *Component*.

This is the main difference between an *Item* and a *Component*. While the former may be offered to the user as a unit to consume or subscribe to, the latter cannot, because it is not an autonomous content. In fact, an *Item* is constituted by a set of *Components* that could be reproduced sequentially, in parallel or alternatively. The *Component* can be downloaded and executed but always in the context of a user's action in which the user is actually requesting the reproduction of an entity (an *Item*) that contains the *Component* as a constitutive element.

```
<tva2:Item>
  <tva2:Component>
    <tva2:Resource crid="CRID://football.ar/Video_FINAL_COPA_AMERICA_2011"/>
  </tva2:Component>
  <tva2:Component>
    <tva2:Resource crid="CRID://football.ar/Stats_Forlan_CA_2011_flash"/>
  </tva2:Component>
</tva2:Item>
```

Listing 6.5 *Item* statement

The debate programme we discussed before is an example of an *Item*, given that the viewer can request its direct reproduction. In contrast, the associated graphs are not, nor the audio of the interview in itself, given that neither of these two elements is offered to the viewer to be consumed alone, as it makes no sense playing them if not together with the main content. They are merely *Components* that can be acquired or obtained to reproduce the *Item* represented by the debate programme.

Referring to the *Components* introduced in Listing 6.3, it makes no sense to offer viewers only the Flash animation file with the statistics if it is not accompanied by the match. In contrast, seeing the goals each of the finalists has scored so far may be of interest to a user, even if he/she does not acquire the final. It is therefore reasonable that the first and last components of those shown in Fig. 6.4 are part of different *Items*; so we will declare an *Item* composed by the first two, as shown in Listing 6.5.

In addition to *Components*, an *Item* can be formed by *sub-items*, which are lower-level elements that, although being classified as *Items*, are part of a higher level. In case an *Item* does not have *sub-items*, it can be considered indivisible content, while if it has them, it would be a set of independent contents that could be offered autonomously. The latter is the case, for example, of a sports interactive application that allows users to see a football match from different angles. There would be a higher-level *Item* that would define the interactive sports experience offered. Under this *Item*, there would be several lower-level *sub-items*, with the match filmed with each camera.

Components or *sub-items* could be coordinated spatially, so that, for example, the video can be confined to a certain area of the screen, while statistics are presented in another area, avoiding overlapping.

Also, within an *Item* it is possible to define time relations between the *Components* (Fig. 6.2). That is, the creator of the package can fully specify the order in which he wants them to be reproduced, so that when one finishes another one follows (a previously determined one), or that after a certain time interval has elapsed from the start of a *Component*, another must be reproduced.

Continuing with the *Item* presented in the example in Listing 6.5, we will assume that the creator of the package wants the statistics of the player to be presented when he scores the second goal of the match (minute 42). This intention is collected in the

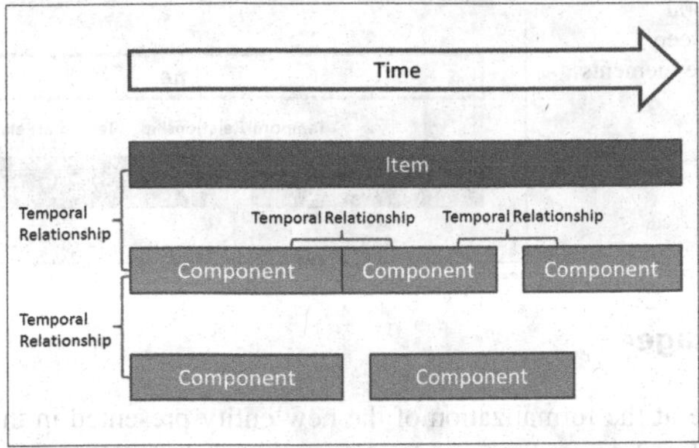

Fig. 6.2 Time relation between an *Item's Components*

```
1 <tva2:Item>
2  <tva2:Relation  source="c_final"  target="c_statistics_flash"
3      href="urn:tva:metadata:extended:cs:TemporalRelationCS:2005:strictContains">
4    <tva2:TemporalInterval>
5      <mpeg7:MediaDuration> PT00H42M </mpeg7:MediaDuration>
6    </tva2:TemporalInterval>
7  </tva2:Relation>
8  <tva2:Component  component_id="c_final">
9    <tva2:Resource crid="CRID://football.ar/Video_FINAL_COPA_AMERICA_2011"/>
10 </tva2:Component>
11 <tva2:Component  component_id="c_statistics_flash">
12   <tva2:Resource crid="CRID://football.ar/Stats_Forlan_CA_2011_flash"/>
13 </tva2:Component>
14 </tva2:Item>
```

Listing 6.6 Declaring an *Item* with synchronized components

metadata shown in Listing 6.6, where we can see a relation of the "*strictContains*" type (line 3) between the *Components* called "*c_final*" and "*c_statistics_flash*" (line 2). This type of relation establishes that the second *Component* is reproduced in full within the reproduction period of the first, and it is only necessary to identify the time span that has to elapse from the moment the first is initiated to activate the second (in this case, 42 min—line 5).

Moreover, there may be more than one version of a particular *Component*, and it is possible that the choice of the one to be reproduced within an *Item* is made in real time depending on the terminal's capabilities, the user's preferences or the instructions he/she provided. Later in this chapter, we will see an example to illustrate this type of situation.

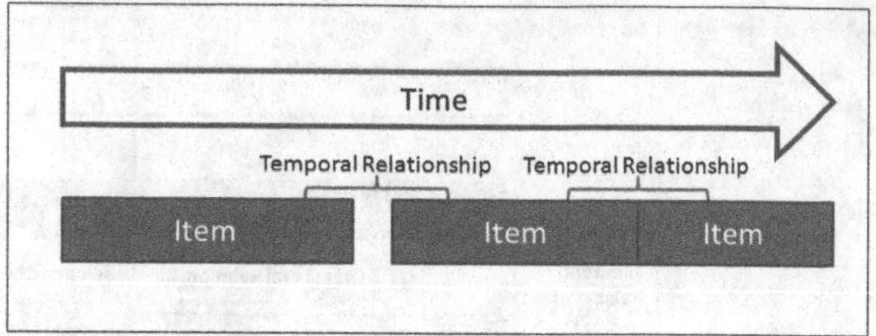

Fig. 6.3 Temporal relationship between Item and Package elements

6.2.4 Package

We thus arrive at the formalization of the new entity presented in this chapter. A *Package* is defined as a collection of contents that, together in a certain combination, either all of them or a subset, provide a richer experience for the consumer. This experience goes beyond the traditional one in which audiovisual contents consist only of audio and video, to involve graphics, applications and other elements as well that make up a group meant to be reproduced together.

Structurally, a *Package* is just a set of *Items*, grouped and organized according to a certain criteria or intention (Fig. 6.3). Combining this with what was illustrated in Fig. 6.2, we can conclude that a *Package* is a grouping of *Components,* among which there can be a temporal and spatial synchronization and which are reproduced according to a coordination designed by the creator of the *Package* that can be affected by the users' preferences, their decisions or the characteristics of their PDRs.

Let us imagine the case of a particular film, which is itself an *Item*. Clearly, there may be other related audiovisual content, as its trailer, or a previous contextualization clip, if necessary, or interviews with the director and actors, or a backstage sequence showing how the movie was filmed, including scenes that were discarded or replaced. Each of these contents may be another *Item*.

The operator or the creator of the content could make a *Package* with all of them, so that the experience of enjoying the programme becomes more valuable to the viewer than simply watching the movie. To this end, it would be necessary for the creator to establish a reproduction order deciding, for example, to reproduce in the first place the trailer and then the informative clip and the interviews, given that they are elements that constitute content to be played before the movie. Then the movie would follow and finish with the *backstage* material. Thus, the user, who was interested in the film when advertised and gave his/her PDR the order to acquire it, will surely be benefited by having at his/her disposal a set of contents related to it, which will certainly rate positively.

When the PDR tries to locate the movie, it discovers that it is part of a *Package* and follows the process of locating and acquiring all *Items* that comprise it, making them available to the user to be reproduced in the order provided in the definition of the *Package*. If a given operator, because of the lack of broadcasting rights or timeliness, does not offer the additional contents of the movie, it would be enough not to broadcast the information declaring that the movie is part of a *Package*.

```
1 <tva2:Package crid="CRID://football.ar/Package/Final_package_CA2011">
2   <tva2:Item item_id="i_previous_goals">
3     <tva2:Relation  source="i_previous_goals"  target="i_final"
4             href="urn:tva:metadata:extended:cs:TemporalRelationCS:2005:meets" />
5     <tva2:Component component_id="c_previous_goals">
6       <tva2:Resource crid="CRID://football.ar/PreviousGoals_FINAL_CA_2011"/>
7     </tva2:Component>
8   </tva2:Item>
9   <tva2:Item  item_id="i_final">
10    <tva2:Relation  source="c_final"  target="c_statistics_flash"
11      href="urn:tva:metadata:extended:cs:TemporalRelationCS:2005:strictContains">
12      <tva2:TemporalInterval>
13        <mpeg7:MediaDuration> PT00H42M </mpeg7:MediaDuration>
14      </tva2:TemporalInterval>
15    </tva2:Relation>
16    <tva2:Component  component_id="c_final">
17      <tva2:Resource crid="CRID://football.ar/Video_FINAL_COPA_AMERICA_2011 "/>
18      <tva2:Anchor>
19        <tva2:Condition require="Second_Goal"/>
20        <tva2:TemporalLocation>
21          <TimePoint> T00:42:00 </TimePoint>
22        </tva2:TemporalLocation>
23      </tva2:Anchor>
24    </tva2:Component>
25    <tva2:Component  component_id="c_statistics_flash">
26      <tva2:Descriptor>
27        CONTENT EXAMPLE IN LISTING 6.2
28      </tva2:Descriptor>
29      <tva2:Resource crid="CRID://football.ar/Stats_Forlan_CA_2011_flash"/>
30    </tva2:Component>
31  </tva2:Item>
32 </tva2:Package>
```

Listing 6.7 Declaring a *Package*

Returning to the example we have described throughout the chapter, in Listing 6.7 we can see a collection of several of the illustrated fragments that we have gathered to compose an example of a *Package*.

In addition to what has already been described, we can see a new relation between the two *Items* that form the package (previous goals and the final), in which the suggested sequence of viewing is declared (the "*meets*" relation—line 5—indicates that the second is played just after finishing the first).

6.2.4.1 PackageTable

In Chaps. 2 and 4, we already mentioned that all the relevant information in the TV-Anytime context (contents, users, environment, etc.) is ultimately structured into tables. Thus, we have, for example, tables about programme descriptions and locations, tables about user descriptions and tables about content purchase models. To no surprise, the descriptive metadata of the different packages that are offered to the user is built around a new table introduced in Phase 2, the *PackageTable*, to structure one or more packages by combining in a coordinated way different *Components* and *Items*.

6.2.5 A Programme with an Associated Package

Among the possibilities offered by the usage of *packages*, we have the capacity to associate a *Package* to a programme. With this, like an "*attractor*", we can announce to viewers interested in a programme that, although they have the option of consuming the content on its own, it has an associated *Package* and they could request its acquisition to enjoy it as a whole.

This instrument is introduced with the aim of providing another path for the user to access the package. That is, the viewer is interested in a programme and then finds out that this content has certain applications or images associated. Listing 6.8 illustrates precisely this.

In that listing, there is a description of a programme called "*Educational Laboratory Classes*" (line 6), which has an associated *Package* called "*EducActive*" (line 17). It can be seen that in the basic description metadata of the programme (lines 5–13), there is a *<RelatedMaterial>* element (line 7) whose role is to declare additional contents related to the one described. In this case, that element informs us that the relation is that of an "*associated package*" (*<HowRelated>* element in line 8) and gives us the CRID of the package (line 10).

Between lines 15 and 28, there is a basic description of that *Package* just like any other content, specifying that the content type is a *Package* (line 25) and mentioning that it is associated to a main content (in the *<HowRelated>* element in line 19 under *<RelatedMaterial>* in line 18) whose CRID is provided in line 21.

Further down, between lines 31 and 35, it is suggested that a *PackageTable* should be present with the declaration of the structure of that *Package*.

6.3 Conditional Reproduction

As we have been showing throughout the chapter, both the terminal's software and the user can influence the customization of the audiovisual experience in the consumption of a *Package*, through the possibility of selecting among the *Items of a Package* (or among the *Components* of an *Item*) which one will be reproduced.

To implement this selection process (sometimes automatically), the creator of the *Package* is provided with the mechanisms to define a decision tree through which the user or device can chose among different options that depend on the usage environment, the terminal's capabilities, the user's preferences or how he/she wants to experience the content.

```
<TVAMain  xsi:type="tva2:ExtendedTVAMainType" >
<ProgramDescription>
   <ProgramInformationTable>
      <ProgramInformation programId="CRID://edu.es/ClassesLab">
         <BasicDescription>
            <Title> Educational Laboratory Classes</Title>
            <RelatedMaterial>
               <HowRelated href="urn:tva:HowRelatedCS:AssociatedPackage"/>
               <MediaLocator>
               <mpeg7:MediaUri>CRID://edu.es/Pkg/09-10-2011</mpeg7:MediaUri>
               </MediaLocator>
            </RelatedMaterial>
         </BasicDescription>
      </ProgramInformation>
      <ProgramInformation programId="CRID://edu.es/Pkg/09-10-2011">
         <BasicDescription  xsi:type="tva2:ExtendedContentDescriptionType">
            <Title> EducActive </Title>
            <RelatedMaterial>
               <HowRelated href="urn:tva:howrelatedCS:PackageMainContent"/>
               <MediaLocator>
                  <mpeg7:MediaUri> CRID://edu.es/ClassesLab </mpeg7:MediaUri>
               </MediaLocator>
            </RelatedMaterial>
            <tva2:ContentProperties>
               <tva2:ContentType href="urn:tva:ContentTypeCS:Package"/>
            </tva2:ContentProperties>
         </BasicDescription>
      </ProgramInformation>
   </ProgramInformationTable>
</ProgramDescription>
<tva2:PackageTable>
   <tva2:Package  crid="CRID://edu.es/Pkg/09-10-2011">
      PACKAGE DECLARATION
   </tva2:Package>
</tva2:PackageTable>
</TVAMain>
```

Listing 6.8 Educational programme with associated package

To illustrate this mechanism, we present the example in Listing 6.9 in which, besides the statistics of the player in F*lash* format, we now introduce the same statistics as a *Java* application. Each version constitutes a different *Component* (lines 27–30 for the first one and 31–34 for the second).

Each *Component* includes a *<Condition>* element that specifies a condition which must be true for the content to be reproduced. In line 28 the condition for the F*lash* application is declared, which requires a "*flash*" rule to be true for the condition to be true and the content to be reproduced with the F*lash* statistics. In line 32 the condition for the *Java* application is declared, which requires a "*java*"

```
1 <tva2:Item>
2   <tva2:Choice choice_id="flash_or_java">
3     <tva2:Selection select_id="flash">
4       <tva2:Descriptor>
5           CONTENT EXAMPLE IN LISTING 6.2
6       </tva2:Descriptor>
7     </tva2:Selection>
8     <tva2:Selection select_id="java">
9      <tva2:Descriptor>
10      <tva2:ObjectDescription>
11        <tva2:ContentDescription>
12          <tva2:TargetingInformation>
13            <tva2:TerminalInformation>
14              <tva2:SystemInformation>
15                <tva2:VirtualMachine
16                         href="urn:tva:metadata:extended:cs:VirtualMachineCS:2005:2">
17                      <Name xml:lang="en"> Java VM </Name>
18                </tva2:VirtualMachine>
19              </tva2:SystemInformation>
20            </tva2:TerminalInformation>
21          </tva2:TargetingInformation>
22        </tva2:ContentDescription>
23      </tva2:ObjectDescription>
24    </tva2:Descriptor>
25   </tva2:Selection>
26  </tva2:Choice>
27  <tva2:Component component_id="c_estadisticas_flash">
28    <tva2:Condition require="flash"/>
29    <tva2:Resource crid="CRID://football.ar/Stats_Forlan_CA_2011_flash"/>
30  </tva2:Component>
31  <tva2:Component component_id="c_estadisticas_java">
32    <tva2:Condition require="java"/>
33    <tva2:Resource crid="CRID://football.ar/Stats_Forlan_CA_2011_java"/>
34  </tva2:Component>
35 </tva2:Item>
```

Listing 6.9 Item declaration with component selection

rule to be true for the condition to be true and the content to be reproduced with the *Java* statistics.

The selection mechanism is implemented through a *<Choice>* element (line 2), which contains a *<Selection>* element for each of the possibilities (line 3 for the first one and line 8 for the second one). The content of each *<Selection>* element will be a descriptor which specifies a characteristic that must be present in the receiver. If it is, the *<Selection>* identifier (which constitutes each of the abovementioned rules) will be true.

If the receiver has the capacity of executing F*lash* applications (lines 4–6 which reference Listing 6.2), then the "*flash*" rule of that *<Selection>* element will be

```
<tva2:Item>
  <tva2:Choice choice_id=" Goal_Selection" minSelections="0" maxSelections="1">
    <tva2:Selection select_id="First_Goal">
      <tva2:Descriptor>
        <tva2:ObjectDescription>
          <tva2:ContentDescription>
            <Title> First goal in the Copa América 2011 final </Title>
          </tva2:ContentDescription>
        </tva2:ObjectDescription>
      </tva2:Descriptor>
    </tva2:Selection>
    <tva2:Selection select_id="Second_Goal">
      SIMILAR CONTENT TO LINES 4-10 FOR THE SECOND GOAL
    </tva2:Selection>
    <tva2:Selection select_id="Third_Goal">
      SIMILAR CONTENT TO LINES 4-10 FOR THE THIRD GOAL
    </tva2:Selection>
  </tva2:Choice>
  <tva2:Component>
    <tva2:Resource crid="CRID://football.ar/Video_FINAL_COPA_AMERICA_2011"/>
    <tva2:Anchor>
      <tva2:Condition require="First_Goal"/>
      <tva2:Descriptor>
        <tva2:ObjectDescription>
          <tva2: Description> The final's first goal </tva2:Description>
        </tva2:ObjectDescription>
      </tva2:Descriptor>
      <tva2:TemporalLocation>
        <TimePoint> T00:11:03 </TimePoint>
      </tva2:TemporalLocation>
    </tva2:Anchor>
    <tva2:Anchor> SIMILAR CONTENT FOR THE SECOND GOAL </tva2:Anchor>
    <tva2:Anchor> SIMILAR CONTENT FOR THE THIRD GOAL </tva2:Anchor>
  </tva2:Component>
</tva2:Item>
```

Listing 6.10 User selection

true, and the "*c_flash_statistics*" *Component* can be reproduced, which has a condition that depends on that rule.

If the receiver has the capacity of executing *Java* applications (lines 9–24), then the "*java*" rule for that *<Selection>* element will be true, and the "*c_java_statistics*" *Component* can be reproduced, which has a condition that depends on that rule.

Next, in Listing 6.10, another example of content selection and reproduction is shown, also regarding football, where the necessary statements for the user to have the possibility of selecting what he/she wants to reproduce are presented.

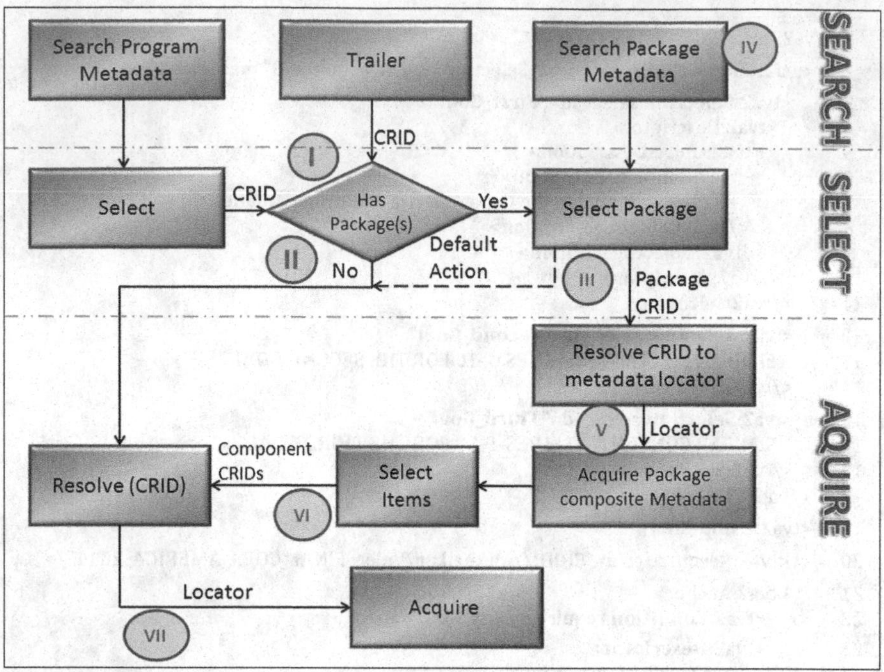

Fig. 6.4 Inclusion of *Packaging* into the resolution process

It is an *Item* of a *Package* about the Copa America 2011 final, related to the example in Listing 6.4. The intention is to offer the user the final of the tournament, allowing a direct access to the moments when the three goals were scored.

Through the <*Choice*> element in line 2, the user is offered the possibility of choosing if he/she wants to see one of the three goals (<*Selection*> elements in lines 3, 12 and 15). In line 20 the *Component* is declared, which represents the final match, together with <*Anchor*> elements (lines 21, 32 and 33) which lead to the moments of the match when the goals were scored (e.g. minute 11 of the <*TemporalLocation*> element in line 28 for the first goal).

These <*Anchor*> elements depend conditionally on certain rules that are true or false according to what the user chose in the initial <*Choice*>. For example, in the case of the first goal, the <*Anchor*> which leads to it depends on the "*First_Goal*" rule in the condition in line 22, which is true only if the user made that selection.

6.4 Package Location Resolution

In light of what was seen in previous chapters, particularly Chap. 3, regarding the existing location resolution mechanism for individual contents based on CRIDs, we should wonder how this procedure is affected with the introduction of *packages*, so that a unified method is provided to resolve and acquire any kind of content.

Figure 6.4 shows how the *Packaging* technology of TV-Anytime Phase 2 is composed of all that was described in Phase 1, presented mainly in Chap. 3. In this figure, there are a series of stages (I to VII) which go from queries (or interest signs) of users to the final result which consists of the reproduction of the contents, whether associated to a *Package* or not:

I. In this stage the user shows interest for a programme (e.g. when watching a trailer) whose CRID is present in the available metadata, or he/she looks for a given content and is presented with different alternatives, among which he/she selects one, from which the corresponding identifying CRID is extracted. The first thing to assess is if this programme is associated to a *Package*.
II. In case it is not associated to a *Package*, the resolution process is the same as the one described in Phase 1, that is, the CRID is resolved to a locator and the content is acquired.
III. However, if the selected content is associated to a *Package*, the user is offered the possibility of selecting it. If this happens (the default option is not to choose it), the CRID of the *Package* is extracted from the metadata.
IV. It is also possible to reach this point through a direct search of content *packages*. The user will select one among the different options presented, and that is how the CRID of the *Package* he/she is interested in is obtained.
V. The CRID of the *Package* is resolved and the metadata describing the composition and the structure of the *Package* is obtained.
VI. The viewer is offered different reproduction options for him/her to select (or the selection is automatic according to the characteristics of the environment). As a result, the CRIDs of the *Components* which participate in the reproduction are obtained.
VII. All the abovementioned CRIDs are resolved, and the *Package's* components are acquired through the resulting locators.

If we remember the case of the viewer who was interested in the debate between political leaders which was exemplified earlier, after watching an advertisement of the programme, maybe the user orders its acquisition, triggering the location and the acquisition process for that programme. However, at the same time, he/she would also be activating the prior stages for the acquisition of all the components of the package that the programme is associated to. That is, the PDR would capture the text and graphs following the steps we just presented.

6.5 Summary

In this chapter, we have presented the mechanism designed by TV-Anytime for content packaging, that is for grouping different multimedia elements whose aim is to be consumed together.

This combined reproduction involving multiple related assets, possibly subject to a temporal/spatial synchronization defined by the creator of the package, aims to enrich the viewer's experience and allows content creators to incorporate innovative products to their offer, beyond traditional programmes composed of audio and video, moving to consider other formats more or less familiar to all viewers: photos, Web pages, interactive applications, simulations, etc.

Additionally, appropriate mechanisms are also defined for the reproduction of the contents of the package not to be a static and deterministic experience, but such that its creator can specify variations conditioned by the users, either manually from their own decisions or arising from the evaluation of conditions involving their personal data, the characteristics of their equipment or the results of their previous actions.

In the next chapter, we will leave aside the introduction of tools to facilitate the creation of new value-added services, and we will describe other contributions of the TV-Anytime standard, this time of a technical nature. Specifically, we will present different aspects of metadata transport in unidirectional environments, including a set of procedures to facilitate management at destination.

Metadata Transport in Unidirectional Environments

7

7.1 Introduction

The specifications developed by TV-Anytime describe in full detail the information structures that help to implement a system of unambiguous content references (Chap. 3) and the characterization of such contents through standardized metadata (Chaps. 4, 5 and 6), as well as how both tools are combined to provide a context that facilitates the construction and deployment of intelligent services.

However, there are a number of procedures (sometimes essential, sometimes advisable) to take into account in order to develop the services described in the introduction that are not regulated in any part of the standards seen so far and that affect, for example, the effective transport of metadata, the synchronization of the metadata's time information with the actual hours for the start or end of programmes, the signalling of changes to update that metadata and the transport of the audiovisual contents themselves.

The purpose of TV-Anytime is to provide a framework that is totally independent from the transport mechanism used in the content distribution network, and, to this end, it only describes what requirements are demanded of that transport mechanism. These requirements are the set of information and signalling elements that must be provided to the software applications that handle the processing of the diverse TV-Anytime information that is involved in the deployment of these services.

In this chapter, we will specifically address the transport of metadata between the operator and the user's receiver and will outline certain mechanisms that TV-Anytime standardizes to facilitate that delivery of information. Specifically, we will focus on unidirectional environments, in which the receiver can only read the information from a broadcast channel. In this case, we will describe a set of facilities that TV-Anytime provides for the management of an efficient submission of metadata from the operator to the user.

A. Gil Solla and R.G. Sotelo Bovino, *TV-Anytime*, X.media.publishing,
DOI 10.1007/978-3-642-36766-3_7, © Springer-Verlag Berlin Heidelberg 2013

7.2 Generic Features of the Platform

The most basic television distribution model covered by TV-Anytime specifications is constituted by a unidirectional environment, where there is only one broadcast channel from the platform operator to the user. It could be a traditional television network or a television distribution platform via IP networks, but with no return to the broadcaster.

In this simple model, there is no return channel from the user to the distribution platform, neither to send information to the operator nor to receive additional data, possibly customized, from it. Therefore, all information, including metadata, is transported to the user through the broadcast channel, whichever it may be. This information should be available for applications when needed. Therefore, given that the distribution system does not notify the operator when a receiver gets connected, and there is no way to know whether information has been received correctly, the transmission of the metadata must happen cyclically, at regular intervals, typically in the form of a carousel. This is the mechanism that traditional TV networks follow to send both the signalling that allows decoding transport streams and non-resident interactive applications.

Moreover, the available bandwidth is usually a limited resource, which is used primarily to send contents for which the operator obtains some kind of income. Therefore, the transmission of metadata must be performed as efficiently as possible, occupying only the necessary bandwidth, for which TV-Anytime provides some optimization mechanisms we will discuss below.

For unidirectional environments, TV-Anytime states that the underlying transport system must provide certain information to higher-level services in charge of implementing the TV-Anytime features. This information, described in full detail in Sect. 7.7, must allow a receiver to find out what metadata is available and how to acquire it and also how to properly receive timely information about existing updates. In any case, TV-Anytime does not regulate how the transport mechanism should provide this information, nor the syntax, format or semantics, leaving these matters within the scope of the standards governing each distribution network.

Sending information in XML format (the default format used as presented in Chap. 4) is significantly inefficient, since it consists of broad self-descriptive textual descriptions, whose aim is to be clear for people to read and simple to process for the applications that handle them. Additionally, not all the information elements in a TV-Anytime document are equally relevant, necessary at the same time, consulted with the same regularity, nor updated with the same frequency.

Therefore, to improve the efficiency of this unidirectional context where the descriptions could span several days and be of considerable size, and given that bandwidth is a limited resource that must be optimized, TV-Anytime defines a series of mechanisms to facilitate the submission and later processing of the metadata that describes contents. These tools are part of a set of processes that can be seen in Fig. 7.1, of which the intermediate ones are the only ones subject to some form of regulation in the TV-Anytime specifications.

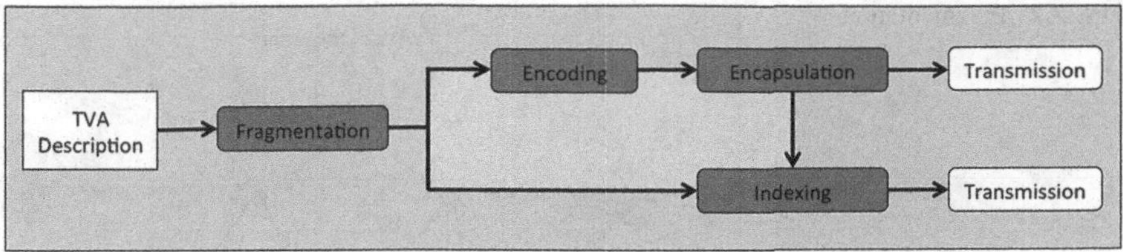

Fig. 7.1 Auxiliary procedures to submit information

These processes, which are shaded in orange in Fig. 7.1, are as follows:

- *Fragmentation*. It is a procedure designed to allow breaking a TV-Anytime document down into a series of smaller, self-contained and consistent units, called fragments, which are sent individually.
- *Encoding*. The aim of this process is to facilitate sending the metadata fragments efficiently (in terms of bandwidth), encoding them using a binary representation. The different encoded fragments are transported (individually or in groups) in a container structure specifically designed in the TV-Anytime standard.
- *Encapsulation*. This mechanism allows adding to previous containers information on the fragments carried inside them to facilitate the task of monitoring updates without having to inspect all fragments individually.
- *Indexing*. Finally, this tool allows adding some indexing information to containers that facilitates the processing of large fragment streams by receivers, making it possible to quickly locate the desired information within large descriptions.

7.3 Fragmentation

Fragmentation is a procedure to decompose a TV-anytime document into a series of smaller consistent and self-contained units named fragments. A fragment is the smallest part of a given description that can be independently transmitted to a terminal and must be consistent in the following ways:

- It has to be able to be transmitted and updated independently from other fragments.
- It must be processed independently from the order in which these fragments are received.
- Its decoding and aggregation must lead to a description which, although it may be partial, must always be valid.

The group of all the fragments which form a certain TV-Anytime document is transmitted in a unidirectional context as a stream of information named *TV-Anytime fragment metadata stream*. In this stream, there is an entry point, a *TVA-init* message, which must be acquired in the first place and contains relevant information for decoding the following messages. The initial message is followed by a fragment containing the *<TVAMain>* root element (or *<ExtendedTVAMain>*

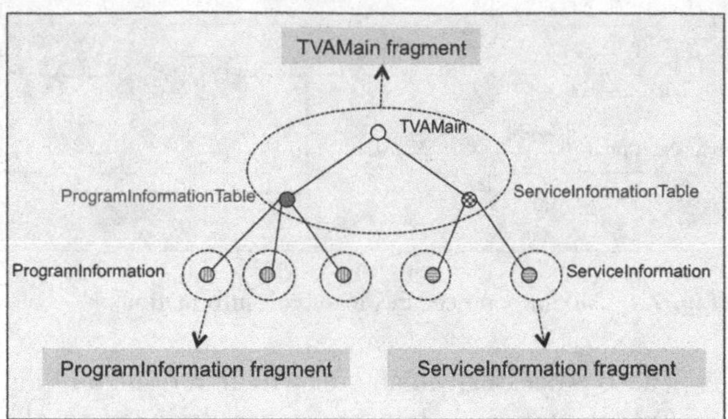

Fig. 7.2 Fragmentation

if Phase 2 metadata is involved), a fragment that must be present in any partial description (see Fig. 7.2).

Considering that the fragment is the smallest indivisible part that can be transmitted, any change in the elements or attributes contained in the fragment implies the need to retransmit the whole fragment to update it. That is, there is no mechanism which allows the transmission of fragment parts.

7.3.1 Fragment Types

In the TV-Anytime standard, a broad set of fragments is defined, all under the same name as the element they transport. Among them, we highlight the following given their importance, although there are others which transport different kinds of information that we have not dealt with in the previous chapters:

TVAMain. This is the only compulsory fragment in a fragment stream, and, clearly, it represents the starting point to create a TV-Anytime description from a given stream. Instead of *<TVAMain>*, the *<ExtendedTVAMain>* fragment can appear which represents an extended description with Phase 2 structures.
Inside, there will be the basic table structure described in Chap. 4, although without its contents, which will be sent inside the corresponding fragments.

ProgramInformation. This fragment transports the *<ProgramInformation>* element (part of the *ProgramInformationTable*), which, as seen in Chap. 4, is the basic structure that contains the descriptive information about a content identified by its CRID. It is a self-contained element, except for possible references to people or organizations declared in the *CreditsInformationTable* (whose entries can be reutilized in many places).

GroupInformation. It contains a *<GroupInformation>* element (part of the *GroupInformationTable*), which informs about most of the contents that form a group according to some criteria. It is also self-contained, except for what has been explained in the *ProgramInformation* fragment.

Schedule. This fragment carries inside a *<Schedule>* element (part of the *ProgramLocationTable* as seen in Chap. 4), which describes a series of audiovisual events (described by <*ScheduleEvent*> elements) which will be broadcast consecutively on a channel. As expected, similar fragments exist for the other known contents of the *ProgramLocationTable* described in Chap. 4 (i.e. *OnDemandProgram, OnDemandService, BroadcastEvent* and *PushDownloadProgram*).

ServiceInformation. It contains a <*ServiceInformation*> element (part of the *ServiceInformationTable*), which describes a television service (channel).

PersonName, OrganizationName. These fragments carry elements of the same name (members of the *CreditsInformationTable*), which transport declarations about people and organizations in full detail, assigning references to them which may be used in other descriptions to avoid unnecessary repetitions.

PurchaseInformation. It transports a <*PurchaseInformation*> element (part of the *PurchaseInformationTable*), which informs about relevant details for the purchase of a given content.

Review. It contains a <*Review*> element (part of the *ProgramReviewTable*), which represents a critic to a specific audiovisual content, identified by its CRID.

ClassificationScheme. It transports the corresponding element (part of the *ClassificationSchemeTable*), which defines a set of terms that belong to a controlled classification, used to assign specific values to content attributes.

SegmentInformation. It carries inside a <*SegmentInformation*> element (i.e. a component of the <*SegmentList*> element, which is in turn a part of the *SegmentInformationTable*) and describes a segment of an audiovisual content (starting point, length, description, etc.)

SegmentGroupInformation. It transports a <*SegmentGroupInformation*> element (part of the <*SegmentGroupList*> element, which belongs in turn to the *SegmentInformationTable*), which describes groups of many elements (references to <*SegmentInformation*> elements), for instance advising about how they should be consumed.

Package. It transports a <*Package*> element (part of the *PackageTable*), which describes a package that groups and coordinates many audiovisual contents.

InterstitialCampaign. It contains an <*InterstitialCampaign*> element (part of the *InterstitialCampaignTable*), which describes a group of advertisements from an advertising campaign.

InterstitialBreak. It carries inside an <*InterstitialBreak*> element (part of the *InterstitialTable*), which describes a group of advertisements that compose an advertising break.

CouponDescription. It contains a <*CouponDescription*> element (part of the *CouponTable*), which represents the description of promotional coupons to encourage the consumption of a given content.

TargetingInformation. It contains a <*TargetingInformation*> element (part of the *TargetingInformationTable*), which informs about how adequate a given content is for a certain type of audience.

7.4 Encoding

The second process mentioned, *Encoding*, is aimed at increasing the efficiency (in terms of bandwidth) when sending metadata in unidirectional contexts. It consists, basically, of sending it in a binary format, for which the *BiM* method (ISO/IEC 15938–1, 2002) defined in the MPEG-7 standard is proposed, mainly due to interoperability reasons, although establishing different restrictions to adapt it to a unidirectional context.

In any case, the information about the encoding method that was really used and other similar technical matters must be available before decoding the metadata fragments, and that is why the initial message (*TVA-init*) is defined. This message must be sent by the operator in the metadata transport mechanism and must be the first structure acquired by the receiver, as it contains essential information to decode the fragments. This initial message, which will be the only one within a metadata fragment stream, will include information such as:

- Identification of the encoding method (for instance, *BiM*)
- Details of the compression mechanism, normally based on *Zlib*
- Specification on the type of character encoding (e.g. ASCII, UTF-8, UTF-16)
- Information about whether this stream of metadata fragments carries indexing information and, if this is the case, the version of the indexing mechanism

The encoding mechanism proposed, *BiM*, is originally designed for the efficient transmission of fragments of an XML document, compressing them and adding the necessary information for their combination at destination. To this end, it defines some transmission units named *FragmentUpdateUnits* which, besides the fragment, include information about what must be done with it (add it to the document, delete it or update an existing one, etc.) and where in the document's tree this fragment must be placed. This allows for an easy reconstruction of the original document from the fragments, in case this is necessary.

7.4.1 Containers

TV-Anytime does not regulate in any way how the metadata must be transported from the operator to the user, giving complete freedom for the different platforms to choose the mechanisms they consider appropriate. The only contribution of TV-Anytime with respect to this is a generic container structure to send the information, individually or grouping many structures in a single message. These containers represent the TV-Anytime structure or outer cover, within which all the information to transmit is stored.

Although the standard does not specify how to convey these containers, it is true that they have been designed to make easier the transport process through typical cyclic information delivery mechanisms in digital television networks, for example through data carousels or object carousels from the MPEG DSM-CC standard.

In a first approach, two types of containers were defined in this part of the TV-Anytime standard:

- Data containers: to transport metadata fragments and encapsulation information (described in the next section)
- Index containers: devised mainly to transport indexing information (indexes, index lists, sub-indexes on different codes, etc.), although they may also contain fragments

The type of the containers sent in the information stream (as well as their identifiers and version numbers) are not data that appears within the container itself. That information must be clearly signalled in the transport network for the receiver to identify it easily and keep the sections it is interested in.

Inside a container, we can find two parts: an informative header and a body where many structures are sent. Each structure contains fragments, indexes, index lists, encapsulation information, etc. The header will inform about the number of structures sent and their types, identifiers and lengths, assigning a pointer at the beginning (see Fig. 7.3).

7.5 Encapsulation

Thirdly, *Encapsulation* is a mechanism that allows the receiver to know the identifiers and the version numbers of the fragments that a container transports, without having to open and analyse them individually.

The encapsulation mechanism consists, basically, of adding a (single) information structure to containers (see Fig. 7.4) that receivers will consult to learn the details of the rest of the structures transported in the container. This declaration of identifiers and version numbers enables the receiver to make a simple query to monitor the updates in the content of a container.

7.6 Indexing

Finally, *Indexing* is a mechanism designed to facilitate the processing of large streams of fragments by receivers with less resources. Certainly, TV-Anytime documents can have a considerable size, structuring information from multiple channels throughout an extended period of time, which makes it possible for the search of particular information inside to become a time-consuming task, especially considering that television receivers are not devices with resources to spare.

Therefore, receiving adequate indexing information allows them to easily locate the desired information within large descriptions. Indexes will provide a shortcut to certain fragments of the document: those containing nodes with a given index key value according to that index.

Thus, receivers, according to their resources, can choose to store the received metadata and offer it to the user through the navigation mechanisms they implement, or they can use the indexing information provided by the operator to generate that presentation (or even an intermediate solution that combines both possibilities).

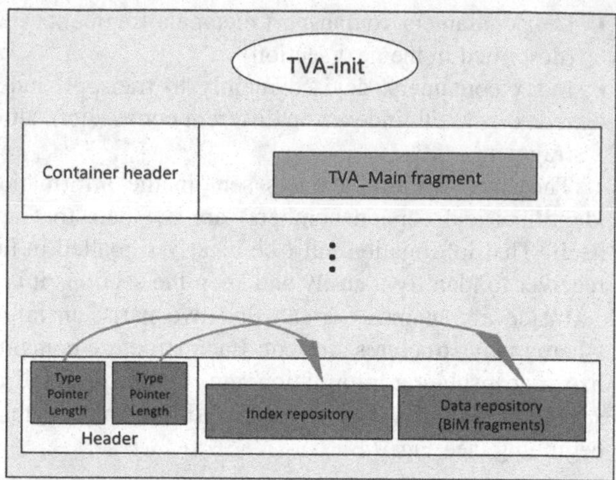

Fig. 7.3 Container stream

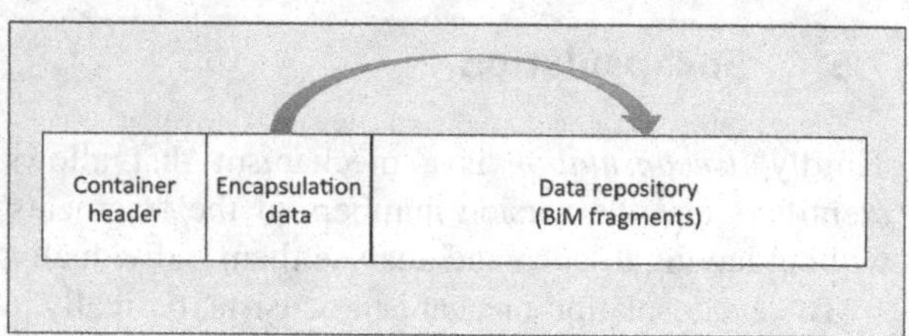

Fig. 7.4 Encapsulation

In any case, indexing information is completely optional, and the receiver can access the entire document without it, although probably more slowly.

The indexing mechanism defined by TV-Anytime is intended for cyclical information transport systems, like the carousels of digital TV networks, but it does not depend, in any case, on a particular mechanism; it should be able to be implemented in any of the ones currently available.

Roughly speaking, the procedure for defining an index consists in adding various information structures to containers through which one or several index keys will be identified (basically, elements or attributes of metadata structures). Certain values (or range of values) will be defined for these keys, and they will be attached pointers to fragments containing information in which those keys have the specified values. These pointers may take the form of identifiers of the nodes in question or be expressions of the *XPath* language (W3C-XPath, 1999), specifically created by W3C to identify certain nodes (elements, attributes, etc.) within an XML document.

Although it is usual for indexes to point at fragments within the container itself (which is why it is known as an indexing container), it is also possible that they point at data containers that only carry fragments. In this case, indexes will point at the encapsulation information of this new container, which in turn will lead to the fragments that carry the indexed metadata (see Fig. 7.5).

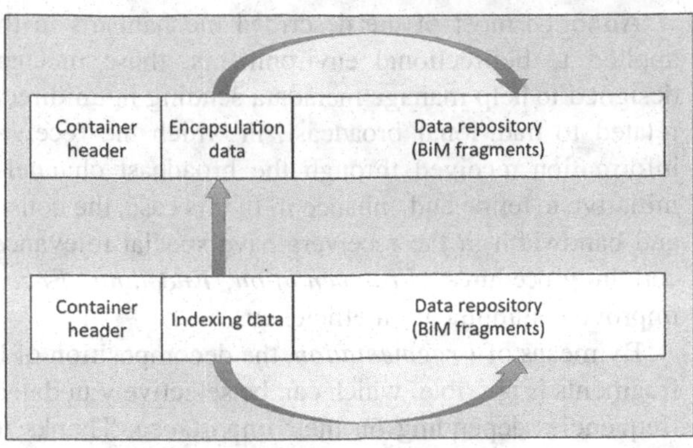

Fig. 7.5 Indexing

7.7 Requirements for the Transport Mechanism in a Unidirectional Environment

In the case of unidirectional environments, although TV-Anytime does not regulate at all how the underlying transport system must carry out its task, it does state that somehow this system must provide some information to higher-level services in charge of implementing the TV-Anytime functionalities. Among them, we can highlight that the transport mechanism will have to carry out the following tasks:

- Carry the metadata and deliver it to the programmes waiting for it, asynchronously, even when the transport takes place through different channels, which must be transparent to the software applications requesting the information.
- Provide a method to find out what kind of TV-Anytime metadata is available and how to get it. This includes location resolution tables (seen in Chap. 3) as well as content description metadata (seen from Chap. 4 on). As for the latter, it must provide the list of TV-Anytime metadata fragments, their access points, the appropriate signalling about updates, etc.
- Provide locators for specific instances of broadcast contents.
- Facilitate mechanisms to insert new metadata, including references and consumption rights management.
- Allow for the continual and repeated broadcast of TV-Anytime information structures, with the frequencies considered convenient in each case.
- Provide support for the selective update of different metadata elements, without the possibility of inconsistencies emerging, even if some of them get lost.

7.8 Summary

In the first few chapters, we described the metadata standardized by TV-Anytime for the construction of value-added services. Now we have introduced details about the standardized aspects regarding how that information gets to the receiver.

Although most of the described mechanisms in the previous sections can be applied to bidirectional environments, those mechanisms have been specially designed to help manage metadata sending in unidirectional environments, mostly related to traditional broadcast, in which the receiver is limited to reading the information received through the broadcast channel and is unable to take the initiative to refine and enhance it. In this case, the constraints of available resources and bandwidth in the receivers have special relevance; so TV-Anytime provides certain procedures (*Fragmentation*, *Encoding*, *Encapsulation* and *Indexing*) to improve communication efficiency.

By means of *Fragmentation*, the decomposition of large descriptions into small fragments is possible, which can be selectively updated as needed, and at different frequencies depending on their importance. Thanks to *Encoding*, the amount of information to be sent is reduced by using efficient compression algorithms.

Meanwhile, *Encapsulation* makes easier for receivers to ascertain the contents of containers and to detect any updates without having to open, read and process them. Finally, *Indexing* facilitates the task of finding the information they need, without having to completely overhaul all received structures, by offering direct links to descriptions that meet certain conditions, regarded as especially interesting by the operator.

In the next chapter, we will deal with different facilities that TV-Anytime standardizes in order to help develop metadata provision services through bidirectional networks. In other words, we will describe what TV-Anytime provides to allow for the deployment of services to which a receiver can connect to expand the metadata received through the broadcast channel, make new enquiries, send users' profiles, etc.

Metadata Provision Services in Bidirectional Environments

8

8.1 Introduction

Most standardization work carried out within TV-Anytime Phase 1 was built assuming as a reference a limited connectivity of the user's receiver, supposing only the existence of a unidirectional channel between the operator and the viewers' homes. However, this was not always the case, and, already in Phase 1, there were some sections of the specification that dealt with the standardization of different aspects concerning communication between the receiver and the outside through a bidirectional access network (e.g. the Internet) through which it was possible to make requests to the operator or third parties and receive responses from them.

This is the case of most of the contents of this chapter, where we will describe some guidelines that TV-Anytime establishes to standardize the communication with external servers (from the operator or third parties) that provide metadata provision services on demand.

In the case of bidirectional contexts, that is when both the capabilities of the receiver and the characteristics of the network to which it is connected allow a permanent communication with the outside world, it is clear that the possibilities of services the user can be provided multiply. This greater diversity of services is based not only on the availability of a larger volume of on-demand contents through the interaction channel but also on the ability to access different sources of metadata about the contents, including third-party services that do not have access to the broadcast channels of television networks, and, of course, also on the ability to build specific queries to narrow down the user's field of interest, or refine those queries interactively. Last, but not least, we must not forget about the ability to implement powerful processing algorithms in the service providers' servers, which are far more powerful than the user's home receivers with regard to memory and CPU.

This section will deal specifically with the regulations that TV-Anytime documents establish about the communication between the user's receiver and metadata provision services offered, whether by the content provider or by third

A. Gil Solla and R.G. Sotelo Bovino, *TV-Anytime*, X.media.publishing,
DOI 10.1007/978-3-642-36766-3_8,

parties, through a return channel connected to a bidirectional network. These regulations can only standardize aspects related to the following:

- The provision of metadata about programme characteristics: origin, length, participants, broadcast data, reviews, etc. Sending this information through a return channel makes it possible to access a wider and more extensive set of data, given that the bandwidth restrictions typical of broadcast channels no longer apply.
- The search for content based on criteria defined by the user: actors, directors, time and date of the plot, genre, etc.
- The resolution and delivery of content referencing information, that is information about the location of contents, for example the *ContentReferencingTable* presented in Chap. 3.
- The submission of different information about the user's profile and his/her consumption history to the service provider, with the purpose of feeding personalization services that may customize future responses, content offers or functionalities of the services provided.

The context in which we will move will be that of a request always started by the user, and connecting to a Web service (called metadata service) over an IP network, using typical Internet transport protocols. This request can logically be made by a set-top box or a smart television set provided with the necessary capabilities, but it can also be carried out by other kinds of devices that usually lack the capability to connect to television networks, such as smartphones or digital tablets. Its ultimate aim may not be showing us the information directly or store it but implementing value-added services derived from the metadata obtained from the queries to the abovementioned services.

The sequence of stages that a device must follow in order to access a metadata service of these characteristics can be seen in Fig. 8.1.

Logically, the first two steps (the discovery of how to access the service and what its capabilities are) must only be carried out the first time a receiver is accessing the service.

The information exchanged with the server when using the service will basically consist of some of the metadata structures established in the previous chapters. For example:

- If a customer wishes to obtain from the service reviews or expert opinions about a given content, he/she will send the content's CRID to the service together with the indication of the kind of request, and, in return, he/she will receive a table with reviews, that is the *ProgramReviewTable*.
- If a customer wishes to obtain information about programmes that will be aired on a specific channel in the next few days, a request with the kind of query will be sent, specifying the channel and the period. As a response, he/she will receive a *ProgramLocationTable* and a *ProgramInformationTable* with the information about programmes airing on that channel.
- If a customer wishes to get the list of programmes that comply with specific criteria regarding elements of metadata that describe them, he/she will send a request, for example, specifying that the genre is "*Action*" and the star is

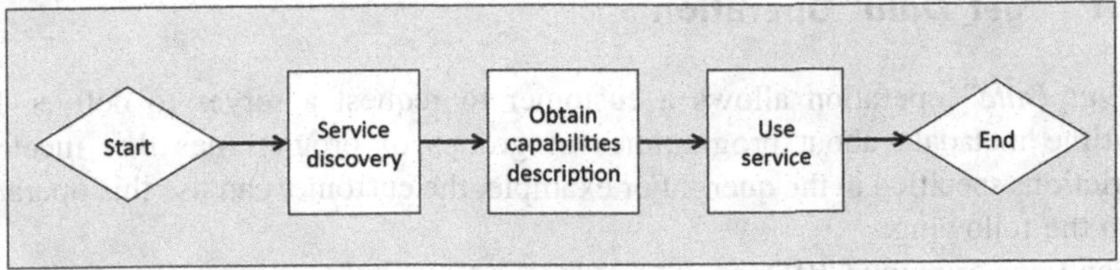

Fig. 8.1 Stages in the use of metadata services

"*Tom Cruise*". The service will send back a list of known films whose metadata comply with the request, using the *ProgramInformationTable* and the *ProgramReviewTable*.

- If a customer wishes to send the information about his/her profile to a server, the user will make the corresponding request, accompanying instances of the *<UserPreferences>* and *<UsageHistory>* structures.

It is clear from this list that a key element in the use of the service is the specification of the kind of operation the user wants to request. Section 8.2 will deal with the query types specified in the TV-Anytime standard. To walk on firm ground, avoiding responses rejecting the operation because it is not available among the capabilities of the service the user wishes to use, it is necessary to know these capabilities in detail, provided that not all services will offer the same functionalities. Section 8.3 will deal with this in depth.

However, of course, it all starts with finding out the address (URL) from where the service can be accessed. Section 8.5 will deal briefly with the discovery of metadata services.

8.2 Query Types

In this context, the queries requested of a TV-Anytime metadata service are known as "operations", a name that comes from the WSDL standard (W3C-WSDL, 2001). They are similar to remote procedure calls with perfectly defined sets of possible input information and responses for each operation.

The data types used in the different operations belong to the namespace "*urn:tva:transport:2008*", whose assigned identifier within the TV-Anytime standard is "*tns*". Besides, within the *XML Schema* where the standardized information structures are defined, the "*tva2*" identifier that corresponds to the namespace "*urn:tva:metadata:extended:2010*" is also extensively used, and all the vocabulary used to define TV-Anytime Phase 2 metadata falls under its scope.

The kinds of operations defined in TV-Anytime to consult metadata servers are:

- "*get_Data*": for requests that require certain information from the server
- "*submit_Data*", "*upload_Personal_Data*" and "*clear_Personal_Data*": for requests whose aim is sending information to the server or asking it to delete it

8.2.1 *"get_Data"* Operation

A "*get_Data*" operation allows a customer to request a server to deliver TV-Anytime metadata about programmes or groups of programmes that meet the restrictions specified in the query. For example, the customer can use this operation to do the following:

- Send one or many CRIDs to request location resolution information or descriptive metadata of the indicated contents
- Send certain property values of a given content to request programmes that meet the criteria to be sent back
- Send certain time values and/or channel identifiers to request programmes broadcast according to that data to be sent back

All of these queries may involve multiple restrictions combined according to several logical conditions (conjunction, disjunction, equality, belonging, order, etc.). However, contrary to what usually happens in formal queries to databases, a TV-Anytime metadata server is not forced to respect strictly the issued restrictions. The server can send back information it deems similar but adequate, which allows us to use smart algorithms that provide some added value besides the sheer syntactic comparison.

One part of the query will consist of specifying the list of metadata tables the customer wishes to receive as a response. According to the kind of query, the user may request the submission of one or various tables, such as the *ContentReferencingTable*, *ProgramInformationTable*, *ProgramLocationTable* and *ProgramReviewTable*.

For example, Listing 8.1 shows a request of information about movies containing in the title the string "*Titanic*" (line 4) and directed by "*James Cameron*" (lines 6, 7 and 8, where the "*V83*" identifier corresponds to the role of director).

As seen in the example, the requirement requested in the query is the conjunction of two predicates (AND operator in line 3), where the first predicate is simple (the title of the content being "*Titanic*") and the second is a conjunction of several predicates (the director's name being "*James*" and his surname "*Cameron*").

As Listing 8.1 shows, the customer requests tables *ProgramInformationTable* (line 13) and *GroupInformationTable* (line 16) as a response, both ordered by the CRID and using an ascending criterion (lines 14 and 17).

Usually, the answer to the "*get_Data*" operation will be logically a *ContentReferencingTable* (to inform us on how to acquire this content) or a *TVAMain* document containing the requested tables. Nonetheless, partial answers containing only certain fields identified in the request can also be requested (an option thought for clients with severe CPU and memory limitations), or even specifying interest only for data structures that have been changed since a certain date.

Listing 8.2 shows a request in which only the fields "*Title*" (line 11) and "*Genre*" (line 12) from the *ProgramInformationTable* (line 9) and fields "*Title*" (line 17) and "*PublishedStart*" (line 18) from the *ProgramLocationTable* (line 15) are requested. Furthermore, the query is for programmes broadcast only in channels "*tve1*" (line 4) and "*a3tv*" (line 5).

```
<tns:get_Data>
 <QueryConstraints>
  <PredicateBag type="AND">
   <BinaryPredicate fieldID="tvaf:Title" fieldValue="Titanic"/>
   <PredicateBag type="AND" contextNode="tvac:CreditsItem">
     <BinaryPredicate fieldID="tvaf:Role" fieldValue=":role:V83"/>
     <BinaryPredicate fieldID="tvaf:GivenName" fieldValue="James"/>
     <BinaryPredicate fieldID="tvaf:FamilyName" fieldValue="Cameron"/>
   </PredicateBag>
  </PredicateBag>
 </QueryConstraints>
 <RequestedTables>
   <Table type="ProgramInformationTable">
     <SortCriteria fieldID="tvaf:CRID" order="ascending"/>
   </Table>
   <Table type="GroupInformationTable">
     <SortCriteria fieldID="tvaf:CRID" order="ascending"/>
   </Table>
 </RequestedTables>
</tns:get_Data>
```

Listing 8.1 Example of a "*get_Data*" operation

```
<tns:get_Data>
 <tns:QueryConstraints>
   <tns:PredicateBag type="OR">
     <tns:BinaryPredicate fieldID="tvaf:ServiceURL" fieldValue="tv://tve1"/>
     <tns:BinaryPredicate fieldID="tvaf:ServiceURL" fieldValue="tv://a3tv"/>
   </tns:PredicateBag>
 </tns:QueryConstraints>
 <tns:RequestedTables>
   <tns:Table type="ProgramInformationTable">
     <tns:RequestedFields>
       <tns:IdentificationByFieldId fieldID="tvaf:Title"/>
       <tns:IdentificationByFieldId fieldID="tvaf:Genre"/>
     </tns:RequestedFields>
   </tns:Table>
   <tns:Table type="ProgramLocationTable">
     <tns:RequestedFields>
       <tns:IdentificationByFieldId fieldID="tvaf:Title"/>
       <tns:IdentificationByFieldId fieldID="tvaf:PublishedStart"/>
     </tns:RequestedFields>
   </tns:Table>
 </tns:RequestedTables>
</tns:get_Data>
```

Listing 8.2 Example of a partial "*get_Data*" operation

8.2.2 *"submit_Data"* Operation

This operation is much simpler than the "*get_Data*" one, and it is thought specially for clients to send a <*UsageHistory*> structure to the server (Sect. 4.2.3).

The information sent must always be anonymous, and its use is exclusively aimed at allowing the server to analyse aggregated consumption data in order to enhance its programming.

8.2.3 *"upload_Personal_Data"* Operation

The "*upload_Personal_Data*" operation has the same objective as the "*submit_Data*" operation but aimed at broadcasting personal information stored in an <*ExtendedUserDescription*> structure (Sect. 4.4.3); so it requires a secure connection.

In this case, the data sent could be used to feed targeting processes, for instance to recommend new contents.

8.2.4 *"clear_Personal_Data"* Operation

Finally, the "*clear_Personal_Data*" operation is aimed at ordering the server to delete from its database certain information that was previously sent through the "*upload_Personal_Data*" operation.

The parameters of the request allow the customer to specify whether all the available information about the user should be deleted or only some tables (e.g. the *BiographicInformation* table, belonging to the new *targeting* information from Phase 2, or the *UsageHistory* table, which records the user's consumption history), or even only information sent during a certain period of time.

8.3 Description of Service Capacities

Taking into account what has been analysed so far, it is clear that the complexity of the queries may vary radically according to the nature of the operations requested of the metadata provision service. Therefore, it seems reasonable to think that not all services will offer the same functionalities, but that there will be a considerable diversity resulting from the ambition of the service, its data sources, commercial objectives, etc.

For example, some services will only offer information about the characteristics of programmes, while others will also provide the necessary information to resolve their location or even segmentation information. Some servers can request the submission of a programme's CRID for any type of query, while others could be more flexible (and probably more sophisticated) and allow the customer to specify only some characteristics of the searched content or to select sorting criteria for the results.

To make the generation of queries easier and guarantee their viability in this multiple-functionality scenario, metadata provision services will provide, subject to the customer's request, a description of their capacities. To that end, there exists an associated operation for each of the abovementioned operations (except for "*clear_Personal_Data*", which does not need an explanation) which provides a detailed description of its capacities. These operations are named in an intuitive way, by using the string "*describe_*" as a prefix ("*describe_get_Data*", "*describe_submit_Data*" and "*describe_upload_Personal_Data*").

The last two are very simple: they merely involve asking the server what type of information it accepts together with the privacy policy that will be applied to the information it receives.

On the other hand, the "*describe_get_Data*" operation sends back plenty of details about everything that can be requested of such a service through the "*get_Data*" operation. Among other things, the result of the operation will inform about:

- An informative text description (understandable by people) of the service's characteristics
- The types of tables available to elaborate the response
- If possible, the fields whose inclusion may be requested in a partial answer
- The corresponding *RAR* registers (*Resolving Authority Record*) available, in case there is location resolution information available
- The authorities (part of the CRID) for whom metadata is available
- The television services (channels) for which information is available
- The fields of each table through which searches can be requested, or, if the service's functionality allows it, through which the sorting of results can be requested
- If the service can provide customized results

Listing 8.3 depicts a typical example of a response to a "*describe_get_Data*" operation.

We can see there that the returned structure is named *<describe_get_Data_Result>* (line 1) and it informs that this service provides information about programmes with CRID from the "*rtve.es*" authority (line 3). Specifically, it delivers data in the form of *ProgramInformationTable* (line 6), *GroupInformationTable* (line 8), *ProgramReviewTable* (line 10) and *SegmentInformationTable* (line 12). Moreover, for the first two the user can request sorting the results according to the title and the genre (lines 6 and 8).

8.4 Transport Protocols

We have already explained above what information is exchanged between the client and the server to communicate the metadata related to the service provided. We will now see how this communication is achieved.

```
<describe_get_Data_Result serviceVersion="3" xmlns="urn:tva:transport:2010">
 <AuthorityList>
   <Authority> rtve.es </Authority>
 </AuthorityList>
 <AvailableTables xmlns:tvaf="urn:tva:transport:fieldIDs:2010">
   <Table xsi:type="ProgramInformationTable" canSort="tvaf:Title tvaf:Genre"
          canQuery="tvaf:fragmentID tvaf:fragmentVersion" />
   <Table xsi:type="GroupInformationTable" canSort="tvaf:Title tvaf:Genre"
          canQuery="tvaf:fragmentID tvaf:fragmentVersion"/>
   <Table xsi:type="ProgramReviewTable"
          canQuery="tvaf:fragmentID tvaf:fragmentVersion"/>
   <Table xsi:type="SegmentInformationTable"
          canQuery="tvaf:fragmentID tvaf:fragmentVersion"/>
 </AvailableTables>
 <UpdateCapability versionRequest="true" invalidResponse="false"/>
</describe_get_Data_Result>
```

Listing 8.3 Example of a response to a "*describe_get_Data*" operation

To send and receive TV-Anytime information over TCP/IP networks about the operations described above, the typical Internet protocols are used, the well-known HTTP and SOAP (W3C-SOAP, 2007), according to the structure shown in Fig. 8.2, whose request-response paradigm is very well suited to the nature of the point-to-point operations defined by TV-Anytime.

This means that TV-Anytime messages which describe the requested operations (for instance, the ones shown in Listings 8.1 and 8.2) are wrapped in SOAP messages, which in turn are inserted in an HTTP message's body so they can be sent according to TCP/IP protocols.

The final result of the message sent through the TCP/IP network can be something similar to what is shown in Listing 8.4, where we can see that a request for a "*get_Data*" operation is sent (line 10), containing two CRIDs (lines 13 and 14) for which location resolution information is requested, in particular, the *ContentReferencingTable* (line 17).

The fragment describing the operation is in turn contained in SOAP's *<Body>* and *<Envelope>* elements (lines 8 and 9). The result is finally sent as the body of an HTTP message, whose header goes from line 1 to 6.

8.5 Service Discovery

As stated at the beginning of this section, the first step to access an external metadata service always consists of finding the address where the service is available, to which one must connect to send requests. Without it, little can be done.

This discovery phase of the service could be implemented in a static way, for example encoding one or many URLs into the receiver's software, asking the user

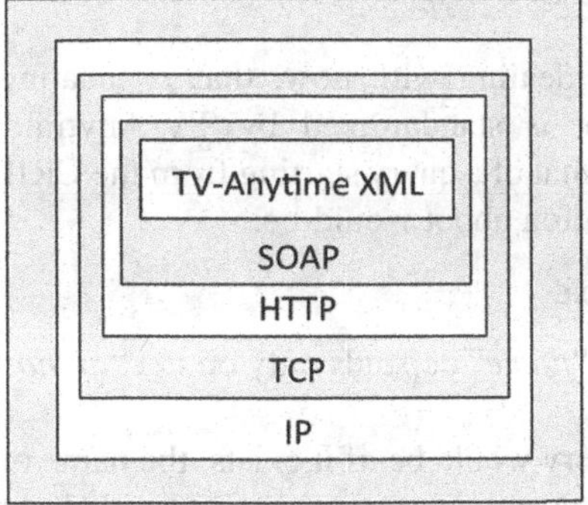

Fig. 8.2 Stack of data submission protocols

```
POST /tva/md-service HTTP/1.0
Host: www.example.com
Content-Type: text/xml; charset="utf-8"
Content-Length: nnnn
Accept-Encoding: deflate
SOAPAction: "get_Data"

<?xml version="1.0" encoding="UTF-8"?>
<Envelope xmlns=" http://schemas.xmlsoap.org/soap/envelope/">
  <Body>
    <get_Data xmlns="urn:tva:transport:2008"
              xmlns:tvaf=" urn:tva:transport: fieldIDs:2010">
      <QueryConstraints type="OR">
        <Predicate fieldID="tvaf:CRID"   fieldValue="crid://tve1.com/Lost"/>
        <Predicate fieldID="tvaf:CRID"   fieldValue="crid://C4.com/House/all"/>
      </QueryConstraints>
      <RequestedTables>
        <Table type="ContentReferencingTable"/>
      </RequestedTables>
    </get_Data>
  </Body>
</Envelope>
```

Listing 8.4 Example of an HTTP message

to input that information directly or even sending the location details of the service through the broadcast channel.

However, in a bidirectional network, there is the possibility of implementing more sophisticated mechanisms to discover services. For instance, a first approach would be something similar to what was presented in Chap. 3 when we dealt with how to find location resolution services. There, we described the use of a DNS server which implements the extension defined in RFC 2782 (IETF RFC 2782, 2000) to provide the resolution for other services. In particular, the format of a query of this type was:

```
_Service._Protocol.Name
```

In the case we are dealing with now, that is locating a metadata provision service, the name that is standardized by TV-Anytime is "*_gmet*" (for "*get metadata*"), and the format of a query starting from the CRID of a given programme we want to get information about would be:

```
_gmet._tcp.name
```

where the format of "*name*" depends only on the "*authority*" field of the specific CRID.

The result of this query would be, if it exists, the name of the machine (and TCP port) where the metadata provision service is provided. And we say "if it exists" because, clearly, nothing guarantees that the creator of that CRID provides an additional metadata provision service.

A second approach would try to find that service regardless of a specific CRID, which means that it would be a service independent from the creator of the CRID. In this regard, TV-Anytime considers the possibility that some yellow pages services exist where TV-Anytime metadata services can be registered and announced, for example through mechanisms standardized by W3C, such as UDDI (UDDI, 2005) or *WS-Inspection* (WS-Inspection, 2001), which can be used separately or together.

For instance, in the case of UDDI, metadata service providers would be registered in what is called the *UDDI Business Registry,* and customers looking for that service would look into one of the nodes of that registry (which have internationally well-known addresses) to get the information. To help the providers of such metadata services to describe and classify their service, the TV-Anytime standard has defined and registered certain models (known as "*tmodels*" in the UDDI terminology) to organize and structure the information that characterizes the service.

In the case of *WS-Inspection*, the only thing TV-Anytime adds is that the *WS-Inspection* descriptive file must be located in the root of the specified Web server under the name "*inspection.wsil*". Only with that information, a client could connect to the server indicated in the metadata and retrieve the service description contained in the abovementioned file.

8.6 Profile Sharing

As stated in the introduction to this chapter, the contribution to the standardization of metadata provision services in bidirectional networks described so far is the result of the work done in TV-Anytime Phase 1. Among the possibilities mentioned so far in this chapter, we find the use of "*submit_Data*" and "*upload_Personal_Data*" operations so that the user is able to send information about his/her socio-demographic profile and consumption history to a service provider.

TV-Anytime Phase 2 intended to go a step further in this aspect, introducing an extension that allows for the exchange and update of this information about personal profiles among different service providers, in such a way that it facilitates the provision of advanced audiovisual content customization services.

The standardization of this extension provides as a result the description of the access interface to a Web service, to which information can be requested about the different parts of a user's profile (from the group of user profiles managed by it), or similar information can be sent to be stored or to update a previous copy.

The benefits of going deeper into this strategy to favour the dissemination of users' personal profiles (as long as it is authorized) are important, both for service providers (who will have access to more information to provide customized services according to the users' interests and needs) and for creators and operators (who will have a better knowledge of their audiences to create and schedule future contents), or even for users themselves (who will trust the providers' proposals more because they are better informed, or will even have an easier time transporting their personal profiles between devices or locations).

Regarding the transport of messages used to make use of this access interface that will be described next, we simply wish to mention that the mechanism suggested for current bidirectional networks (i.e. the Internet) is the one already introduced in a previous section (Sect. 8.4) to access general metadata provision services, that is the combination of the HTTP and SOAP protocols normally used on the Internet for similar tasks.

8.6.1 Exchanged Information

The Web service that will implement the functionalities sought will manage a group of personal profiles, on which it will work upon receiving either of the two specified operations, "*Query*" and "*Modify*", which we will deal with later. These operations will carry out their task on the users' information organized by means of an *<ExtendedUserDescription>* structure, described in Chap. 5, as an extension of the *<UserDescription>* structure introduced in Chap. 4. This structure is made up of the following elements:

- *<UsageHistory>*, a Phase 1 structure that stores different user actions in relation to certain audiovisual contents
- *<UserPreferences>*, a Phase 1 structure that gathers different user preferences, categorized as:
  - *<BrowsingPreferences>*, which groups the user's preferences about how to consume contents
  - *<FilteringAndSearchPreferences>*, which describes the user's preferences regarding audiovisual contents, based on their classifications (*<ClassificationPreferences>*), creation data (*<CreationPreferences>*) or origin details (*<SourcePreferences>*)
- *<UserInformation>*, a Phase 2 structure that gathers biographical and demographic information about the user (*<BiographicInformation>*) and the possible accessibility issues that may be relevant to customize content offers (*<AccessibilityInformation>*)

- *<UsageEnvironmentDescription>*, a Phase 2 structure that gathers information about the characteristics of the user's receiver, the network it is connected to and other current conditions (time, location, weather conditions, etc.)

All this information will compose the user's profile that will be managed by the Web service, which can be consulted as well as completely or partially modified.

8.6.2 Standardized Operations

The two standardized operations to specify requests to a personal profile management Web service are:

- "*Query*", which requests a response with certain information about a profile
- "*Modify*", which sends certain information to modify a stored profile (or to create a new one)

We will see below that each operation can be made up of several queries.

Both operations include as a first informative element an identifier for the resource (user profile) on which the operation is to be carried out. This identifier is sent in an element called *<ResourceID>* (or *<EncryptedResourceID>* if the user wants to send it as hidden information) and its format is a URI that unambiguously identifies each resource (profile).

Likewise, the description of both operations is based on an element called *<Select>* (one for each issued query), whose mission is to identify the part of the user's profile which the query is about, be it to request such information or to identify what part of the profile is to be modified. In other words, the *<Select>* element will point, for example, to a *<UserPreferences>*, *<FilteringAndSearchPreferences>* or *<BiographicInformation>* element, according to what kind of information is to be requested or modified. To this end, inside the *<Select>* element, an *XPath* expression can be used to point to the selected element; alternatively, an abbreviated expression can be used to that aim, providing an identifying code from a set that is predetermined in the specification, which aims at the most common items. These predetermined identifiers can be seen in the left column in Fig. 8.3 accompanied to the right by the equivalent *XPath* expression, which points to the selected item within the user's profile. The method used (*XPath* expression or predefined identifier) is indicated as an attribute to the *<Select>* called "*type*", whose value can be "*xpath*" or "*abbreviated*" (default value).

On the other hand, the responses to these operations must carry one or more instances of an element called *<Status>* (e.g. an element for each of the queries of an operation). Each *<Status>* element contains, at least, one "*code*" attribute whose value must be *"OK"* or *"Failed"* to reflect the result of the query it makes reference to. If it is considered necessary, within *<Status>* you may find another *<StatusDescription>* element containing more specific information, usually of interest in case the query fails.

Fig. 8.3 Predetermined contents of a <*Select*> element

Identifier	Xpath expression for identified element
tva:profile:UserSearchPreferences	/TVAMain/ExtendedUserDescription/UserPreferences/FilteringAndSearchPreferences
tva:profile:UserBrowsingPreferences	/TVAMain/ExtendedUserDescriptions/UserPreferences/BrowsingPreferences
tva:profile:UserActionHistory	/TVAMain/ExtendedUserDescriptions/UsageHistory/UserActionHistory
tva:profile:UserName	/TVAMain/ExtendedUserDescription/UserInformationTable/BioGraphicInformation/Name
tva:profile:UserAge	/TVAMain/ExtendedUserDescription/UserInformationTable/BioGraphicInformation/Age
tva:profile:UserGender	/TVAMain/ExtendedUserDescription/UserInformationTable/BioGraphicInformation/Gender
tva:profile:UserLanguage	/TVAMain/ExtendedUserDescription/UserInformationTable/BioGraphicInformation/Language
tva:profile:UserLocation	/TVAMain/ExtendedUserDescription/UserInformationTable/UsageEnvironment/NaturalEnvironment/Location

8.6.2.1 *"Query"* Operation

The *"Query"* operation is used to request certain information about a specific user profile from a service. As stated before, its first argument is an identifier for the resource (profile) about which the information is requested, which is sent in the <*ResourceID*> element.

Then, one or more <*QueryItem*> elements are added, each one of them indicating a specific query. Each <*QueryItem*> element contains a <*Select*> element which describes the query it is making. Also, each <*QueryItem*> element may carry an attribute called "*changedSince*" by means of which one can specify that only information that has been modified since the date indicated as the value of that attribute must be returned.

For example, Listing 8.5 shows an example of a "*Query*" operation, referenced as *"Q1"* (line 1), made up of three different queries (three <*QueryItem*> elements in lines 3, 6 and 9), to find out certain information about the profile whose identifier is *"http://serprov.es/aefc12bd35"* (line 2).

The fist query is specified between lines 3 and 5; it is called "*preferences*" (which is the value of the "*itemID*" attribute in line 3), and it requests the preferences of the profile (<*FilteringAndSearchPreferences*> structure, identified by the abbreviated method in line 4) that may have changed since October 12, 2011 (value of the "*changedSince*" attribute in line 3).

The second query is called "*location*" (line 6), and it requests the location where the user currently consumes contents (abbreviated identifier in line 7).

The third and last query is called "*history*" (line 9), and it requests the history of the user's actions (abbreviated identifier in line 10) that took place since last October 25, 2011 ("*changedSince*" attribute in line 9).

The response to this operation could very well be the one shown in Listing 8.6, where its connection to operation "*Q1*" is identified in line 2 ("*queryIDRef*" attribute). There, we can see a positive result to the "*preferences*" query (<*Status*> element with a "*code*" attribute with "*OK*" value in line 4).

Along with this indicator of the result of the query comes a <*Data*> element which contains a *TVAMain* table where the preferences that have changed since the

```
<Query queryID="Q1">
 <ResourceID> http://serprov.es/aefc12bd35 </ResourceID>
 <QueryItem itemID="preferences" changedSince="2011-10-12T00:00:00">
   <Select type="abbreviated"> tva:profile:UserSearchPreferences </Select>
 </QueryItem>
 <QueryItem itemID="location">
   <Select type="abbreviated"> tva:profile:UserLocation </Select>
 </QueryItem>
 <QueryItem itemID="history" changedSince="2011-10-25T00:00:00">
   <Select type="abbreviated"> tva:profile:UserActionHistory </Select>
 </QueryItem>
</Query>
```

Listing 8.5 Example of a "*Query*" operation

```
1 <QueryResponse xmlns="urn:tva:profile:2010" xmlns:mpeg7="urn:tva:mpeg7:2008"
2                xmlns:tva="urn:tva:metadata:2010" queryIDRef="Q1"
3                timeStamp="2011-10-14T12:00:00">
4  <Status code="OK" requestIDRef="preferences"/>
5  <Data itemIDRef="preferences">
6   <TVAMain xml:lang="en" publisher="C4.com" rightsOwner="C4.com"
7            publicationTime="2011-10-13T11:30:00" >
8     <tva:UserDescription>
9       <tva:UserPreferences>
10        <tva:UserPreference>
11          <mpeg7:FilteringAndSearchPreferences preferenceValue="66"
12                   xmlns:mpeg7="urn:mpeg:mpeg7:schema:2001">
13            <mpeg7:ClassificationPreferences>
14              <mpeg7:Genre href="urn:mpeg:GenreCS">
15                <mpeg7:Name> Soccer </mpeg7:Name>
16              </mpeg7:Genre>
17            </mpeg7:ClassificationPreferences>
18          </mpeg7:FilteringAndSearchPreferences>
19        </tva:UserPreference>
20      </tva:UserPreferences>
21    </tva:UserDescription>
22  </TVAMain>
23 </Data>
24 </QueryResponse>
```

Listing 8.6 Example of a response to a "*Query*" operation

specified date are included. In this case, the only notification involves a new rating of the "*Soccer*" genre (lines 14–16).

The "*timeStamp*" attribute in line 3 provides the date when the response is sent, which can be used as a reference point for future updates (using it as a value for the "*changedSince*" attribute).

8.6.2.2 *"Modify"* Operation

The "*Modify*" operation, on the other hand, is used to request a server to modify some information stored in a user's profile, which includes both giving it an initial value and eliminating it altogether.

Apart from the abovementioned *<ResourceID>* element, used to identify the resource to be modified, this operation contains one or many *<Modification>* elements, one for each modification that is to be made in that profile. Each one of these *<Modification>* elements will include a clause (*<Select>* element) to identify the kind of information that is being modified and a *<NewData>* element with the new information to be added.

In turn, each *<Modification>* element may have a "*notChangedSince*" attribute to specify that this modification must be discarded if the resource has changed since a given date, thus avoiding possible concurrence problems.

Listing 8.7 shows an example of a "*Modify*" operation, called *"M1"* (value of the "*modifyID*" attribute, line 2). In this figure, we can see that the profile identified by "*http://serprov.es/aefc12bd35*" (line 3) is modified. The modification is called "*genre*" (value of the "*itemID*" attribute, line 4), and it consists of changing the user's preferences, establishing a new rating to the *"Sports"* genre in line 12.

In any case, this modification will have to be discarded if those preferences have changed since October 12, 2011, as stated by the "*notChangedSince*" attribute (line 4).

The response to this operation could very well be the one shown in Listing 8.8, where its connection to operation *"M1"* is indicated in line 2 ("*modifyIDRef*" attribute). In this case, the response to the modification request called *"genre"* is negative, as indicated by the "*Failed*" value of the "*code*" attribute of the *<Status>* element in line 2. The additional *<StatusDescription>* element (line 3) provides some additional information about the cause of the failure.

8.7 Summary

This chapter has introduced details about the TV-Anytime standardization regarding possible metadata provision services managed by third parties, which are accessible through a bidirectional network.

If the receiver is connected to a bidirectional network, the access to external information provided by third parties multiplies the possibilities of the deployed services. In this case, we have seen that TV-Anytime standardizes several aspects of the access to that universe of external metadata (aspects related to the discovery of the services, the protocols to communicate with them and the range of operations that can be requested of providers, including a complete specification of the formats of the messages to be exchanged).

As presented before, this range of operations contains elements to request the execution of the operations that are offered, but also to know in detail what these operations are, and the options offered by the provider in each of them, with the purpose of making it more likely to succeed in their execution.

```
<Modify xmlns="urn:tva:profile:2010" xmlns:mpeg7="urn:tva_mpeg7:2005"
          xmlns:tva="urn:tva:metadata:2010"  modifyID="M1">
 <ResourceID> http://serprov.es/aefc12bd35 </ResourceID>
 <Modification itemID="genre" notChangedSince="2011-10-12T12:00:00">
   <Select type="abbreviated"> Genre </Select>
   <NewData>
     <TVAMain xml:lang="en" publicationTime="2011-10-12T12:00:00">
       <tva:UserDescription>
        <tva:UserPreferences>
          <mpeg7:FilteringAndSearchPreferences>
            <mpeg7:ClassificationPreferences>
              <mpeg7:Genre href="urn:tva:metadata:cs:ContentCS:2005:3.1.1.9"
                           preferenceValue="9">
                <mpeg7:Name xml:lang="en"> Sports </mpeg7:Name>
              </mpeg7:Genre>
            </mpeg7:ClassificationPreferences>
          </mpeg7:FilteringAndSearchPreferences>
        </tva:UserPreferences>
       </tva:UserDescription>
     </TVAMain>
   </NewData>
 </Modification>
</Modify>
```

Listing 8.7 Example of a "*Modify*" operation

```
<ModifyResponse xmlns="urn:tva:profile:2010" modifyIDRef="M1">
 <Status code="Failed" requestIDRef="genre">
   <StatusDescription xml:lang="en"href="urn:tva:profile:cs:StatusCS:2005:7">
       InvalidData
   </StatusDescription>
 </Status>
</ModifyResponse>
```

Listing 8.8 Example of a response to a "*Modify*" operation

Finally, Phase 2 focuses especially on the exchange of the users' personal profiles among providers, with the purpose of furthering their knowledge of the audience in order to improve the services provided.

The next chapter will deal with TV-Anytime's contribution to the standardization of the procedures to allow the remote programming of a receiver through a bidirectional network such as the Internet.

Remote Terminal Programming 9

9.1 Introduction

To finish describing the most important aspects of the TV-Anytime standard, in this chapter, we will deal with a part devoted to regulating several mechanisms aimed at making the remote programming of terminals easier, that is to allow users to instruct them remotely to order operations that must be performed upon audiovisual contents the device can access through the distribution networks it is connected to.

In the different parts of the TV-Anytime standard, there are many sections related directly or indirectly to this functionality, among which we find the three cases we are going to describe, all of them regulated in TV-Anytime Phase 2.

A first case is derived from the facilities provided to make easier the interaction between devices and applications that follow the directives of the TV-Anytime standard and those whose way of operating and data models do not follow these specifications. The regulated aspects, centred on the exchange of information, consider, among other things, the indications about what should be done with this metadata, which supposes a way of remote programming (for instance, recording the content described by the metadata).

A second aspect is aimed at enabling a procedure to allow the direct remote programming of a PDR in our home, for example, through the office computer or our smartphone from any place. The TV-Anytime standard offers a procedure through an email service to do this.

Last, but not least, we will deal with the most complex case which describes a procedure to program an NDR (*Network Digital Recorder*) belonging to the operator and located in its facilities. It is, definitely, about the remote use of a recorder that belongs to the service provider, programming it to record a given content for us (which it will supposedly later send to one of our devices). There can be many reasons, for example because we cannot make the recording in our PDR, because we do not have enough space or because our PDR does not have access to the distribution network where the content is available, or simply because we are not at home and our PDR does not allow remote access to program the recording.

A. Gil Solla and R.G. Sotelo Bovino, *TV-Anytime*, X.media.publishing,
DOI 10.1007/978-3-642-36766-3_9, © Springer-Verlag Berlin Heidelberg 2013

9.2 Data Exchange Format

9.2.1 Objective

A collateral aspect of TV-Anytime's standardization (in Phase 2) regarding the remote programming of receivers is related to the interaction between devices and applications that follow the guidelines of this standard and those whose way of operating and data models do not follow them. To this aim, it is clear that there are both past and future worlds beyond the TV-Anytime regulations, and that audiovisual services that provide interesting functions incompatible with TV-Anytime products exist and will exist. Because of this, the interaction between these services and TV-Anytime devices has interesting advantages that make it advisable to have some kind of standardization to facilitate an operational communication between both worlds.

In this regard, TV-Anytime standardizes a data-packaging format to send information from applications of devices that do not follow TV-Anytime's data and operation models to devices that are compatible with this standard. We are talking both about content description metadata and location resolution information to facilitate their acquisition. This would allow, among other things, a system that is not capable of performing certain tasks with the information to be able to translate it into the TV-Anytime format and send it to a system that can perform the task.

In the case of a user finding certain information on a service that does not have the capacity to resolve and acquire the content (e.g. a Web page), this could make it possible to have an option in that page to package the results of that search in the format we are discussing and request its submission to a TV-Anytime device, possibly with some indication of what to do with it. This would prevent the user from having to repeat the search in a TV-Anytime system to, for instance, request a recording. Of course, this could only occur if the creator of the original service had enabled such a feature.

But this mechanism could also be of interest in certain cases to exchange information between providers and customers that are compatible with TV-Anytime. We can think of TV-Anytime providers with no access to a television broadcast system; or special client devices, beyond televisions or *set-top boxes*, such as a phone or a digital tablet, that cannot receive television signals; or that the data is the result of a simple adaptation of information provided by selection and location services outside TV-Anytime world.

9.2.2 Packaging Structure

As one could easily guess, the information to be exchanged is packaged using an XML structure, whose root element is called *<CoreData>*. This root element contains one or several elements called *<SelectedContent>*, each of them describing an individual piece of information (that characterizes or facilitates the location of a given content) that is sent in the message.

Each of the <*SelectedContent*> elements has the following characteristics:

- It includes an "*Id*" attribute that stores the CRID of the content being described. It may also be accompanied by an *IMI*, which points to a specific copy of the content, as described in Chap. 3.
- It may carry a <*TVAMain*> element to describe the referenced content, which can include information on specific instances of that content.
- It may also contain a <*ContentReferencingTable*> element, if what is being sent is location information of the referenced content.
- It optionally contains a <*WSIFServerAddress*> element, which carries the URL of a Web server that contains in its root a *WS-Inspection* file, as a means to make additional queries about the content.
- It can also contain an <*Action*> element that describes the action that the receiver must perform on the content it receives information about. The different possibilities that can be indicated in this element are collected in a new classification scheme called "*CoreDataActionTypeCS*", which gathers a set of instructions such as "*recordReplace*", "*recordAllowDuplicates*", "*recordIfNotYetExists*", "*remind*" and "*recommend*". The default action, if the element does not exist, will be the first of the possibilities described above. In addition, this action can be accompanied by an indication about whether it is supposed to be a new action to be added or if it is an existing action that needs to be cancelled.

In Listing 9.1 we can see a simple example of this type of packaging.

There, some information is sent about two contents (the two <*SelectedContent*> elements that start in lines 4 and 28, respectively).

A basic description of the first content (*CRID://C4.com/House/S1/E1*) is sent through the <*TVAMain*> element (line 6) as well as a reference table with location resolution information (line 17). Therefore, the action that the receiver must perform is the default one: recording that content replacing any previous copies. To help in this task, an *IMI* is sent along with the CRID (line 5), whose name indicates that we are interested in an HD copy.

In the case of the second content described in Listing 9.1 (i.e. *CRID://C4.com/House/S1/E2*), no description is provided inside the corresponding <*SelectedContent*> element (empty <*TVAMain*> element in line 29), but we see the URL of a server from which a *WS-Inspection* file with more information on the content can be found (line 30).

Also, the action to be performed by the receiver is specified: it must recommend the content to the user (content of the <*Action*> element in line 31, with the action indicated in the <*Type*> element in line 32 and described in text in line 33—"*recommend*").

```
<?xml version="1.0" encoding="UTF-8"?>
 <CoreData xmlns="urn:tva:CoreData:2010" xmlns:tva="urn:tva:metadata:2010"
           xmlns:CR="urn:tva:ContentReferencing:2010">
  <SelectedContent Id="CRID://C4.com/House/S1/E1"
                   instanceMetadataId="imi:C4.com/house/hd">
   <tva:TVAMain version="03" xml:lang="en" publisher="..." publicationTime="...">
    <tva:ProgramDescription>
     <tva:ProgramInformationTable>
      <tva:ProgramInformation programId="CRID://C4.com/House/S1/E1">
        <tva:BasicDescription>
         <tva:Title> House </tva:Title>
        </tva:BasicDescription>
       </tva:ProgramInformation>
     </tva:ProgramInformationTable>
    </tva:ProgramDescription>
   </tva:TVAMain>
   <CR:ContentReferencingTable version="1.0">
    <CR:Result CRID="crid://C4.com/House/S1/E1"
           status="resolved" complete="true" acquire="any">
     <CR:LocationsResult>
      <CR:Locator>
        dvb://1.4ee2.3f4;4f5~@2011-10-19T22:00:00.00+01:00/PT01H00M
      </CR:Locator>
     </CR:LocationsResult>
    </CR:Result>
   </CR:ContentReferencingTable>
  </SelectedContent>
  <SelectedContent Id="CRID://C4.com/House/S1/E2">
   <tva:TVAMain />
   <WSIFServerAddress> http://www.C4.com/WS </WSIFServerAddress>
   <Action instruction="create">
    <Type href="urn:tva:CoreData:cs:CoreDataActionTypeCS:2005:5">
     <tva:Name xml:lang="en"> recommend </tva:Name>
    </Type>
   </Action>
  </SelectedContent>
 </CoreData>
```

Listing 9.1 Example of a "*CoreData*" structure

9.3 Remote PDR Programming

9.3.1 Objective

The second standardization process described in TV-Anytime's Phase 2 on the remote programming of devices is meant to allow the user to control his/her home receiver (the PDR or a similar device) remotely.

Even though this control can materialize in different aspects (request information on stored contents, order searches, delete items, check pending tasks, etc.), finally, the only standardized feature in this first version of the standard is related to

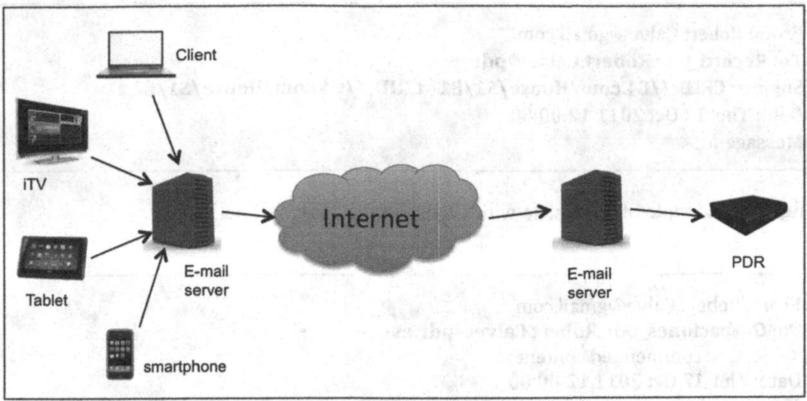

Fig. 9.1 Sending emails to a PDR

instructing the receiver to schedule the recording of contents, possibly with the sole purpose of showing the path that future functionalities in this regard may follow.

On the one hand, it is clear the interest of the possibility given to the users to order their home device to record contents when they are not at home, for example from a computer at work or from their *smartphone* wherever they may be.

But this mechanism can also be used by a service provider to program the user's PDR to automatically acquire contents it thinks may be of interest to the user (with the necessary authorization by the user, who has probably signed up for this service). That is, the service provider can not only send recommendations of programmes that it thinks the user might like, but it could also order the user's PDR to record them automatically, if the user cannot do it on his/her own.

To send these orders to the PDR, TV-Anytime standardizes a simple procedure based on sending email messages to the receiver.

9.3.2 Remote Programming by Email

The procedure to remotely order a PDR to record a given content will therefore consist of sending an email (to a particular email address assigned to the PDR) that identifies the content that should be recorded (Fig. 9.1), following the syntax and semantics specified in RFC 822 (IETF RFC 822, 1982).

The first possibility, the simplest, consists of specifying the CRID of the content the user wants to have recorded in the "*Subject*" field of the message (or several CRIDs, separated by spaces, if ordering the recording of several contents).

We can see a simple example of this in Listing 9.2, where an order to record two contents is sent to the PDR's email address (*Record_pdr.Robert.Calve@pdr.es* in line 2). Both contents are fully identified by their references in line 3, *CRID://C4.com/House/S1/E1* and *CRID://C4.com/House/S1/E2*.

Another more elaborate possibility consists of including a <*CoreData*> structure as described in Sect. 9.2 in the body of the HTTP message, specifying with the

```
From: Robert.Calve@gmail.com
To: Record_pdr.Robert.Calve@pdr.es
Subject: CRID://C4.com/House/S1/E1  CRID://C4.com/House/S1/E2
Date: Thu, 12 Oct 2011 12:00:00
Message-Id:
```

Listing 9.2 Example of a message with CRIDs in the "*Subject*" field

```
1 From: Robert.Calve@gmail.com
2 To: Grabaciones_pdr.Robert.Calve@pdr.es
3 Subject: Recommended content
4 Date: Thu, 12 Oct 2011 12:00:00
5 Message-Id:
6 Content-Type: text/xml; charset=UTF-8

7 <?xml version="1.0" encoding="UTF-8"?>
8 <CoreData xmlns="urn:tva:CoreData:2010" xmlns:tva="urn:tva:metadata:2010"
9           xmlns:xsi:schemaLocation="urn:tva:CoreData:2010 tva_core_data_8_v141.xsd">
10  <SelectedContent id="CRID://C4.com/House/S1/E1">
11    <tva:TVAMain version="03" xml:lang="en" publisher="..." publicationTime="...">
12      <tva:ProgramDescription>
13        <tva:ProgramInformationTable>
14          <tva:ProgramInformation programId=" CRID://C4.com/House/S1/E1">
15            <tva:BasicDescription>
16               <tva:Title> House </tva:Title>
17            </tva:BasicDescription>
18          </tva:ProgramInformation>
19        </tva:ProgramInformationTable>
20      </tva:ProgramDescription>
21    </tva:TVAMain>
22    <Action>
23       <Type href="urn:tva:CoreData:cs:CoreDataActionTypeCS:2005:3">
24          <tva:Name xml:lang="en"> recordIfNotYetExists </tva:Name>
25       </Type>
26    </Action>
27  </SelectedContent>
28 </CoreData>
```

Listing 9.3 Example of an email message with a body

"*Content-Type*" field that the content of the body is of the "*text/xml*" type. In this case, the CRIDs defined in this structure have precedence over those which may appear in the "*Subject*" field of the message.

In Listing 9.3, we can see an example of this second possibility, where the PDR is ordered to record one of the abovementioned contents (line 10), but this time only in the case this recording does not exist yet (lines 23 and 24). In this case, as we can see in line 3, the "*Subject*" field of the message is merely informative.

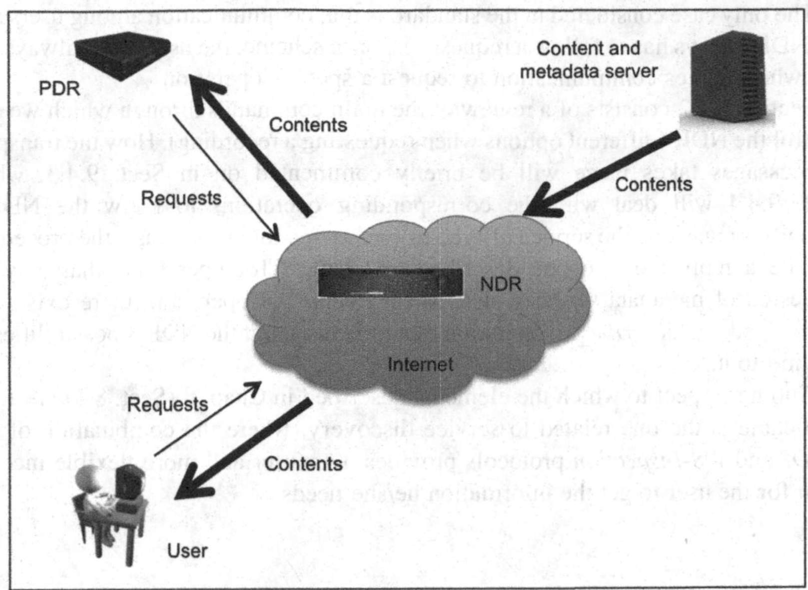

Fig. 9.2 NDR access scenario

9.4 Remote NDR Programming

9.4.1 Objective

The last case to be analysed about remote programming procedures in TV-Anytime refers to the possibility of using devices outside the user's home (possibly provided by a service managed by third parties) to record the indicated contents and subsequently deliver them to our equipments. These external devices which can be managed remotely are named *Network Digital Recorders* (NDRs).

This would allow us, for instance, not only to make sure that the requested recordings are being made when nobody is at home and we cannot program our receiver remotely (e.g. through the mechanisms described in the previous section) but also to acquire the desired contents whenever there is no space left in our device, or when, for whatever reason, our receiver does not have access to the distribution network through which the desired content can be accessed, or when we just want to record two contents at the same time and our device lacks that capability.

As shown in Fig. 9.2, the anticipated scenario allows us to give instructions to an NDR through a network (possibly, the Internet) from a computer or from our own PDR, request the recording of a given content, and have it sent to any of the abovementioned devices. In this regard, TV-Anytime standardizes how to declare this service to make it accessible for users, how users can discover it and find out its characteristics and how they must use it according to their objectives.

The only case considered in the standard is that communication among users and the NDR always has to follow a request-response scheme, the user being always the one who initiates communication to request a specific operation.

Section 9.4.2 consists of a review of the main commands through which we can control the NDR (different options when requesting a recording). How the transport of messages takes place will be briefly commented on in Sect. 9.4.3, while Sect. 9.4.4 will deal with the corresponding operations to know the NDR's capacities regarding the service offered to customers. In this last case, the procedure will be a replica of the one described in Chap. 8 for operations that may be requested of metadata services, that is, for every "*X*" operation, there exists the corresponding "*describe_X*" operation that informs about the NDR's possibilities in relation to it.

Another aspect to which the elements described in Chap. 8 (Sect. 8.5) are fully applicable is the one related to service discovery, where the combination of the *UDDI* and *WS-Inspection* protocols provides a smarter and more flexible mechanism for the user to get the information he/she needs.

9.4.2 Controlling an NDR

Given that the aim is also to regulate communications through a network, the mechanism used to perform control operations over an NDR is similar to what was described in Chap. 8 for requests made to metadata provision services. It has to do with establishing a point-to-point communication with a remote device and sending it the request for an operation, with well-defined input, output and behaviour, similar to remote procedure calls.

In this case, the defined operation is called "*control_NDR*", and it offers the requesting party different possibilities to specify the objective of that control, such as:

- Request the NDR to record what is being broadcast at that moment on a certain channel
- Provide a CRID (and maybe an *IMI*) for the NDR to look for and record that content
- Check the status of scheduled recordings in the NDR or order their cancellation

To this end, the *<control_NDR>* element that describes the operation will contain another element defining it. The element may be *<RecordRequest>*, *<RecordStatus>*, *<RecordCancel>* or *<RecordListRequest>*. Their meanings are evident in view of their names, and their respective contents will be different in each case, as we will observe below.

The NDR's response will consist of an element named *<Control_NDR_Result>* that will contain inside a different element according to the kind of request, that is it can be *<RecordRequestResult>*, *<RecordStatusResult>*, *<RecordCancelResult>* or *<RecordListRequestResult>*. We shall see their structures below as well.

```
1 <RecordRequest>
2   <SubscriptionId> 3456-4567-5677-4321 </SubscriptionId>
3   <ContentId CRID="CRID://C4.com/House/S1/E1"/>
4   <Locator> dvb://1.4ee2.3fa;4f5 </Locator>
5   <Locator> dvb://1.3fc4.431;9bC </Locator>
6 </RecordRequest>
```

Listing 9.4 Example of a "*RequestRecord*" operation

9.4.2.1 "*RecordRequest*" Operation

The appearance of the *<RecordRequest>* element inside the *<control_NDR>* element indicates that the operation is a recording request (and subsequent delivery of the content to the requesting party).

This is a compound element, within which various elements can appear that make clarifications to the recording operation. This operation may take place on a certain channel, specifying the channel and the period of time to record, or it may simply be defined by the content's CRID, in which case the NDR will have to find it among its sources of information and acquire it.

The elements that constitute a *<RecordRequest>* are as follows:

- *<SubscriptionId>*, to reference the user's subscription to this service, which gives him/her the right to request the operation.
- *<ContentId>*, to identify the content to be recorded by its CRID (and maybe *IMI*). If the element is not present, whatever is broadcast on the channel identified in the next element will be recorded.
- *<Locator>*, to identify the channel from where the desired content is to be recorded.
- *<DeliveryMediaFormat>*, to specify recording encryption or bit rate details.
- *<ProtocolSet>*, to specify the protocols to deliver the recorded content to the user. Downloading and control protocols can be specified (control makes sense in some cases (udp) and in others it does not (ftp)). The default values are "*rtp*" and "*rtsp*".
- *<StartTime>*, the start time of the recording, if a channel is specified instead of the CRID.
- *<EndTime>*, the end time of a recording, if a channel is specified.
- *<FilteringAndSearchPreferences>*, to indicate the user's preferences, only used if a CRID is specified and the NDR has some freedom to choose the content among various alternatives.

For instance, Listing 9.4 shows a simple case of a recording request made by a user that is identified in line 2. The user specifically requests the content "*CRID://C4.com/House/S1/E1*" (line 3) and indicates that the NDR must look for this content in the channels specified in the two*<Locator>*elements in lines 5 and 6.

The response sent back by the NDR for this operation will be a *<RecordRequestResult>* element, made up of a *<RecordRequestOK>* element if the operation is accepted (which does not guarantee its success), or a

```
1 <RecordRequestResult serviceVersion="12">
2  <RecordRequestOK>
3    <RequestId> 45U753-452 </RequestId>
4    <Time2Call> 2011-10-15T20:00:00 </Time2Call>
5    <RecordingCharge currency="EUR"> 2 </RecordingCharge>
6    <ConservationDelay> PT12H </ConservationDelay>
7  </RecordRequestOK>
8 </RecordRequestResult>
```

Listing 9.5 Example of the result of a "*RequestRecord*" operation

<RecordRequestError> element if the operation is rejected because it cannot be completed.

If the operation is accepted, the *<RecordRequestOK>* element will in turn contain several elements:

- *<RequestId>*, an identifier for the operation, to make reference to it in subsequent requests
- *<Time2Call>*, estimated date and time when the content is believed to be available
- *<RecordingCharge>*, the price charged to the user for this recording
- *<ConservationDelay>*, the period of time during which the recording will be kept (the user shall download it during this time)

For instance, Listing 9.5 depicts a possible response accepting the request shown in Listing 9.4. The acceptance of the operation is indicated in line 2, the identifier assigned to the request is *45U753-452* (line 3), the estimated time of availability is "*2011-10-15T20:00:00*" (line 4), the price of the recording is €2 (line 5) and the recording will be kept for 12 h (line 6).

However, if the operation is rejected, the *<RecordRequestResult>* element will include a *<RecordRequestError>* element, which will contain a string providing certain information about the reason ("*unknownCRID*", "*unavailableServiceURL*", "*unknownSubscriptionId*", etc.), whose explanation is usually unnecessary.

9.4.2.2 "*RecordStatus*" Operation

The appearance of the *<RecordStatus>* element inside the *<control_NDR>* element indicates that the customer wants to know if a recording operation that was previously accepted has already been completed or not.

In this case, the only information that should be provided is the identifier of the operation to be checked, which is done by sending as a parameter the identifier received in the response to the corresponding *RecordRequest* operation in which the recording was requested.

For example, Listing 9.6 shows an operation that asks about the status of the recording ordered in Listing 9.4, whose identifier (the "*requestId*" attribute with value *"45U753-452"*) was returned in the response shown in Listing 9.5.

The response to this operation will consist of a *<RecordStatusResult>* element, which will contain a *<Running>* element (indicating that the recording is still

```
<RecordStatus requestId="45U753-452"/>
```

Listing 9.6 Example of a "*RecordStatus*" operation

```
1 <RecordStatusResult requestId="45U753-452">
2   <ContentAvailable>
3     <ContentURL> ftp://servicioPDR.es/house.avi </ContentURL>
4     <ConservationDeadline> 2011-10-17T20:00:00 </ConservationDeadline>
5   </ContentAvailable>
6 </RecordStatusResult>
```

Listing 9.7 Example of the result of a "*RecordStatus*" operation

```
<RecordCancel requestId="45U753-452"/>
```

Listing 9.8 Example of a "*RecordCancel*" operation

pending), a *<ContentAvailable>* element (indicating that the content is already available) or a *<Failure>* element that indicates the operation has failed.

If the response is *<Running>*, it will contain in turn a *<Time2Call>* element with the estimated moment it will become available.

If the response is *<ContentAvailable>*, it will have in it a *<ContentURL>* element (with the link to access the content) and a *<ConservationDeadline>* element with the time when the recording will expire.

If the response is *<Failure>*, it will contain a string with a brief explanation of the reason ("*unknownRequest*", "*cancelledBroadcast*" or "*cancelledByNDR*", whose meaning is clear).

For instance, Listing 9.7 shows a possible response to the request in Listing 9.6. The response indicates that the content is already available (line 2) and provides an FTP link to retrieve it (line 3), indicating up to when it will be available (line 4).

9.4.2.3 "*RecordCancel*" Operation

The inclusion of the *<RecordCancel>* element inside the *<control_NDR>* element indicates that the customer wishes to cancel a recording operation which was previously accepted.

In this case, the only information he/she needs to provide is the identifier of the operation to be cancelled, which he/she received in the response to the *RecordRequest* operation in which the recording was requested.

For example, Listing 9.8 shows the operation to cancel the recording ordered in Listing 9.4, whose identifier was returned in the response shown in Listing 9.5.

```
<RecordCancelResult> OK </RecordCancelResult>
```

Listing 9.9 Example of the result of a "*RecordCancel*" operation

```
<RecordListRequest>
  <SubscriptionId> 3456-4567-5677-4321 </SubscriptionId>
</RecordListRequest>
```

Listing 9.10 Example of a "*RecordListRequest*" operation

The response to this operation will be a *<RecordCancelResult>* element whose content will be a string indicating the result ("*OK*", "*unknownRequest*" or "*removedAfterRecording*", whose explanation is unnecessary again).

For instance, Listing 9.9 shows a possible response to the request in Listing 9.8.

9.4.2.4 *"RecordListRequest"* Operation

The inclusion of the *<RecordListRequest>* element inside the *<control_NDR>* element indicates that the customer wants to know the list of recording operations that have been accepted so far by the NDR.

In this case, the only information that needs to be provided is the user's subscription identifier, which is sent as the content of a *<SubscriptionId>* element that goes inside the *<RecordListRequest>* element.

For example, Listing 9.10 shows one such request.

The response to this operation will consist of an element named *<RecordListRequestResult>*, which will contain a sequence of *<RecordRequestStatus>* elements (one for each recording that was requested and accepted). This *<RecordRequestStatus>* element is of the same type as the *<RecordStatusResult>* element described above.

For instance, Listing 9.11 shows a possible response to the request in Listing 9.10, where the information regarding the only recording that was requested is presented, informing that the broadcast has been cancelled (line 3).

9.4.3 Transporting Messages

The transport over IP networks of XML structures representing the operations and responses described so far has the same requirements and characteristics as the communication related to the metadata provision services described in Chap. 8 (see Sect. 8.4). Therefore, the transport of the messages we have just introduced is achieved as well by means of the combination of the HTTP and SOAP protocols, particularly suited for the request-response nature of this type of point-to-point communication. Therefore, Fig. 8.5, which showed the stack of protocols used there, is perfectly applicable to this case.

```
<RecordListRequestResult>
  <RecordRequestStatus requestId="45U753-452">
     <Failure> cancelledBroadcast </Failure>
  <RecordRequestStatus>
</RecordListRequestResult>
```

Listing 9.11 Example of the result of a "*RecordListRequest*" operation

Listing 9.12 displays the HTTP message sent in the case of the *RecordCancel* operation shown in Listing 9.8.

There, we can see that the identification of the operation itself occupies only line 15, which is the main part of the *<control_NDR>* operation (line 10), which in turn is wrapped by a SOAP message sent with the HTTP protocol.

9.4.4 Describing Service Capabilities

As described in Sect. 8.6, it is fair to think of a heterogeneous scenario in which NDR service providers may diversify the scope of the functionalities provided according to their investments and the intended audience's objectives. For example, some NDRs may simply provide the recording capacity; meanwhile, others can allow choosing the format, signal encoding details or the content's delivery protocol.

Given this diversity, it is fundamental to provide a mechanism for customers to get to know the capabilities of the services they have access to in order to make sure they can do what the user may require of them. To this end, besides the "*control_NDR*" operation, the service must always offer the corresponding "*describe_control_NDR*" operation, which will inform the user about the details and variations of the operation, without needing any input parameter. Both operations constitute what is known as a "*port*", which will be accessible at a common URL.

The response to this operation will be a message containing the *<describe_control_NDR_Result>* element, which will include the following elements:

- *<Name>*, with a string informing the name of the service
- *<Description>*, with a brief text description of the service
- *<SubscriptionURL>*, which includes the URL where the user can find out the conditions of the subscription
- *<ServiceURLList>*, with a list of channels the NDR receives and can, therefore, make recordings from
- *<ConversionList>*, with a list of the conversion possibilities (original and final formats) that may be requested of the NDR

```
POST /tva/remote-service HTTP/1.0
Host: www.uvigo.es
Content-Type: text/xml; charset="utf-8"
Content-Length: nnnn
Accept-Encoding: deflate
SOAPAction: "control_NDR"

<?xml version="1.0" encoding="UTF-8"?>
 <Envelope xmlns="http://schemas.xmlsoap.org/soap/envelope/">
   <Body>
     <ndr:Control_NDR xmlns:NDR="urn:tva:ndr:2010"
                      xmlns:tva="urn:tva:metadata:2010"
                      xmlns:mpeg7="urn:tva:mpeg7:2008"
                      xmlns:xsi="http://www.w3.org/2001/XMLSchema-instance"
                      xsi:schemaLocation="urn:tva:ndr:2010 tva_ndr_9_v141.xsd">
        <RecordCancel requestId="45U753-452"/>
     </ndr:Control_NDR>
   </Body>
 </Envelope>
```

Listing 9.12 HTTP message of a "*RecordCancel*" operation

- *<ProtocolSetList>*, with a list of the protocols that the NDR may use to deliver the recordings
- *<PlayWhileRecording>*, with an indicator stating whether the service is capable of starting to deliver the information before ending the recording or not
- *<SupportForFilteringAndSearchPreferences>*, with an indicator stating whether the service allows the indicated preference structure to help in the selection of contents to be recorded

Listing 9.13 indicates a possible response to this operation requesting the description of the service's capabilities.

It can be observed there that only one channel can be recorded (identified in line 12), that a conversion of the recording can be made to deliver the audio in AMR format (lines 19 and 20) and the video in MPEG-4 format (lines 24 and 25), that the recordings can be delivered to the user by means of the "*udp*/*rtsp*" protocols (lines 33 and 34) and, finally, that it is possible to start delivering the content while it is being recorded (line 37).

9.5 Summary

In this chapter, we have presented the standardizing efforts of TV-Anytime in relation to the remote access to terminals, whose aim is to enable the remote querying and programming of these devices, especially through IP networks.

Throughout the previous pages, three different mechanisms have been presented, of increasing complexity and functionality. First, we have seen a simple mechanism created to send certain encapsulated information from non-TV-

```
<?xml version="1.0" encoding="UTF-8"?>
<ndr:describe_control_NDR_Result xmlns:ndr="urn:tva:ndr:2010"
                                 xmlns:tva="urn:tva:metadata:2010"
                                 xmlns:mpeg7="urn:tva:mpeg7:2008"
                        xmlns:xsi="http://www.w3.org/2001/XMLSchema-instance"
                        xsi:schemaLocation="urn:tva:ndr:2010 tva_ndr_9_v141.xsd"
                        serviceVersion="148">
  <Name xml:lang="en"> Audiovisual recording service </Name>
  <Description xml:lang="en"> Remote free recording service </Description>
  <SubscriptionURL>http://www.NDRservice.es/subscription.php</SubscriptionURL>
  <ServiceURLList>
    <ServiceURL> dvb://1.8.f </ServiceURL>
  </ServiceURLList>
  <ConversionList>
    <ConversionOffer>
      <DeliveryMediaFormat>
        <tva:BitRate variable="false">3500000</tva:BitRate>
        <tva:AudioAttributes>
          <tva:Coding href="urn:mpeg:mpeg7:cs:AudioCodingFormatCS:2001:6">
            <tva:Name xml:lang="en">AMR</tva:Name>
          </tva:Coding>
        </tva:AudioAttributes>
        <tva:VideoAttributes>
          <tva:Coding href="urn:mpeg:mpeg7:cs:VisualCodingFormatCS:2001:3.1">
            <tva:Name xml:lang="en">MPEG-4 Visual Simple Profile</tva:Name>
          </tva:Coding>
        </tva:VideoAttributes>
      </DeliveryMediaFormat>
    </ConversionOffer>
  </ConversionList>
  <ProtocolSetList>
    <ProtocolSet>
      <DeliveryProtocol href="urn:tva:ndr:cs:DeliveryProtocolTypeCS:2005:udp"/>
      <ControlProtocol href="urn:tva:ndr:cs:ControlProtocolTypeCS:2005:rtsp"/>
    </ProtocolSet>
  </ProtocolSetList>
  <PlayWhileRecording> true </PlayWhileRecording>
</ndr:describe_control_NDR_Result>
```

Listing 9.13 Message describing capabilities

Anytime systems which enables us to attach to this operation some indications of what the receiver should do with it. Among these indications, we can specify the order to record a given content referenced by that information, what constitutes an indirect way of remote programming.

A second approach permits the direct programming of the user's home receiver through IP networks by means of a simple procedure of sending emails to the PDR with the references of the contents to be recorded. This simple procedure could be used by the user or by a service provider with authorization to schedule our recordings for us.

Finally, the most complete mechanism presented enables the programming of an NDR connected to a network, a service provided by the operator or by an external provider, so that users can make recordings in another device when their own cannot do it for any reason.

Conclusions 10

10.1 A Broad Regulatory Framework

Throughout the previous chapters, we have presented the TV-Anytime standard broadly, describing the many mechanisms and metadata structures it provides to enable the development of value-added audiovisual services.

The parts of the standard we have tried to explain in this book can be classified into three sections, which we will summarize now.

On the one hand, TV-Anytime provides a simple referential framework to unambiguously identify and refer to any audiovisual content within our reach. The reference through CRIDs presented in Chap. 3 allows us to accurately describe the different programmes we handle, to safely avoid the usual confusions that result from the frequent similarity in their names. Furthermore, TV-Anytime provides a simple, standardized mechanism for operators to make public the necessary data to locate the referenced contents, a mechanism which allows receivers to acquire the desired programmes with little or no help from the users. This mechanism considers the information structures necessary for the user's devices to locate and access contents, both in unidirectional contexts (programmes received in the available broadcast channels) and in bidirectional networks (e.g. online contents available in Internet servers).

A second class of tools standardized by TV-Anytime (and maybe the most important one) is the repertoire of descriptive metadata used to characterize contents. In Chap. 4, we offered a broad perspective on the different structures provided by TV-Anytime to describe contents, regarding both their core, unchanging characteristics and the qualities that can vary from copy to copy, due to the format of the container, the characteristics of the distribution, the purpose of the broadcast, etc. The identification and description of the different parts of a given content also give us the necessary tools to segment programmes and with it go beyond the traditional linearity of television to make true the possibility of a selective and individual visualization. Since the pairing of a given content with the more appropriate viewers is an omnipresent concern in the objectives of

A. Gil Solla and R.G. Sotelo Bovino, *TV-Anytime*, X.media.publishing,
DOI 10.1007/978-3-642-36766-3_10,

TV-Anytime, the standard adopts from MPEG-7 (and expands) certain additional metadata to describe users effectively and allow for the development of comparison processes that measure the degree of similarity between contents and viewers. Moreover, TV-Anytime also tries to go one step beyond content itself to deal with their combination or use for specific purposes. Chapters 5 and 6 gave us good examples of this, showing the rich and diverse possibilities in environments such as synchronized packaging of many contents, targeting or dynamic customized advertising according to viewers.

Finally, we must highlight the area on procedures, in which TV-Anytime makes many contributions (expressed in Chaps. 8 and 9) aimed at making the communication between different devices easier so as to access and exchange information through bidirectional networks, program user or third-party devices remotely, or even enable exchange mechanisms with systems that do not apply the standards described here. It is equally important in this section to mention a set of procedures like *Fragmentation*, *Encoding*, *Encapsulation* and *Indexing* (presented in Chap. 7) meant to make the submission of information to a receiver flexible to facilitate its processing. These mechanisms enable a selective submission of metadata and provide a system of index-linked references which reduces both the bandwidth required and the necessary computational capacity to process large volumes of data.

Together with all that has been presented in this book, there are many aspects to which TV-Anytime makes some kind of contribution in its specifications, but they have not been mentioned in this book for several reasons, such as the lack of contributions aimed at enabling new business models or the need to go into detail about related technologies for their adequate understanding. Among them, the most important ones are related to the management and protection of rights over a given content (to set conditions about its consumption or export), or the metadata protection mechanisms in bidirectional network transactions, for example, to guarantee the origin and integrity of the messages received, or to hide them from others through encryption (mechanisms based on the use of the typical security protocols used on the Internet, such as TLS—*Transport Layer Security* (IETF RFC 2246, 1999)).

10.2 An Ambitious Regulatory Framework

The true importance of TV-Anytime's set of standards is not the number of standardized aspects, but the multiple possibilities it opens up by facilitating the development and deployment of new business models in the audiovisual industry.

Throughout this book, we have presented some of these new business models, we have suggested many others, and we hope to have fed the reader's imagination by planting the seed for most of the new services that will be conceived.

The aim of TV-Anytime is to provide tools to make the most out of the great computational capacity modern PDRs (or smart televisions) have, to go beyond the current scenario (limited almost exclusively to the recording and reproduction of contents) and to head towards a new scene where the flexibility of digital technology allows us to manipulate information and reason on its meaning.

This increase in the PDRs' intelligence must materialize on the one hand in the deployment of new services that provide unprecedented functionalities, because now the receiver can automatically perform a vast number of tasks that before (if possible) required the user's intervention because there were no formal information elements that could be processed by a computer algorithm. This must lead to a scenario where the PDR will provide valuable notifications beyond simple reminders of preprogrammed events, carry out smart content searches—possibly with concatenated stages enriched by information additional to that provided by the user—take the initiative to acquire contents of interest to users, etc.

But TV-Anytime also wants to set the foundations for the development of one of the most outstanding characteristics of this new television: the condition of being customizable, a quality that is found in the antipodes of the nature of this medium since its birth. The new information processing capacity will allow the PDR to provide us with customized contents (and advertising), whether requested by us or not, with the format, composition and time availability that are more suited to our preferences, devices or current circumstances.

To this end, to allow an individual consumption and enjoyment, it is necessary in any case for new services to be able to take into consideration the elements involved in this experience (contents, users and environments) and perform matching analysis to later select among the most attractive alternatives in each case. TV-Anytime tries to set the foundations for the development of frameworks that allow precisely this: to take into account the information so that it is possible to develop smart services, aware enough of the characteristics of their environment to choose the right options when they have to make decisions.

10.3 A Necessary Regulatory Framework

Although television still occupies a privileged position in our ecosystem of leisure and communication channels, it is undeniable that this medium is going through a significant period of change. After many years of placid technological immobility, a myriad of new concepts has shaken the foundations of this market over the last decade (flat screens, digital transition, video on demand through the Internet, *Catchup-TV*, *Over-the-top*, MHP, HbbTV, second screens, etc.), spreading uncertainty among some operators only used to fighting for the viewers' favouritism for their programming.

Surviving this new scenario of multiple formats, protocols and interoperability inevitably requires significant investments to keep the services provided to the user up to date. It is essential that the decisions made over these investments are supported by steady elements that guarantee a lasting background, at least for a period of time that feeds the hope of amortization.

It is there where standards such as TV-Anytime play an important role, standardizing this common background that guarantees interoperability and leads to some economies of scale in which to develop with some certainty the new services enabled by the flexibility of digital technology.

Whether this objective is finally achieved or not depends mainly on the support received by the players involved in this market (operators, device manufacturers and service developers) and, above all, by those who must generate the descriptive metadata, which is what this reasoning framework is based on. Without its universalization, it is not possible to aim at the effective deployment of new business models meaningful enough to constitute the suggested revolution.

The authors of this book are certain that the services outlined throughout this work will sooner or later appear in the audiovisual scenario. The uncertainty lies solely in knowing whether it is going to be a hard, uncoordinated labour promoted by private initiatives or, on the contrary, a smoothly conducted change empowered by unifying standards.

Bibliography

AIMC. (Nov, 2012). *AIMC*. Obtained from "Asociación para la Investigación de los Medios de Comunicación" (AIMC): http://www.aimc.es.

AIMC. (November, 2010). *Internet, en medio de los medios*. Obtained from AIMC: http://www.aimc.es.

ETSI TS 102 727. (January, 2010). "Digital Video Broadcasting (DVB); Multimedia Home Platform (MHP) Specification 1.1.2, V1.1.1". European Telecommunications Standards Institute (ETSI).

ETSI TS 102 728. (September, 2011). "Digital Video Broadcasting (DVB); Globally Executable MHP (GEM), Specification 1.3 (including OTT and hybrid broadcast/broadband), V1.2.1". European Telecommunications Standards Institute (ETSI).

ETSI TS 102 822–1. (January, 2006). "Broadcast and Online Services: Search, select, and rightful use of content on personal storage systems (TV-Anytime); Part 1: Benchmark Features", V1.3.1. European Telecommunications Standards Institute (ETSI).

ETSI TS 102 822–2. (November, 2007). "Broadcast and Online Services: Search, select, and rightful use of content on personal storage systems (TV-Anytime); Part 2: Phase 1 - System description", V1.4.1. European Telecommunications Standards Institute (ETSI).

ETSI TS 102 822-3-1. (November, 2011). "Broadcast and Online Services: Search, select, and rightful use of content on personal storage systems (TV-Anytime); Part 3: Metadata; Sub-part 1: Phase 1 - Metadata schemas", V1.7.1. European Telecommunications Standards Institute (ETSI).

ETSI TS 102 822-3-2. (July, 2010). "Broadcast and Online Services: Search, select, and rightful use of content on personal storage systems (TV-Anytime); Part 3: Metadata; Sub-part 2: System aspects in a uni-directional environment", V1.6.1. European Telecommunications Standards Institute (ETSI).

ETSI TS 102 822-3-3. (November, 2011). "Broadcast and Online Services: Search, select, and rightful use of content on personal storage systems (TV-Anytime); Part 3: Metadata; Sub-part 3: Phase 2 - Extended Metadata Schema", V1.5.1. European Telecommunications Standards Institute (ETSI).

ETSI TS 102 822-3-4. (November, 2011). "Broadcast and Online Services: Search, select, and rightful use of content on personal storage systems (TV-Anytime); Part 3: Metadata; Sub-part 4: Phase 2 - Interstitial metadata", V1.5.1. European Telecommunications Standards Institute (ETSI).

ETSI TS 102 822–4. (November, 2011). "Broadcast and Online Services: Search, select, and rightful use of content on personal storage systems (TV-Anytime); Part 4: Phase 1 - Content referencing", V1.6.1. European Telecommunications Standards Institute (ETSI).

ETSI TS 102 822-5-1. (November, 2011). "Broadcast and Online Services: Search, select, and rightful use of content on personal storage systems (TV-Anytime); Part 5: Rights Management and Protection (RMP); Sub-part 1: Information for Broadcast Applications", V1.6.1". European Telecommunications Standards Institute (ETSI).

A. Gil Solla and R.G. Sotelo Bovino, *TV-Anytime*, X.media.publishing,
DOI 10.1007/978-3-642-36766-3, © Springer-Verlag Berlin Heidelberg 2013

ETSI TS 102 822-5-2. (January, 2006). "Broadcast and Online Services: Search, select, and rightful use of content on personal storage systems (TV-Anytime); Part 5: Rights Management and Protection (RMP) Sub-part 2: RMPI binding", V1.2.1. European Telecommunications Standards Institute (ETSI).

ETSI TS 102 822-6-1. (November, 2011). "Broadcast and Online Services: Search, select, and rightful use of content on personal storage systems (TV-Anytime); Part 6: Delivery of metadata over a bi-directional network; Sub-part 1: Service and transport", V1.7.1. European Telecommunications Standards Institute (ETSI).

ETSI TS 102 822-6-2. (January, 2006). "Broadcast and Online Services: Search, select, and rightful use of content on personal storage systems (TV-Anytime); Part 6: Delivery of metadata over a bi-directional network; Sub-part 2: Phase 1 - Service discovery", V1.3.1. European Telecommunications Standards Institute (ETSI).

ETSI TS 102 822-6-3. (November, 2011). "Broadcast and Online Services: Search, select, and rightful use of content on personal storage systems (TV-Anytime); Part 6: Delivery of metadata over a bi-directional network; Sub-part 3: Phase 2 - Exchange of Personal Profile", V1.5.1. European Telecommunications Standards Institute (ETSI).

ETSI TS 102 822–7. (October, 2003). "Broadcast and Online Services: Search, select, and rightful use of content on personal storage systems (TV-Anytime); Part 7: Bi-directional metadata delivery protection", V1.1.1. European Telecommunications Standards Institute (ETSI).

ETSI TS 102 822–8. (November, 2011). "Broadcast and Online Services: Search, select, and rightful use of content on personal storage systems (TV-Anytime); Part 8: Phase 2 - Interchange Data Format", V1.5.1. European Telecommunications Standards Institute (ETSI).

ETSI TS 102 822–9. (November, 2011). "Broadcast and Online Services: Search, select, and rightful use of content on personal storage systems (TV-Anytime); Part 9: Phase 2 - Remote Programming", V1.5.1. European Telecommunications Standards Institute (ETSI).

ETSI TS 102 851. (January, 2010). "Digital Video Broadcasting: Uniform Resource Identifiers (URI) for DVB Systems". European Telecommunications Standards Institute.

ABNT NBR 15606. (July, 2011). Ginga, ABNT NBR 15606, 2011 Esp. Associação Brasileira de Normas Técnicas (ABNT).

IETF RFC 1591. (March, 1994). "Domain Name System Structure and Delegation". (J. Postel, Ed.)

IETF RFC 2246. (January, 1999). "The TLS protocol version 1.0". (C. A. T. Dierks, Ed.)

IETF RFC 2782. (February, 2000). "A DNS RR for specifying the location of services (DNS SRV)". (P. V. A. Gulbrandsen, Ed.)

IETF RFC 822. (August, 1982). "STANDARD FOR THE FORMAT OF ARPA INTERNET TEXT MESSAGES". (D. H. Crocker, Ed.)

INFOADEX. (2011). *Estudio INFOADEX de la Inversión Publicitaria en España 2010*. INFOADEX.

ISO/IEC 15938–1. (2002). "Information technology - Multimedia content description interface - Part 1: Systems". Moving Picture Expert Group.

ISO/IEC 15938–2. (2001). "Multimedia Content Description Interface - Part 2: DDL". Moving Picture Expert Group.

ISO/IEC 21000–2. (October, 2005). "Information technology - Multimedia framework (MPEG-21) - Part 2: Digital Item Declaration". Moving Picture Expert Group.

ISO/IEC 21000–7. (April, 2006). "Information technology - Multimedia framework (MPEG-21) - Part 7: MPEG-21 Digital Item Adaptation". Moving Picture Expert Group.

Lara, P. R. (2010). "Jóvenes y Televisión generalista en España: ¿Es Internet responsable de una audiencia perdida?". *Juventud y nuevos medios de comunicación* (88).

UDDI. (February, 2005). "Universal Description, Discovery and Integration V3.0.2". (L. e. Clement, Ed.) OASIS.

W3C-SOAP. (April, 2007). "Simple Object Access Protocol (SOAP) V1.2". (M. e. Guggin, Ed.) W3C Consortium.

W3C-WSDL. (March, 2001). Web Services Description Language (WSDL). (E. e. Christensen, Ed.) World Wide Web Consortium.

W3C-XML. (November 26, 2008). "The Extensible Markup Language (XML), 1.0, 5ª Edición". (T. Bray, Ed.) World Wide Web Consortium.

W3C-XML Schema. (October, 2004). "XML Schema Primer, Second Edition". (D. C. Fallside, Ed.) World Wide Web Consortium.

W3C-XPath. (November, 1999). "XML Path Language (XPath)". (S. D. James Clark, Ed.) World Wide Web Consortium.

WS-Inspection. (November, 2001). "The Web Services Inspection Language". (K. e. Ballinger, Ed.) IBM.

Index

A. Gil Solla and R.G. Sotelo Bovino, *TV-Anytime*, X.media.publishing,
DOI 10.1007/978-3-642-36766-3, © Springer-Verlag Berlin Heidelberg 2013